CHIEFS AND LEADING FAMILIES IN
RAJPUTANA

CHIEFS AND LEADING FAMILIES IN
RAJPUTANA

C. S. BAYLEY

GYAN

Published by

Gyan Publishing House
5, Ansari Road
Daryaganj, New Delhi-110002
Phone: 011-47034999, 9811692060
E-mail: books@gyanbooks.com

Distribution Network
gyanbooks.com
India, USA, Canada, UK, Australia, France

ISBN : 978-81-212-3231-9 (PB)
First Published, Calcutta, 1894

2nd Impression 2020

Printed at: Gyan Press, Delhi.

Chiefs and Leading Families in Rajputana
Author: C. S. Bayley

PREFACE.

THE materials for this work projected in 1890 by Colonel G. H. Trevor, C.S.I., Agent to the Governor-General for Rajputana, were collected from the several States of that province through the Political Officers according to certain specified instructions with regard to arrangement. They were afterwards compiled, at Colonel Trevor's request, and put into their present form by Mr. C. S. Bayley, C.S., then Political Agent, Bikanir, who has drawn on the Rajputana Gazetteer for the historical extracts inserted to render clearer the position of the Chiefs and leading families noticed. For purposes of reference, the compilation will, it is hoped, prove useful and supply a recognized want. It must not be regarded as strictly accurate in all details of family history which, as usual, have been supplied from interested sources. They have, however, been checked as far as possible.

INDEX.

JODHPUR.

BIKANIR.

KISHANGARH.

UDAIPUR.

DUNGARPUR.

BANSWARA.

PARTABGARH.

SHAHPURA.

BUNDI.

KOTAH.

SIROHI.

JAISALMER.

KARAULI.

JAIPUR.

ALWAR.

TONK.

AJMER.

CHIEFS AND LEADING FAMILIES

IN

RAJPUTANA.

CHAPTER I.

INTRODUCTION.

[Contributed by Sir Alfred Lyall, K.C.B., to the Gazetteer of Rajputana, dated 1879.]

THE faint outlines which can be traced of the condition of the country now called Rajputana, for one or two centuries before the Muhammadans invaded Upper India, indicate that it was subject for the most part to two or three very powerful tribal dynasties. Of these, the dynasty of the Rahtor family, which ruled at Kanauj, appears to have had the widest dominion; for the early Arabian Geographers make the frontier of Kanauj conterminous with Sind, and Al-Marudi styles the Kanauj monarch one of the Kings of Sind. However this may be, it seems certain that the Kanauj territory extended far westward beyond the Jumna into Rajputana, while much of the south-western part was included within the limits of another great kingdom which had its capital in Gujarat. Other tribal dynasties succeeded; and in the eleventh century, about the period of the first Muhammadan inroad into the interior of Northern India, the leading tribes were the Solankhyas of Anhilwara in Gujarat, the Chauhans at Ajmere, and the Rahtors at Kanauj. The Gehlot clan had established itself in the Mewar country which is still held by the Sesodias, a sept of the Gehlots. The Rahtors and Sodas held the north-western deserts where they are still dwelling, and the Kachhwaha clan had occupied the eastern tracts about Jaipur, now their Chief's capital.

The desert which lies between Sind and Rajputana appears to have sheltered the tribes from any serious inroads of the Arabs who reigned in Sind, but from the north-west their territory was more exposed. Thus the first Musalman invasions found Rajput dynasties seated in all the chief cities of the north and ruling large territories throughout the rich Gangetic plains, at Lahore, Delhi, Kanauj, and Ajudhya. Mahmud of Ghazni marched to Kanauj in 1017 A.D. and reached Muttra; a few years later he subdued Lahore, and in 1024 he made his celebrated expedition to Somnath in Gujarat, marching from Muttra across the Rajput countries to Ajmer. The Solankhyas of Anhilwara were overcome; but the Rajputs barred Mahmud's return by Ajmer, and he was forced to find his way back through the Sind deserts.

In 1170 a furious war broke out between the Solankhyas of Anhilwara and the Chauhans of Ajmer, in which the former were defeated; and about the same time began the famous feud between the Chauhans and the Rahtors of Kanauj. These dissensions weakened the dynasties; nevertheless when Shahabu-d-din began his invasions, the Chauhans fought hard before they were driven out of Delhi and Ajmer in 1193 A.D. Next year Kanauj was taken and the Rahtor princes, utterly broken in the Gangetic Doab, emigrated to the country which they have since ruled in North-Western Rajputana. But Ajmer was still sharply disputed, though Kutbu-d-din, Shahabu-d-din's Governor in India, managed at last to drive back the tribes united to contest his occupation of the middle countries, and to force his way through them again into Gujarat. Ajmer and Anhilwara, the former Rajput capitals, were garrisoned by his troops, and the Musalmans appear gradually to have overawed, if they did not entirely reduce, the open country between and about these two places, having garrisoned the fortresses and secured the natural outlets of Rajputana toward Gujarat on the south-west and the Jumna on the north-east. The effect was probably to press back the clans more into the outlying districts where a more difficult and less inviting country afforded a second line of defence against the foreigner, a line which they have held successfully up to the present day. The existing capitals of the modern States indicate the positions to which the earlier Chiefs retreated. One clan (the Bhatis) had before this founded Jaisalmer in the extreme north-west, having been driven across the Sutlej by the Ghaznavi conquerors. The Rahtors settled down among the sands of Marwar; the Sesodias pushed inward from north-east and south-west concentrating on the Mewar plateau behind the scarps of the Aravalis; while the Jaduns were protected by the hills and ravines that lie along the Chambal. From these and other migrations and settlements grew up gradually, with varying features and constantly shifting territory, the States now governed by the Rajput Chiefs, the non-Rajput States being of a very different and much more recent formation. The larger States represent the acquisitions of the more powerful and predominant clans; the smaller States are either the separate conquests of a sept that parted company from the main clan or the appanage of some Chief who set up independently. They have all, in fact, a very similar origin. When the dominant families of a clan lost their dominion in the fertile regions of the north-west, one part of the clan seems to have remained in the conquered country, while another part, probably the defeated Chief's kinsmen and followers, went off westward and carved out another, though much poorer, dominion. They were gradually hemmed up into parts of the country productive enough to yield food and rent, and defensible against the great armies of the foreigner. Having then made a settlement and built a city of refuge, each clan started on an interminable course of feuds and forays, striving to enlarge its borders at the cost of its neighbour. When the land grew too strait for the support of the Chief's family and of the increased clan, a band would assemble under some new leader and go forth to plant itself elsewhere. In this way the whole of Rajputana appears to have been parted off among the clans which we find there now, and the territories that have been gradually rounded off and consolidated by incessant friction are now called States, under the rule of the Chief of the clan dominant. Of course the original type of tribal dominion has been modified; towns have grown up round the ancient forts and the Chiefs have, in some instances, modernized their status towards the likeness of a territorial King. Nevertheless, on the whole, these States are still essentially the possessions of clans, and, as such, can be defined and distinguished territorially; nor is the political nature or tenure of these States properly intelligible without bearing their origin in mind. Setting aside, then, the two Jat States and the Muhammadan principality of Tonk, we may describe Rajputana as the region within which the pure-blooded Rajput States have maintained their independence under their own chieftains, and have kept together their primitive societies ever since their principal dynasties in Northern India were cast down and swept away by the Musalman irruption. Of the States of Rajputana eighteen belong to the first rank in the Empire, being under treaty with the Imperial Government, and of these eighteen, fifteen are still ruled by the Chiefs of Rajput clans or families, two of the other three belonging to Jat families and one to a Muhammadan dynasty. A sixteenth Rajput State is Shahpura which has no treaty with the Empire, and which differs from the others both as to its origin and as to the nature of its political connections . . . . The Chief of Shahpura holds his lands by distinct grants from two different superiors, the Rana of Mewar and the Empire. The sixteen Rajput States may be arranged according to the different clans which founded them, and to which the ruling family of necessity belongs, in the following manner :—

Clan.	Subdivision or sept.	State.
Rahtor	......	Jodhpur (Marwar). Bikanir. Kishangarh.
Sesodia	......	Mewar (Udaipur). Banswara. Dungarpur. Pertabgarh. Shahpura.
Chauhan	Hara	Bundi. Kotah.
	Deoria	Sirohi.
Jadun	Bhati	Karauli. Jaisalmir.
Kachhwaha	......	Jaipur.
	Naruka	Alwar.
Jhala	......	Jhalawar.

The small Chiefship of Khetri in the Shaikhawati district of Jaipur is held on a double tenure of the same kind as that of Shahpura, as the Chief holds one part of his territory, the pargana of Kot Putli, by a grant made on behalf of the British Government by Lord Lake in 1803 and subsequently confirmed as a free gift in perpetuity. On the eastern border of Rajputana, beyond the States of Bundi and Kotah, are seven estates called the seven Kotris, held by seven Rajput families of the Hara clan which belong to a peculiar political arrangement.* . . . . There are other minor Chiefs of a similar class in different parts of Rajputana, who claim some kind of privileged status and separate jurisdiction under the ruling power of the State within which their lands are included. This claim is usually by virtue of having descended from a distant stock, or of having originally conquered and maintained their lands without aid or commission from the State's ruler, but on their own score and venture; they nevertheless pay tribute to the State's Chief and are subject to his general authority. Such are the Chiefs of Sikar in Jaipur, of Nimrana in Alwar, of Fathgarh in Kishangarh (though he pays no tribute), and of Kushalgarh in Banswara, though the last-mentioned Chief (who also holds lands of Ratlam) has been withdrawn from direct subordination to Banswara. The Bhil Chiefs of the Mewar hill tracts belong to a slightly different category, though they assert internal independence of Udaipur; and the Thakur of Lawa, a small feudatory, has, for peculiar reasons, been declared separate from Tonk, to which he was subordinate up to 1870. Besides these minor or mediatized Chiefships, there are other gradations of status and privilege; but their classification becomes indistinct as it descends, shading off into the great estate-holder and head of a branch family of the Chief's blood, with high rank and formal hereditary privileges rather than separate political jurisdiction. . . . .

The remaining three States of the first class, not being under Rajput Chiefs, are of a different origin and growth. The State of Tonk was formed out of the convention which allowed the famous Amir Khan to hold certain lands which he possessed in 1817; it consists of six separate districts, of which three only are within the administrative province of Rajputana. The Jat States of Bhartpur and Dholpur are the other two; the first is governed by the descendant of the bold and adroit land-holders who raised themselves to the rank and power of territorial Chiefs during the confusion of the eighteenth century; the second, Dholpur, is the territory remaining with a family that had gained distinction earlier, though it first acquired political independence in the same century and under similar circumstances. But, whereas the Bhartpur Chief kept his territory intact, and even increased it during the contest between the Mahrattas and the English at the beginning of this century, the Dholpur Chief in the same period lost a great part of his acquisitions. These two States, lying as they do outside Central India, did not fall within the range of the treaties of 1817-18. These States, therefore, are governed each by a family of the Jat tribe, which gives to that particular tribe a sort of precedence and privilege in the State, but their constitution is by no means tribal in the meaning with which that word applies to the territory of a Rajput clan. In Tonk the descendant of Amir Khan is an autocratic Nawab of the ordinary Indian type.

It has been explained that the existing Rajput States trace their historic descent from the ancient tribal settlements in this part of India; and as they differ in origin from the great majority of States in other parts of the Empire, so do they in political constitution. A Rajput State, where its peculiar structure has been least modified, means the territory over which a particular clan or division of a clan claims dominion for its Chief and political predominance for itself by right of occupation or conquest. A Rajput Chief is the head of a clan which have for many centuries been lords of the soil, or of the greater part of it, lying within the State's limits, and, as a ruler, instead of being an absolute despot, he exercises a jurisdiction more or less limited over an aristocracy consisting principally of his kinsmen and connections, while in the cities and throughout the districts not within the estates of the great fief-holders his authority is absolute. In the Western States, where the original type is best preserved, the dominant clans are still much in the position which they took up on first entry upon the land; and there we find all the territory (with exceptions in favour of particular grantees) still parcelled out among the Rajputs; mainly among the branch families of the dominant clan and their offshoots. . . . . All over the west it would be difficult to find a single important estate not held by a Rajput. The supreme governing authority in a Rajput State is, of course, in the hands of the hereditary Chief of the dominant clan, who is supposed to be the nearest

* See page 55.

legitimate descendant in direct male line from the founder of the State, according to the genealogy of the tribe. . . . . But even primogeniture has been required to qualify up to a low standard of competency; and when direct heirs fail, the Chief may be chosen from any branch of the stock group, the choice sometimes going from one branch to another according to critical needs and circumstances. The right of adoption by a Rajput Chief of his successor according to law and customs, on failure of natural heirs, has been formally recognized by the British Government. . . . . When the succession is disputed the Imperial Government is often forced to step in and arbitrate and decide. The interior economy of a complete Rajput family has often suggested the analogy of feudalism, though in fact there are essential differences. There is, however, a chain of mutual authority and subordination which runs from the Chief by gradations downwards to the possessor of one or more villages. The lands are for the most part divided off and inherited among the branch families of the dominant clan; some considerable estates being held by families of a different clan who have come in by marriage or by anterior settlement in the country. Very large estates are held by the hereditary heads of the branch septs which have spread out from the main stock and by kindred families which are as boughs to the great branches. . . . . . These estates are owned and inherited by Chiefs who much resemble the State Chief in miniature, where they are strong and independent. The relations of these minor Chiefs to the State Chief differ very much in different States; in the best-preserved States of the west and south-west they exercise almost complete jurisdiction each within his own domain proper; and their obedience to any unusual command of the State Chief depends on his power to enforce it. They pay him certain dues or assessed contributions rated upon their income and regulated by immemorial custom; they are bound to render military service against the foreigner and against rebels, to make additional emergent contributions in war time; and their lands are usually rated at so many horsemen or footmen to be furnished yearly for the ordinary public service. The number of followers to be maintained may depend on the value of the land and upon the rank and consequence of the estate-holder. At every succession to an estate the heir is bound to do homage to the Chief and to pay a fine of some value—these acts being essential to entry into legal possession of his inheritance. He also pays some customary dues of a feudal nature and is bound to personal attendance at certain periods and occasions. In the States of the west, belonging to the Rathor and Sesodia clans, the domains of all the subordinate Chiefs are rated at a certain valuation of annual rent-roll; and for every thousand rupees a certain number of armed men must be provided for the State's service. In some States this service has been commuted for cash payment, but the great land-holders have usually resisted this change, which obviously tends to increase the Chief's power and to lessen their own. Disobedience to a lawful summons or order involves sequestration of lands, if the Chief can enforce it; but it is rare that an estate is confiscated outright and annexed to Crown lands, as the whole federation of minor Chiefs would be against such an absorption if there were any practical alternative. So long as the minor Chiefs fulfil their customary obligations, they hold their estates on conditions as well founded and defined as those on which the ruling Chief governs his territory, and their tenure is often just as ancient, and their authority within their own limits often as absolute.

In fact the system upon which the land is distributed among the branch families and other great hereditary land-holders is the basis of the political constitution of a Rajput State and forms its characteristic distinction. And this system is not, speaking accurately, feudal, though it has grown in certain States into something very like feudalism. The tenure of the great clansmen involves military service and payment of financial aids, but its source is to be found in the original clan occupation of the lands and in the privileges of kinship and purity of descent from the original occupants or conquerors. The subordinate Chiefs really claim to be coparceners with the rulers in their right to dominion over the soil and to the fruits of it. Of course this constitutional principle has been much changed in practice in many of the States, especially since the Mahrattas disorganized Rajputana at the end of the last century. In the Eastern Rajput States, which were most exposed to the attacks of Mughal, Mahratta, and Pathan, the clan system has been much effaced politically, and some Chiefs have centralized their power so as to obtain almost absolute jurisdiction over the whole of their territories; moreover, the Rajputs are very few among the population of some of these States. In Kotah the clan system was almost extinguished by Zalim Singh, who brought the land mainly under direct fiscal management and substituted his own armed police for the feudal contingents. In Bundi some relations of the Chief still hold large grants, but without any independent jurisdiction. Bhartpur and Dholpur are Jat States in which the Chief's power is supreme, and in the Muhammadan State of Tonk the Rajput land-holders have been inevitably depressed while the government is of the ordinary Muhammadan type. So that, whereas in the north and west a ruling Chief would hardly break through the compact front which his clansmen could at once oppose to any serious political encroachment and has a dubious jurisdiction within the domains of his leading kinsmen, in the east and south a Chief has his State more or less directly under his own executive power and a people of whom his clansmen form a small part. In the small Eastern State of Karauli, however, the clan system is still vigorous.

Around and below the great minor Chiefs and families are the kinsfolk who belong to the same sept of the clan; and who hold land of more or less extent, either independently of their head or on a sort of grant from him. In Western Rajputana there are large tracts of lands held by groups of Rajput proprietors, who represent a settlement anterior to, or at least coeval with, that of the dominant clan, which settlement may have been either that of an alien clan that has kept its lands undisturbed, or of a distinct sept belonging to the ruling clan. Some of the alien clans have been brought in later by marriage alliances or by having come as a contingent to aid the Chief of the country in some hard-fought war or distant expedition, services for which they received an allotment of land. The heads of these alien families often hold high rank in the State. . . . .

The administrative business of a State usually falls into several different departments, which are under hereditary officials—a very important class, of which the members almost always belong to particular castes and families—rarely to a Rajput clan. In some States the highest offices belong by heritage to a great kinsman of the Chief; though these offices are apt to become honorary, as they have become in Europe, and the real power gets into the hands of very acute instruments of the Chief's good pleasure. It is often imprudent to place much authority in the hands of a leading noble; nor are the Thakurs usually qualified for the transaction of affairs, while they would rather look down upon official duties unless accompanied by very substantial rank and influence. In fact, the condition of internal government in Rajputana much resembles what has passed in Europe; the ruler seeks to strengthen himself at the cost of the nobles; the nobles are on the watch against the encroachments of the ruler; and the officials are the astute men of business, the *gens de la robe* of Europe, expect in law and finance, whose aid in such times has always been so essential to the ruler. . . . . . As the tendency of all office in Rajputana is to become hereditary, and as the right of the children and relations of an official to be provided for in the public service is universally recognized, the Chief is always surrounded by a crowd of qualified claimants. . . . . Several of the official families are descended from persons of the writing or commercial caste, who accompanied the earliest immigration of the ruling Chiefs into the country.

The great estate-holders, called the Thakurs, live most of the year in their forts on their own lands, and in the west they manage their own domains with little State interference, distributing justice and collecting their taxes and rents. When some complainant has interest enough to get an appeal seriously taken up at head-quarters, or when some disorder or deed of notorious violence has created scandal, the ruling Chief interposes vigorously, though the matter is usually settled by a fine or a present. Where the Thakurs are most independent they go little to court, though there is usually a fixed period when each man of rank is bound to attend on his Chief, and on great occasions they all assemble.

Where their separate status and power have been much reduced, they gravitate towards the level of privileged courtiers, whose places in the Chief's presence and at ceremonies are regulated by very minute etiquette. But a turbulent noble of the old school does not much enjoy a visit to court, where there are usually long outstanding accounts to settle with astute officials; he goes there well attended by kinsfolk, and fences himself in his town house, where he occasionally stood a siege in the last generation, and was sometimes murdered. It may be said that all the internal disorders of Rajputana since 1818, which were serious and wide-spread, up to recent years, have been caused entirely by disputes between the ruling Chiefs and their nobles; the Chiefs striving to always depress and break down the power of the great kinsmen, the nobles being determined to restrict the strength of their ruler. The Mahratta invasion and usurpations had much diminished the strength of the State's ruler; on the other hand, the English supremacy is favourable to him, and the inclination of an English Government is naturally toward support of the central administration. Nor has the time of armed resistance by nobles to their Chief yet passed* away in the west and south-west, where a Thakur will still, if aggrieved, hold out as long as he can in the ancestral fort, and if the fort is made too hot for him, take to the wilds with his kinsmen and become an outlaw and leader of banditti. Usually these proceedings end in compromise and reconciliation.

* This was written in 1879.

CHAPTER II.

RAHTOR STATES.

[*Jodhpur—Bikanir—Kishangarh.*]

Origin of the Rahtor States.

As mentioned in the last chapter the original capital of the Rahtor clan was Kanauj. On the capture of this city by Shahabu-d-din in 1194 A.D., the dynasty which according to tradition ruled for fourteen centuries was expelled and Sivaji, the grandson or nephew of Jay Chand the last Chief, started on a pilgrimage to Dwarka. On his way he halted at Pali in Marwar, where, having won the favour of the local Brahmans by repelling bands of marauders, he eventually settled. He and his descendants grew in lands and power until Chanda, the tenth in descent from Sivaji, was strong enough in 1382 to acquire Mandor, then the chief town of Marwar, by marriage from the Parihar ruler. Chanda was succeeded by his son Rirmal and his grandson Jodha, who in 1459 founded the city of Jodhpur which has since been the capital of the Marwar State. From Rao Jodha's fourteen sons and twenty-three brothers are descended the Chiefs and the principal nobles of Marwar and Bikanir, and by them and their followers the dominion of the Rahtors was established throughout the greater part of the territories now comprised in these States. From Raja Udai Singh (1583—1594), the fourth in descent from Jodha, are descended the Chiefs of Kishangarh in Rajputana and of Ratlam and Sitamau in Central India, and from Maharaja Ajit Singh, the great-great-grandson of Udai Singh (1681—1725) are sprung the ruling families of Idar and Ahmadnagar in Gujarat.

JODHPUR.

Present Chief.

I.—The present Chief of Marwar or Jodhpur is **His Highness Raj Rajeshwar Maharaj Adhiraj Maharaja Sir Jaswant Singh Bahadur, G.C.S.I.**, the head of the Rahtor clan. His Highness, who was born at Ahmadnagar in Gujarat in 1838, succeeded his father, the late Maharaja Takht Singh, G.C.S.I., in March 1873. Maharaja Takht Singh, Chief of Ahmadnagar, had obtained the Chiefship of Marwar by the choice of the widows of his predecessor Maharaja Man Singh and of the principal nobles and officials of the State. On the succession of Maharaja Takht Singh, Ahmadnagar was transferred to the Chief of Idar, from which State it had been separated in 1784. Maharaja Jaswant Singh has contracted eight marriages, the first being with the daughter of the Jam of Jamnagar, a Rajput of the Jarecha clan. By Rani Puarji (Pramarji) of Narsingarh in Central India, His Highness has one son, **Maharaj Kunwar Sardar Singh,** who was born in 1879 and is heir-apparent of Jodhpur. The Maharaj Kunwar was married in February 1892 to a daughter of the late Maharao Raja of Bundi.

Near relatives.

The Maharaja has five brothers, of whom the eldest—

(1) **Maharaj Dhiraj Sir Pratap Singh, K.C.S.I.**, is now (1893) forty-nine years of age. He is a Colonel in Her Majesty's Army and an Aide-de-Camp to His Royal Highness the Prince of Wales. He was *Musahib Ala* or Chief Minister of Marwar in 1878 and 1879. In 1880 he accompanied the mission to Afghanistan, and in recognition of his services was created a Companion of the Star of India. On his return, he resumed his duties as Chief Minister of the State, and has since been to England on the occasion of Her Majesty's Jubilee. He was promoted to a Knight Commandership of the Star of India on the 1st January 1886. During Sir Partap Singh's tenure of office the administration of the State has made great progress. Sir Partap Singh receives a fixed salary and holds no *jagir.*

(2) **Maharaj Kishor Singh,** the third brother, aged forty-three years, is Commander-in-Chief of the State forces. He holds a *jagir* of six villages.

(3) The fifth brother, **Maharaj Zalim Singh,** was educated at the Mayo College, and holds the appointment of Assistant *Musahib Ala* (Chief Minister). He has a *jagir* of five villages.

The remaining brother is **Maharaj Bhupal Singh.**

In addition to the above, His Highness has thirteen illegitimate uncles, brothers and nephews who are known by the title of Rao Raja.*

Of the Maharaja's legitimate brothers, Maharaj Bhupal Singh has four sons,† Maharaj Zalim Singh two sons,‡ and Maharaj Kishor Singh one son.§

One deceased brother, Maharaj Zorawar Singh, has left four sons || and another, Maharaj Bahadur Singh, one son.¶

As shown above, the ruling family most closely connected with the Chief of Marwar is that of Idar, after which come in the order named Kishangarh, Ratlam, Sitamau, and Silana, Amjhera, Jhabua, and Bikanir.

His Highness the Maharaja's mother was a lady of the Deolia Partabgarh family. Besides this house, the following Chiefships are also connected by marriage with Jodhpur Jaipur, Bundi, Kotah, Rewa, Sirohi and Jaisalmer.

The following table shows the descent of the ruling Chief and of the most mportant connected families in and out of Marwar :—

- RAO SIVAJI (1211).
  - **Rao Malinath** (1374) founded Malani.
    - **Rao Chanda** (1395).
      - **Rao Rirmal** (1417).
        - Karn (founder of the Karnot sept).
        - Pata (founder of the Patawat sept).
        - Rupa (founder of the Rupawat sept).
        - **Rao Jodha** (1453) (founder of Jodha sept).
          - Rao Bika (founder of the Bikanir State). See p. 14.
          - Keshodas (founder of Jhabua).
          - **Rao Suja** (1491).
            - Udai (founder of the Udawat sept).
              - **Rao Ganga** (1515).
                - **Rao Maldeo** (1531) (founder of the Amjhera family).
                  - **Raja Udai Singh** (1583).
                    - Kishan Singh (founder of the Kishangarh State). See p. 22.
                    - **Raja Sur Singh** (1594)
                      - **Raja Gaj Singh** (1619)—served with distinction under the Empire.
                        - **Maharaja Jaswant Singh** (1635)—played an important part in the struggles between Aurangzeb and his brothers.
                          - **Maharaja Ajit Singh** (1678)—recovered Jodhpur from the Mughals.
                            - Anand Singh (founder of the Idar and Ahmadnagar States).
                              - **Maharaja Bakht Singh** (1751).
                                - **Maharaja Man Singh** (1804)—concluded a treaty with the British in 1817.
                                  - **Maharaja Takht Singh** (1843)—showed a loyal spirit during Mutiny.
                                    - **Maharaja Jaswant Singh** (1873), present Chief.
                    - Ratn Singh (founder of the Ratlam State).
                    - Kesodas (founder of the Sitaman State).
          - Duda (founder of the Mertia sept).
          - Karamsi (founder of the Karamsot sept).
        - Champa (founder of the Champawat sept).
        - Kumpa (founder of the Kumpawat sept).
        - Jaita (founder of Jaitawat sept).
      - Bhim, founder of the Bhiot family.

II.—The leading men of Marwar fall into three classes—(1) the members of the ruling family who are known as Rajwis, (2) the hereditary nobles and Thakurs, and (3) the chief officials. Of these, the first class has already been mentioned.

* *Rao Rajas Sohan Singh, Gulab Singh, Amar Singh, Fath Singh, Moti Singh, Raghunath Singh, Sardar Singh, Jiwan Singh, Bishan Singh, Tej Singh, Kalyan Singh, Bharat Singh, and Bherun Singh.*

† *Maharaj Daulat Singh* adopted by the late Maharaj Madho Singh and *Kunwars Ratn Singh, Pane Singh, and Kishan Singh.*

‡ *Maharaj Bijay Singh* adopted by the late Maharaj Muhabbat Singh ; and *Kunwar Guman Singh.*

§ *Kunwar Arjun Singh.*

|| *Maharaj Fath Singh ; Maharaj Mul Singh* adopted by the Jagirdar of Datti in Malwa ; *Maharaj Sheo Singh* and *Maharaj Akhay Singh.*

¶ *Maharaj Jiwan Singh.*

Tazimi Sardars.

The hereditary nobles of distinction are styled as **Tazimi Sardars**,—that is, nobles who are entitled to the honour of recognition by the Chief in Darbar. They are 144 in number, of whom 122 are Rahtors descended from the ruling stock and 22 are connections by marriage belonging to other clans—Bhatis, Ranawats, Kachhwahas, Chauhans, and Deoras. These last are known as *Ganayats*.

The Tazimi Sardars are again subdivided according to the degree of recognition which they are entitled to receive. Seventy-two Rahtors and ten Ganayats belong to the first division, twelve Rahtors (known as *Sarayats* from their position in Darbar near the staircase) being held superior to the rest. The whole of the first class receive *dohri* (double) *tazim*, the Chief rising at their arrival and departure, and the *Huth-ka-kurab*. On the arrival in Darbar of a noble of this rank, the Maharaja stands up. The Sardar places his sword in front of him, bows and touches the hem of the Chief's garment. The Chief acknowledges the salutation by placing his hand on the nobleman's shoulder and drawing it back to his chest.

In the second division are comprised thirty-eight Rahtors and seven Ganayats, who are also entitled to the *dohri tazim*, but instead of the *Hath-ka-kurab* receive only the *Banh pusao*,—that is to say, the Chief after touching the Sardar's shoulder omits to draw his hand back to his chest. Eight Rahtors and five Ganayats receive only the single *tazim*,—that is, the Chief rises on their arrival only.

The *Jagirs* of Marwar are all younger than the State. There is, however, a class of land-holders known as **Bhumias** who differ from the nobles in that they pay a contribution toward the cost of the army (*faujbal*) and are not liable to military service. The *Bhum* tenure prevails throughout Malani and is common in the parganas of Sanchor and Jalor. The chief *Bhumias'* estates were founded before the Rahtor conquest.

In the case of all the *jagir* estates and some of the *Bhumia* holdings succession is by primogeniture. The *jagirdars* pay to the Darbar an annual revenue known as *rekh* which amounts to 8 per cent. of the annual income. Military service is rendered at the rate of one horseman for each thousand rupees of revenue, and one camel or footman for fractions of one thousand rupees exceeding R750 and R500, respectively. In times of emergency the *jagirdars* are bound to serve the Darbar at their own expense with all their followers.

The only hereditary office-bearer of note is the **Thakur of Pokaran**. This nobleman holds the office of *pardhan* by virtue of which he attests all grants of lands and villages made by the Darbar, and is entitled to a seat on the Khawass or behind the Maharaja on an elephant on all state occasions. Two other persons, though not office-bearers, also perform hereditary duties. **The Thakur of Bagri** marks the new Chief on his installation with blood drawn from his own thumb and binds on the Chief's sword, and the **Barath of the village of Mandiar** invokes blessings at the weddings and installation of a Chief, in return for which service he receives from the Darbar a robe of honour and an elephant.

III.—The following nobles are entitled by their position to separate notice :—

Pokaran.

(1) **Thakur Mangal Singh of Pokaran** is a Rahtor of the Champawat sept descended from a brother of Rao Jodha. The family, which was originally settled at Bhinmal, came to Pokaran in the time of Maharaja Abhay Singh. The estate is situated some 80 miles north of Jodhpur and comprises one hundred villages yielding an annual income of about R93,000. Thakur Mangal Singh was a son of the Thakur of Daspan and was adopted by the late Thakur of Pokaran. He is twenty-two years of age, was educated at the Mayo College, has passed the University Entrance Examination, and is now a member of the Maharaja's Council. He succeeded to the estate in 1877. He has two infant sons, Chain Singh and Sukh Singh. As already noticed, this Thakur is the hereditary *Pardhan* of the State.

Nimaj.

(2) **Thakur Chatar Singh of Nimaj**, a descendant of Rao Suja through the latter's son Udai, holds an estate of ten villages situated at about 60 miles south-east of Jodhpur. The estate yields an income of some R36,000. The Thakur is thirty-nine years of age and was adopted by the late Thakur of Nimaj from the connected family of Ramgarh. He succeeded to the estate in 1870, and has one son Prithwi Singh, aged three years. The nearest relations are members of the Ramgarh, Nawara, Saisra, and Agewa families.

Asop.

(3) **Thakur Chain Singh of Asop**, a descendant of Kumpa, a brother of Rao Jodha, holds an estate some 50 miles north-east of Jodhpur, consisting of 4½ villages yielding an

annual revenue of about R30,000. The estate pays as *rekh* to the Darbar about R3,120. Thakur Chain Singh, who is now thirty years of age, is a son of Thakur Daulat Singh of Barnia, having been adopted by his cousin, Thakur Sheonath Singh. He succeeded to the estate in 1873, and is now a member of the State Council. He has one son, Fath Singh, aged eight years, and two uncles, Bherun Singh and Zorawar Singh.

Rian.

(4) **Thakur Bijay Singh of Rian,** a Rahtor of the Mertia clan, holds eight villages yielding an annual income of about R36,000. One village has been assigned for the support of the Thakur's great-uncle Himmat Singh. The Thakur, who is twenty-two years of age, succeeded his father Thakur Ghamir Singh in 1878. He was educated at the Mayo College. He has one brother, Fath Singh, and four uncles, Lachhman Singh, Bhagwat Singh, Mul Singh, and Rirmal Singh. The families of Bikharnia, Bijathal, Dabri, and Khera are closely connected with Rian.

Awa.

(5) **Thakur Shimbhu Singh of Awa,** a Champawat Rahtor, holds an estate of fourteen villages situated 60 miles south-east of Jodhpur and yielding an annual income of about R16,000. The Thakur, who is twenty-four years of age, was educated at the Mayo College and succeeded his father Thakur Devi Singh on the latter's death in 1876. He has one son, Pratap Singh, aged six years, one brother, Sheodan Singh, who has been adopted by the Thakur of Lambian, and one uncle, Ranjit Singh, who has been adopted by the Thakur of Rohat.

Ras.

(6) **Thakur Fath Singh of Ras,** a Rahtor Rajput, descended through Udaiji from Rao Suja, holds an estate of seventeen villages yielding an income of R40,000, situated 70 miles east of Jodhpur. Two villages, with an income of R2,500, have been assigned to uncles of the Thakur. Thakur Fath Singh, who is now (1893) eighteen years of age, succeeded his father Thakur Partap Singh. His father was a member of the Council up to 1868. The Thakur's brother Bhupal Singh is adopted by the Thakur of Agewa. He has also a brother Balwant Singh, a nephew Hanwant Singh, an uncle Hamir Singh, and a cousin Mahtab Singh.

Raipur.

(7) **Thakur Hari Singh of Raipur** is also descended from Rao Udai. He holds an estate of 38½ villages lying 64 miles east of Jodhpur, the annual income of which is about R44,000. Three of the villages have been assigned for the maintenance of brothers of the Thakur, and three to servants of the estate as a reward for good service. Thakur Hari Singh is the nephew and adopted son of the late Thakur Lachhman Singh, whom he succeeded in 1879. He is now twenty-eight years of age. His nearest relations are his natural father Bhabhut Singh who is also his uncle by adoption, his uncle Bane Singh and his cousins Madan Singh, Ram Singh, Gobardan Singh, and Sohan Singh. The families of Rampura and Lilaya are closely connected.

Kherwa.

(8) **Thakur Fath Singh of Kherwa** is a Rahtor Rajput descended from Rao Jodha, the founder of the State. His estate, which comprises eleven villages with an annual income of about R2,000, lies 46 miles south of Jodhpur. Owing to the minority of the proprietor, the management is at present vested in the Court of Wards. Thakur Fath Singh, who is now four years of age, succeeded his father in 1888. The late Thakur, Lachhman Singh, whose services in the Mutiny gained him the title of Rao Bahadur from the British Government, was, like his predecessor, Thakur Sanwant Singh, a member of the State Council. Thakur Fath Singh who has no near relatives, is connected with the families of Balera, Butis, and Babra.

Bhadrajan.

(9) **Thakur Sangram Singh of Bhadrajan** is also a descendant of Rao Jodha. His estate of twenty-seven villages is situated 44 miles south of Jodhpur and yields an income of about R32,000. Five of the villages have been assigned in maintenance, three of them to brothers of the Thakur and two to servants of the family. Thakur Sangram Singh, who is over forty-nine years of age, succeeded his father Thakur Indra Bhan in 1856. His grandfather, Thakur Bakhtawar Singh, was a *Musahib* (Minister) during the reign of Maharaja Man Singh. The present Thakur has one son, Partap Singh, aged thirty years, and no other near relations. His nearest connection is Thakur Sardar Singh of Rama.

Agewa.

(10) **Thakur Bakhtawar Singh of Agewa,** a descendant of Rao Udai, holds three villages 50 miles to the east of Jodhpur, with an annual income of about R18,000. The Thakur, who is

now fifty years of age, succeeded his father Thakur Sheonath Singh in 1844. He has no near relations, but has adopted Bhupal Singh of Ras and is connected with the families of Ras, Nimaj, Morra, and Lambian.

Kantalia.

(11) **Thakur Arjun Singh of Kantalia** is a Kumpawat Rahtor descended from a brother of Rao Jodha. His estate, which consists of twelve villages with an income of about R14,000, lies 60 miles to the south-east of Jodhpur. The Thakur is thirty years of age and succeeded the late Thakur Gordhan Singh by adoption. His original family was that of Dudor. He has no near relatives, but is connected with the Asop and Chandawal families.

Alniawas.

(12) **Thakur Sheo Singh of Alniawas**, is a Mertia Rahtor descended from Duda, brother of Rao Suja. The Alniawas estate comprises four villages 70 miles east of Jodhpur yielding an annual income of about R13,000. The estate, which is embarrassed, is at present under the management of the Darbar. Thakur Sheo Singh, who is now eleven years old, belonged originally to the Jalsu family and succeeded the late Thakur of Alniawas in 1888. He is now at the Mayo College. The Thakur has no near relatives. The *Jagirdars* of Jalsu and Rian are his nearest connections.

The twelve Sardars mentioned above are all **Sarayats** (page 9). None of them holds any estate under the British Government.

Officials.

The following are the most prominent officials in Marwar:—

(1) **Mahta Sardar Singh,** the Diwan of the State and a member of the Council, is fifty-five years of age. He receives a yearly salary of R12,000 and has two villages with an annual income of R4,375. Mahta Sardar Singh succeeded his father Mahta Bijay Singh, Rai Bahadur, on the death of the latter in September 1892. Mahta Bijay Singh, who originally came from Kishangarh in the reign of Maharaja Man Singh, was formerly Hakim of Nagor. He held the office of Diwan in 1851, 1868, 1872, and from 1876 to his death. His good services and ability were recognized by the bestowal on him of the title of Rai Bahadur by the British Government, and of the single *tazim* by his Chief. The latter honour is enjoyed by the present Diwan, whose duties, however, are of a comparatively unimportant character.

(2) **Munshi Hardayal Singh, Rai Bahadur,** is Superintendent of the Sardars' Court, Secretary to the *Musahib Ala*, a member of the Council, and Superintendent of Malani. He receives a yearly salary of R13,200. Munshi Hardayal Singh, who is by caste a Kayastha, was originally an Extra Assistant Commissioner in the Punjab, and has received the single *tazim* and a gold anklet from the Darbar.*

(3) **Kaviraj Murardan,** a member of the Council, and head of the Faujdari (Criminal) Court, is by caste a Cháran and is Court Poet of Marwar. He is now fifty-six years of age and was formerly head of the Diwani (Civil) and subsequently of the Appellate Court. He has received the honour of the single *tazim* from his Chief. He enjoys a grant of two villages and an annual salary in cash of R8,400.

(4) **Joshi Askarn,** member of the Council, was formerly City Kotwal and Kiladar (Chief Constable and Castellan), and subsequently held charge of the old Record Office. He is a Brahman by caste, and is forty-nine years of age. He has received the single *tazim* and holds two villages in addition to his annual salary of R3,600.

(5) **Hanwant Chand, Bhandari,** a member of the Council, is also Superintendent of the Appellate Court. He was formerly Residency Vakil and afterwards Vakil in attendance on the Agent to the Governor-General. Hanwant Chand, who is fifty-five years of age, is by caste a Bhandari. He holds a grant of one village and receives an annual salary of R4,800.

(6) **Mahta Amrit Lal,** a member of the Council and head of the Dewani (Civil) Court, is a Mahajan by caste. He is fifty-seven years of age and has one village in addition to his annual salary of R3,600. This officer's father, who accompanied the late Maharaja Takht Singh from Ahmadnagar, was formerly Diwan of the State.

(7) **Munshi Hira Lal,** a member of the Council, by caste a Kayastha, is fifty-nine years of age. He is hereditary Raj Munshi or *Kharita-navis* (writer of complimentary letters) and formerly held the offices of Vakil with the Agent to the Governor-General and *Munsarim* (Superintendent) of the Sardars' Court.

* Munshi Hardayal Singh was killed, while these pages were in the press, by a fall from his horse.

(8) **Pandit Sukhdeo Prasad**, B.A., is a member of the Council and Judicial Secretary to the *Musahib Ala*. This officer who is twenty-eight years of age is a Kashmiri Pandit. His father was Pandit Sheonarayan, Private Secretary to His Highness the Maharaja.

(9) **Pandit Jivanand**, a Brahman, thirty-eight years of age, is Assistant Superintendent of the Court of Sardars and was formerly Private Secretary to His Highness the Maharaja of Mandi.

(10) **Munshi Kishori Lal, Rai Bahadur**, Superintendent of Police, a Kayastha by caste, aged forty-two years, was formerly an Inspector of Police in the Ajmere District. He received the title of Rai Bahadur on the 1st January 1892.

BIKANIR.

Chief.

The Chief of the Bikanir State is **His Highness Maharaja Raj Rajeshwar Saroman Sri Ganga Singh Bahadur.** His Highness, who was born at Bikanir on the 13th October 1880, is a Rahtor Rajput and is the adopted son of his elder half-brother, the late Maharaja Dungar Singh. The natural father of both the late and present Chiefs was Maharaj Lal Singh, a descendant of Maharaja Gaj Singh who ruled Bikanir from A. D. 1745 to 1788. The eldest branch and a younger branch of Maharaja Gaj Singh's descendants occupied the *gadi* until the death of Maharaja Sardar Singh, the immediate predecessor and adoptive father of Maharaja Dungar Singh. Maharaja Ganga Singh succeeded to the Chiefship on the 31st August 1887. The Chief, who is betrothed to a daughter of His Highness the Maharana of

Relatives.

Udaipur, is unmarried and his nearest relations are his second cousins, the descendants of Maharaj Dalel Singh, a grandson of Maharaja Gaj Singh. Their relationship stands thus—

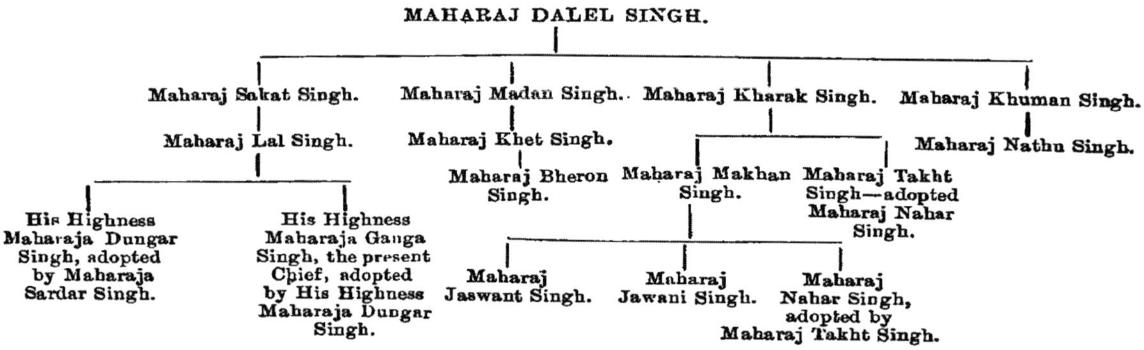

After these the nearest relatives are descendants of Maharaja Gaj Singh through other lines. These are numerous. The present Chief is the fourteenth in descent from Rao Bika, the founder of the State, and the fifteenth in descent from Rao Jodha of Jodhpur, and is the twenty-

Marriages.

first occupant of the Bikanir *gadi.* The only important connections by marriage which have been formed in recent times by the ruling family are those with Udaipur, Alwar, Kachh-Bhuj, Partabgarh, and Rewa. Intermarriages between the Meywar and Bikanir ruling houses have been frequent in the past. The first on record was that of Rao Lunkaran, Rao Bika's successor, with a daughter of Rana Rai Mal, and the last that of Maharana Sardar Singh of Udaipur with a sister of Maharaja Ratn Singh, which took place in 1839. Maharaja Sardar Singh in 1855 married a princess of Alwar, the daughter of Maharao Raja Bani Singh of that State. In the year 1876 Maharaja Dungar Singh married a princess of Kachh, a sister of the present Maharao. In 1832 Maharaja Sardar Singh married a daughter of the Maharawat of Partabgarh and in 1836 he married a niece of the Maharaja of Rewa. In former times also several marriages took place with Jaipur and Jaisalmer. No lady of the Bikanir house has married into Jaisalmer since the reign of Maharaja Sur Singh (1613—1631), who in consequence of the murder by the Bhatis of a son of his niece, the wife of Rawal Bhim, swore that no Bikanir princess should again go to Jaisalmer. This oath has been considered as binding by all his successors. The following is a brief abstract of the pedigree of the ruling family since the days of Rao Jodha :—

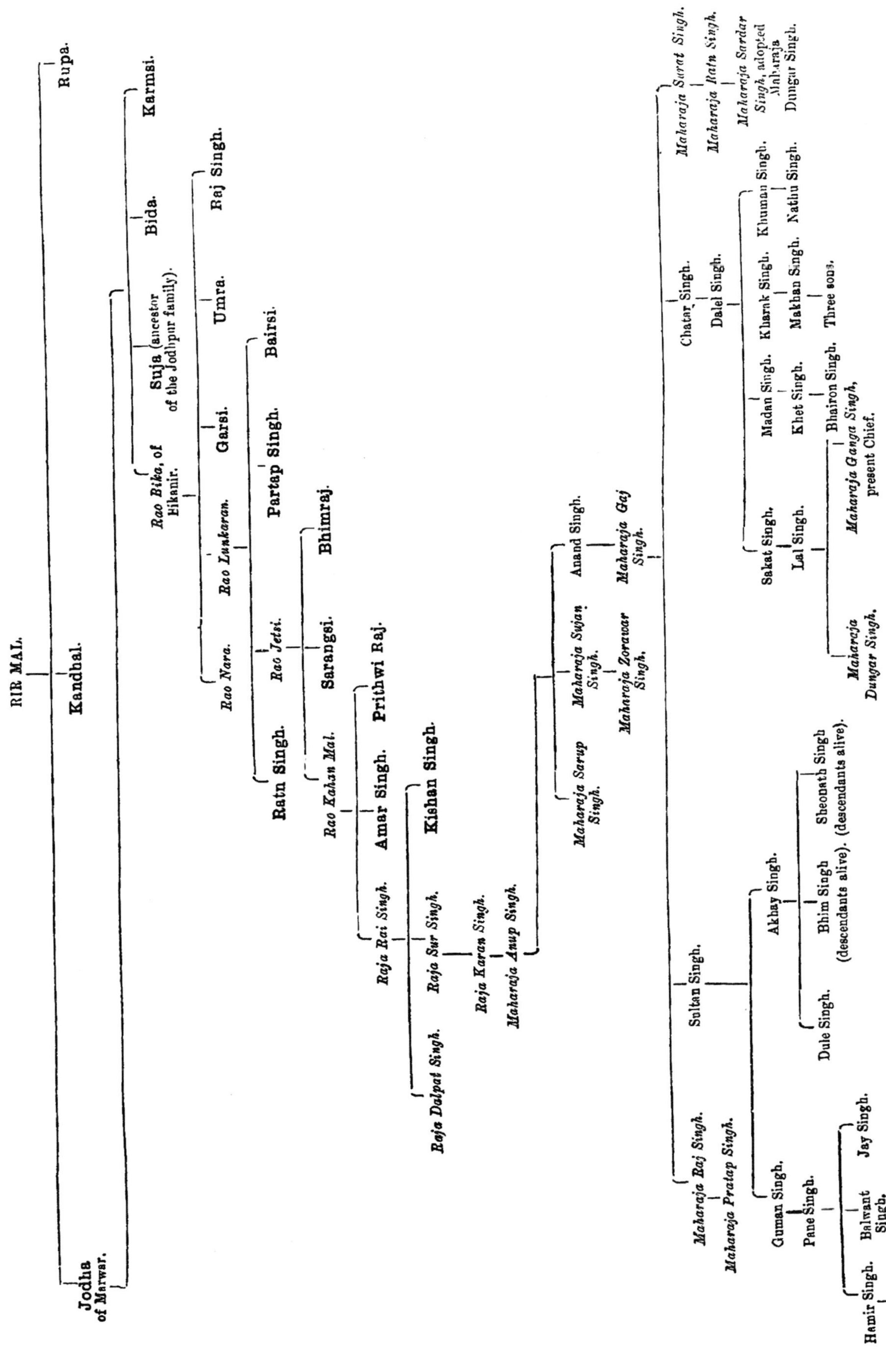

NOTE.—The names in italics are those of Ruling Chiefs | The names in antique are those of persons whose descendants are numerous and of some importance in the State.

Historical outline.

The conquest of the State was commenced in 1465 by Bika, son of Rao Jodha of Marwar, and was carried out mainly by him, his brother Bida, and his uncle Kandhal. Rao Bika founded Bikanir city in 1465. Owing to combinations formed against them by disaffected Thakurs and external enemies, Bika's immediate successors had, until Rao Kalyan Singh succeeded to the *gadi* in 1541, much difficulty in keeping their hold on the territory which he had overrun. Kalyan Singh's efforts to consolidate his dominions were successful, and he left the State in good order to his son Rao Rai Singh. This Chief realized the advantage which would accrue to him from securing the support of the rulers of Delhi, and accordingly did homage at Ajmer to the Emperor Akbar by whom he was employed in Gujarat and the Dakhan. In return for his services he received the title of Raja and a grant of fifty *parganas* in which were comprised not only the whole of the present Bikanir State, but certain territories which are now included in Jodhpur and the Punjab, as well as a *jagir* in Gujarat. His grandson and great-grandson Raja Karn Singh (A. D. 1631—1669) and Raja Anup Singh (A. D. 1669—1698) were also generals of note. The former was long employed in the Dakhan, where he died and where he received from the Mughals the grant of a *jagir* situated in what is now the Nizam's territory. This *jagir* is still held by the Bikanir Chiefs. The title of Maharaja was conferred on Anup Singh by the Emperor Aurangzeb in recognition of the services rendered by him at the siege of Golconda. The present titles of the Bikanir Chiefs were conferred by the Emperor Shah Alam on Maharaja Gaj Singh in 1752.

The first intercourse that is known to have taken place between the British Government and Bikanir occurred in 1808, when Maharaja Surat Singh applied for protection against attacks from Jodhpur. This request was refused, but a prayer for help was granted in 1818 on the occurrence of an insurrection headed by the Thakur of Churu and supported from outside. A formal treaty was then signed with the government of the Marquess of Hastings by which the integrity of Bikanir was guaranteed and the Chief undertook to act in subordinate co-operation with the British Government and to form no connection with other Chiefs or States. Since that time, though there have been occasional internal difficulties, external troubles have ceased. During the Mutiny of 1857 the State rendered loyal service to the Supreme Government and was rewarded in 1861 by the transfer to it from the Sirsa district of the *pargana* of Tibi of which the Darbar had previously claimed possession.

Maharaja Surat Singh took his seat on the *gadi* in the year 1787 and was succeeded in 1831 by his eldest son Maharaja Ratn Singh who died in 1852. His son and successor Maharaja Sardar Singh ruled till his death in 1872, when he was succeeded by his adopted son Maharaja Dungar Singh. The present Chief is the adopted son of Maharaja Dungar Singh.

Leading men.

Hereditary nobles.

The leading men of the State are either hereditary nobles, hereditary office-bearers, or recently-imported officials. Of these the first class falls into four divisions: (1) descendants of families which were in Bikanir before the Rahtor invasion at the end of the fifteenth century; (2) descendants of Bika the first Chief, or of one of his uncles or brothers; (3) descendants of later Chiefs; and (4) descendants of persons related by marriage to former Chiefs. The western and northern portions of the State were held at the arrival of the Rahtors by Bhatis, who had wrested them in former times from the Pramars or Puars. There are at present some families of Puar Rajputs in the State, but these are of later origin and not of much importance. The older families are all extinct. One of the first acts of Rao Bika was to secure the neutrality of the Bhatis by marrying the daughter of their leading Chief, Rao Shaikha of Pungal. The Bhatis were subsequently stripped of a great portion of their possessions including the stronghold of Bhatner. They now hold only fifty-nine villages, of which thirty-one belong to the **Rao of Pungal**. The other leading Bhatis are the **Thakur of Bithnok**, the **Rao of Jaimalser**, and the **Thakurs of Kharbara and Satasar**, but none of them has much influence. A daughter of the late Thakur of Satasar was married to Maharaja Dungar Singh and is now the senior Maharani. The largest estates are at present in the hands of members of the second and third divisions, namely descendants of Rao Bika, of his uncles or his brothers or of subsequent Chiefs. The most important of them is the **Thakur of Mahajan**, a descendant of Ratn Singh, a son of Roo Lunkaran. Next to him come the **Rawat of Rawatsar**, who is descended from Rao Bika's uncle Kandhal, and the **Thakur of Bhukarka**, a descendant of Rao Jetsi, who hold respectively twenty-seven and twenty-eight villages. These, together with the **Thakur of Bidasar,** are known as *Sarayats* from the place near the staircase which they occupy in Darbar. The next largest estates are those of **Jasana, Sidhmukh,** and **Ajitpura,** with twenty-five, eighteen, and sixteen villages respectively held by the Sarangot descendants of Rao Jetsi; **Sankhu,** with twenty-four villages held by Kishen Singhot descendants of Raja Rai Singh; and **Rajpura,** with nineteen villages of which the Thakur is descended from Rao Jetsi through the latter's son Bhim Raj. The descendants of Rao Bika's brother Bida, known as **Bidawats,** hold what is termed the Bidahad territory near Sujangarh, which formerly belonged to the Mohel Rajputs. None of their estates are of great extent, the largest, Bidasar, comprising only twelve villages; but owing to their compact situation and to the strong family feeling which has generally prevailed among their owners, they form in the aggregate a body which has till recently been fairly able to hold its own against oppressions on the part of the Darbar. At the beginning of the present century the principal land-holders of the State were the **Thakur of Mahajan** who, though shorn of a considerable portion of his possessions, is still the premier noble of Bikanir, and the **Thakurs of Bahadaran and Churu.** The two latter were descendants of Kandhal of the Banirot and Saindasot lines, and their estates consisted of about a hundred villages and eighty villages respectively. The Banirots were expelled from Bahadaran by Maharaja Surat Singh in 1818, and the Saindasots from Churu by Maharaja Sardar Singh in 1854 after long-continued struggles with the Darbar. The heads of both families received a few villages by way of maintenance, and are still looked up to as persons of importance. In the third division also are comprised the descendants of Maharaja Gaj Singh, who are known as **Rajwis** and hold some twenty-two villages. These persons are very numerous and their rank entitles them to notice, but they are greatly hampered by debt and are not of any political importance. The most noteworthy of them in recent years was Maharaj Lal Singh, who was for some time President of Maharaja Dungar Singh's Council and, who was the father of that Chief and of his brother, the present Chief. About thirty villages are held by members of the fourth division who are known as **parsangis.** These are also individually unimportant.

The hereditary nobles are distinguished among themselves by their respective positions in Darbar and by the possession of the greater or lesser *tazim*, eighty-three enjoying the latter and twenty-eight the former honour. Succession among the *Tazimi Pattadars** is by primogeniture and, though in some branches partition used to take place, this is no longer the case. As a rule, a grant of villages or of land for cultivation is made to the younger sons. Some villages, and especially those held by Rajwis, are exempt from the payment of revenue. The rest pay revenue which varies in amount in different estates, but is generally about one-third of the income. Originally this liability took the form of providing fighting men for the Chiefs,—cavalry in the case of the larger estates, and camelmen or footmen in that of the smaller. The obligation has now in all cases been commuted for a money payment. All *pattadars* on succeeding to their estates pay one year's revenue as *nazarana* (fee on succession) to the Darbar. They also pay *neota* on a change in the Chiefship, as well as various other occasional charges. In return they receive from the Darbar presents (*rijbakhshish*) when marriages and funerals take place in their own families. Both the *neota* and *rijbakhshish* were till recently of uncertain amount, depending on the pleasure of the Chief and the strength of the Thakur. On the accession of the present Chief, the Council of Regency found it necessary to lay down a definite scale in both cases for its own guidance during the minority. What has been said above in regard to the Pungal, Mahajan, Churu, and Bahadaran estates shows how the Darbar has in the course of continued struggles with the leading nobles strengthened its own position and weakened theirs. Colonel Powlett in his Gazetteer has expressed his opinion that there is no State in Rajputana in which the old feudal tenure has so nearly passed away and the power of the Chief is so absolute as in Bikanir. It has thus come about that no single noble is in a position to resist or even very seriously trouble the Darbar, though as lately as 1884 a combination of several rendered it necessary to send a brigade from Nasirabad to restore order. None of the nobles of Bikanir holds any estate from the British Government.

Hereditary office-bearers.

The hereditary office-bearers are the descendants of the men who accompanied Rao Bika from Jodhpur or of those who were introduced by subsequent Chiefs. Rao Bika's principal

* The grant by which an estate is held is termed a *patta*, and the grantee is styled a *pattadar*.

companions were Mahta Lal Singh and Lakhani Baid, Bar Singh Bachawat, Baga Mushraf, Gopal Bararia, Salaji Rathi, Napa Sankhla, and Bela Parihar. The Baids have frequently held the highest offices in the State, such as those of Diwan and Vakil, and have received much honour from the Darbar. Thakursi Baid was Diwan in the time of Raja Rai Singh and was subsequently Governor of Bhatner fort. His descendant Hindu Mal was Vakil at Delhi in 1833 and received from Maharaja Ratn Singh the title of Maharao which is still held by the head of the family. Members of the family held the office of Diwan under Maharajas Ratn Singh, Surat Singh, Sardar Singh, and Dungar Singh.

The descendauts of Bar Singh Bachawat rose to considerable importance, but were exterminated by Raja Sur Singh (1613—1631) with the exception of one boy, who was absent with his mother's family at Udaipur. From him is descended Mahta Rai Panna Lal, C.I.E., Diwan of Meywar. (See page 36.)

The descendants of Baga Mushraf still hold the office of *Mushraf* or head of the stables. Of the Bararias several are still living and are considered to have a claim to employment. One of them is now Darogha of the *Modi-khana* (Commissariat). Salaji Rathi's descendants hold at present several minor posts. One held the office of *Lekhan* (writer of grants) under Raja Rai Singh, and his son Kalyan Das was Diwan to Raja Sur Singh. Mahta Makan Rai of the same family was Diwan to Maharaja Anup Singh, and Ram Lal Dwarkani to Maharaja Sardar Singh. The descendants of Napa Sankla held the post of *Kiladar* (Castellan) of Bikanir till the time of Raja Sur Singh whose displeasure they incurred. Many of them were killed and the rest fled to Marwar. Bela Parihar was the founder of a numerous family, of which two branches have been continuously employed, the first in the care of the Raj horses and the other in personal attendance on the Chiefs. They are known as Sahnis and Parihars respectively.

When Raja Rai Singh went to Jaisalmer in 1595 to marry the daughter of the Rawal, he brought back with him two officials of note, Karamsi Rakhicha, whom he placed in charge of his wardrobe and jewellery, and Kallaji Tosniwal Kothiari. To the former family belonged Madan Chand, Diwan to Maharaja Ratn Singh, and Lachi Ram and his sons Man Mal and Gyan Mal, who were all Diwans to Maharaja Sardar Siugh on several occasions. A son of the last-named, Mahta Mangal Chand, is at present a member of the Council of Regency. Kallaji was an inhabitant of Nagor and was placed on his arrival in Bikanir in charge of the fixed establishments (*Karkhanajat*).

Raja Sur Singh on his return from his marriage at Phalodi was accompanied by Urja Kolhar and Sidhayach Kishnaji. The former of these was placed in charge of the Raj *Daftar* or Secretariat and his descendants are considered to have a claim to service. To the latter was assigned the care of the library which is one of some celebrity. His descendants hold villages in the State. The title of *Kaviraj* (or Court Poet) was conferred on them by Maharaja Sardar Singh, who also granted them the honour of the greater *tazim*. Since the arrival of the family in the State the compilation of the annals of Bikanir has been entrusted to them. The principal source of information in all matters relating to Bikanir history is the *kayant* composed by Dayal Das who died recently at a very advanced age.

Raja Karn Singh married a lady from Rampur, and brought with him Khianji Rampuria to whom was entrusted the duty of copying all State grants. This duty is still performed by his descendants.

With Maharaja Anup Singh came the ancestor of the present hereditary copyists of *kharitas* or complimentary letters, and of the Darbar Treasurer. Other minor officials are descended from persons who were brought into the State by Maharajas Gaj Singh and Surat Singh.

Of the new officials of the State the most important have been lent by the British Government or have been introduced during the minority of the present Chief.

The account of the hereditary nobles given in the preceding paragraphs has shown that no single member of this class is now of very great importance. The following may, however, be mentioned :—

Individual nobles.

Mahajan.

(1) **Thakur Hari Singh of Mahajan**, a Rahtor Rajput of the Ratn Singhot family of the Bikawat clan, is the premier noble of Bikanir. His estate, which lies in the northern portion of the Lunkarnsar *pargana*, consists of ninety-seven villages, of which the estimated annual value is R64,000.* It pays a yearly revenue

* The incomes of the pattadars are roughly estimated and cannot be relied upon as accurate.

to the State of ₹15,257. The present Thakur, Hari Singh, is seventeen years of age and is being educated at the Mayo College, Ajmer. The last Thakur but one, Amar Singh, was suspected of being concerned in a supposed attempt to poison Maharaja Dungar Singh in 1874 and was deposed by the Darbar, the estate being made over to his eldest son, Ram Singh. Thakur Ram Singh, who received and afterwards forfeited the title of Rao Raja, held the estate till 1883, when he was removed and banished under the orders of the Government of India for his share in the revolt against the Chief which took place in that year. Being childless Thakur Ram Singh was allowed to adopt his brother Sheonath Singh's son, Hari Singh, the present Thakur. Thakur Ram Singh, who resided during his banishment with his sister's husband, His Highness the late Maharawal Bairi Sal of Jaisalmer, was allowed to return to Bikanir in 1888, but is obliged to live at the capital. Thakur Hari Singh's nearest relatives are his adoptive father Thakur Ram Singh, his real father Thakur Sheonath Singh, and his uncles Thakurs Bakhtawar Singh and Bhupal Singh. The last named was for a time Commandant of the Imperial Service Troops of the State. The estate is under the management of the Court of Wards.

Rawatsar.

(2) **Rawat Man Singh of Rawatsar** is a Rahtor Rajput of the Kandhlot clan descended from Kandhal, uncle of Rao Bika and brother of Rao Jodha of Jodhpur. His estate consists of twenty-eight villages and lies to the west of the Nuhar Tahsil. The annual income is about ₹30,000, and the revenue payable to the Darbar is ₹10,481. The estate with the title of Rawat was conferred on Raghu Das for his services in the Dakhan and Gujarat with Raja Rai Singh. The late Rawat, who was sixteenth in descent from Kandhal, was the son of Rawat Ranjit Singh, who died in 1885. He died recently (1893) at the age of about twenty-two years and was succeeded after a short interval by his posthumous son Man Singh. The estate is under the management of the Court of Wards.

Bhukarka.

(3) **Thakur Nathu Singh of Bhukarka,** a Rahtor Rajput of the Sarangot family of the Bikawat clan, holds an estate consisting of thirty-three villages in the north of the Nuhar Tehsil. The estimated income of the estate is ₹24,700 and the revenue payable to the Darbar is ₹8,401. The Thakur is about fifty-four years of age. He succeeded his father Thakur Khet Singh in 1874. The estate is said to have been originally conferred by Raja Rai Singh on Sarang, the ancestor of the family, in recognition of the good advice which he gave to his Chief to fight under Akbar in Kashmir where Raja Rai Singh rendered conspicuous service. Subsequently in 1735 Thakur Kishan Singh was instrumental in helping Maharaja Zorawar Singh to repel an attack from the Chiefs of Jodhpur and Nagor. The present Thakur has one son, Kan Singh.

Bidasar.

(4) **Thakur Hukm Singh of Bidasar,** a Rahtor Rajput of the Keshodasot family of the Bidawat clan, is the head of the descendants of Bida. His estate, which consists of twelve villages only, is situated near Sujangarh in the region which formerly belonged to the Mohel Rajputs and is now known as the Bidahad. The estate, which pays ₹5,570 as revenue to the Darbar, has an annual income of about ₹13,000. The present Thakur, Hukm Singh, is fifteen years of age and is being educated at the Mayo College. He succeeded his father Thakur Bahadur Singh in 1883, the latter having been deposed for his share in the coalition against the Darbar which took place in that year. Thakur Bahadur Singh, who is a man of much intelligence, lived in banishment at Deoli until 1888, since which time he has been permitted to reside in Bikanir. He holds no paid office, but performs several useful honorary duties, especially in connection with the "Walter Krit Rajputra Hit Karini Sabha."* The estate is under the management of the Court of Wards.

Pungal.

(5) **Rao Mahtab Singh of Pungal** is a Bhati Rajput of the Pungaliya clan and is descended from Rao Shaikha, who, as noticed above, was in possession of all the western portion of the State when the Rahtor invasion took place, and whose daughter Rao Bika married. The estate which is situated on the borders of Jaisalmer and Bahawalpur now consists of thirty-one villages and yields an annual income of about ₹22,000. It pays no revenue to the Darbar. The present Rao, a young man of about twenty-six years of age, is a son of the Thakur of Karnisar, a junior branch of the Pungal family. He was adopted by the late Rao Raghunath Singh,

* Since this was written Thakur Bahadur Singh has been appointed a member of the Council of Regency.

who died in 1890, and who though he never occupied any prominent position in the State, was much respected.

Churu.

(6) **Thakur Lal Singh of Churu** is a Rahtor Rajput of the Saindasot family of the Kandhlot clan. As already mentioned, the Churu estate was formerly one of the three most important in Bikanir and consisted of about eighty villages. The heads of the house were generally in opposition to the Darbar which, owing to their distance from head-quarters, was not in a position to control them effectively. The late Thakur was finally reduced to subjection in 1856 and was deprived of his estate, five villages being given to him for maintenance. The income of these is small and they are not liable to payment of revenue. The present Thakur is about forty-seven years of age and much respected. He has been a member of the Council of Regency since 1890. He has three sons. His first cousin, Thakur Pane Singh of Buchawas, is Superintendent of the *Girai* or Police Department.

Sandwa.

(7) **Thakur Moti Singh of Sandwa,** a Rahtor Rajput of the Manohar Dasot family of the Bidawat clan, has an estate consisting of ten villages which yield an annual income of about R12,500. The revenue payable to the Darbar is R4,300 a year. Thakur Moti Singh succeeded his adoptive father Thakur Hir Singh in 1892. The late Thakur was implicated in the disturbance of 1883 and his fort was demolished. He was subsequently allowed to rebuild it. At the time of his death he was a member of the Council of Regency.

Bae.

(8) **Thakur Jagmal Singh of Bae,** a Rahtor Rajput of the Sarangot family of the Bikawat clan, holds an estate of fifteen villages which yields an income of about R22,550 and pays an annual revenue of R7,201. The estate is situated in the north-eastern portion of the State between Sardarshahr and Bahadaran. The *pattadar* was appointed a member of the Council of Regency on the accession of the present Chief and held that post till his resignation in 1890.

(9) **Thakur Jiwraj Singh,** a Tanwar Rajput, holds four and a half villages, chiefly in the Dungargarh Tahsil, which yield a revenue of about R7,500 and pay no revenue to the Darbar. This Thakur was the uncle (mother's brother) of the late Chief, Maharaja Dungar Singh, and so became a person of some prominence. His daughter has recently been married to His Highness the Maharaja of Jaipur. (See page 72.)

Of the **Rajwis** no single individual calls for special notice. The head of the family by seniority is Maharaj Pane Singh, a great-grandson of Maharaja Gaj Singh. This Chief left a number of sons, and at his death the eldest, Maharaja Raj Singh, succeeded him. After the funeral rites had been performed, some of the other brothers, including the second, Sultan Singh, who had recently tried to capture Raj Singh, fled. Maharaja Raj Singh died ten days later and was succeeded by his son Pratap Singh, a boy of six years of age. Surat Singh, Maharaja Raj Singh's third brother, managed the affairs of the State and very shortly afterwards on the death of Maharaja Pratap Singh in 1787 established himself on the *gadi*. His elder brother of the whole-blood, Chatar Singh, made no objection. The Chiefship remained in this line till the death of Maharaja Sardar Singh, who adopted Maharaja Dungar Singh, a descendant of Maharaja Gaj Singh's third son, Chatar Singh. The children of the elder branch, descendants of Sultan Singh, have thus remained excluded from the succession. Sultan Singh himself after leaving Bikanir fled to Udaipur, where he died, leaving two sons, Guman Singh and Akhay Singh. These subsequently came to Bikanir and received a revenue-free grant of villages.

Individual office-bearers.

Of the hereditary office-bearers the most important is (1) **Mahta Mangal Chand,*** a son of Man Mal and grandson of Lachhi Ram Rakhicha, both of whom were Diwans to Maharaja Sardar Singh. Mahta Mangal Chand is now about thirty-seven years of age. He was formerly a member of the Council of Maharaja Dungar Singh and on the constitution of the Council of Regency he was appointed a member of it, a position which he still holds. Of the **Baid** family the only one who holds office at present is (2) **Maharao Sawai Singh,** who is in charge

* Mahta Mangal Chand died on the 11th February 1894, while this work was in the press.

of the wardrobe and *toshakhana* (treasure house).* The other leading members of the family are (3) **Rao Chatar Singh** and (4) **Mahta Abhay Singh**. The following persons among others who are now holding office belong to families which are considered to have a claim to employment: (5) **Dalu Ram Modi**, head of the Accounts Department; (6) **Kaviraj Bheron Dan**, Commandant of the Army (formerly a member of the Council of Regency); (7) **Man Mal Kochar**, Tahsildar of Sardarshahr; (8) **Lakshmi Chand Kochar**, Vakil at Jaipur; (9) **Indraj Mal Kochar**, Tahsildar of Lunkarnsar; (10) **Dharm Chand Mushraf**, head of the stables; (11) **Jethmal Sahni**; (12) **Sugan Chand Kothiari**; (13) **Amba Dan Charan**, son of Dayal Das, author of the *Kiyant;* (14) **Tej Karn Rampuria**; (15) **Sugan Chand Mahta**; and (16) **Man Singh Mahta**.

New officials.

Of the new officials it will suffice to notice the following:—

(1) **Sodhi Hukm Singh, Rai Bahadur**, a *Jagirdar* of the Punjab, Vice-President of the Council of Regency. This gentleman, who had been in Government employ since 1866, had been Mir Munshi to the Lieutenant-Governor of the Punjab from June 1875 to May 1886 and had been an Extra Assistant Commissioner in that Province since 1873, was on the 14th December 1888 appointed, on the recommendation of Sir James Lyall, Vice-President of the Council. He received the title of Rai Bahadur on the 1st January 1893.

(2) **Munshi Sohan Lal, Rai Sahib**, Additional Member of the Council and Revenue Officer, served in various capacities under the Government of the Punjab from 1861—1884, at the end of which period he was Deputy Superintendent of Settlement in Jalandhar. He was appointed Revenue Officer in Bikanir on the 1st April 1884 and Additional Member of the Council on the 14th July 1888. The title of Rai Sahib was conferred on him on the 24th May 1893.

(3) **Kazi Hamidulla** was from 1855 to 1857 employed in the Ambala Settlement and was afterwards a Munshi in the Bhartpur Political Agency. In 1859 he came to Bikanir on the invitation of Maharaja Sardar Singh. He subsequently filled the offices of Vakil at Jodhpur and Abu, of Criminal Judge and of Nazim, and was eventually appointed a Member of the Appellate Court on the 26th December 1887.

(4) **Seth Milap Chand**, son of Multan Chand, Oswal, of Ajmere, was employed from 1859 to 1866 in various capacities in the Alwar State. After that he served for two years in the Department of Revenue arrears in the Kotah State, was subsequently Gumashta to Rai Bahādur Seth Mul Chand of Ajmer. He came to the Bikanir State in 1883 as Customs Officer, and was a Member of the Council of His Highness the Maharaja from 1884 to 1887 as well as Officer of Accounts. In 1887 he was reappointed as Customs Officer.

(5) **Seth Nemi Chand**, brother to Seth Milap Chand, was Civil Judge in Bikanir from the 15th April 1884 to the 1st April 1886, when he was appointed Customs Officer. In the following year he was appointed Officer of Accounts. In August 1891 he was transferred as Nazim to Suratgarh. Seth Nemi Chand was a member of the Council of Regency from the 9th September to the 26th November 1887.

(6) **Thakur Chiman Singh**, son of Thakur Shimbhu Singh, formerly a member of the Jaipur Council, and nephew of Thakur Fath Singh of Naila, some time Diwan of Jaipur, was appointed head of the Fixed Establishments on the 18th December 1890. (See page 79.)

(7) **Pandit Ram Chandra Dube**, an inhabitant of Benares, educated at the Government College, Benares, was from 1881 to 1887 a Sanskrit teacher in the Government College at Ajmer, and was appointed on the 14th November 1887 to be tutor to the Maharaja of Bikanir. He subsequently received the additional title of Assistant Guardian to His Highness.

(8) **Munshi Muhammad Ikbal Husain**, a native of Delhi, was appointed Mir Munshi in the Loharu State in 1858 and was subsequently Vakil for that State at Hisar. In November 1868 he took service in Bikanir, where he has held various appointments. In March 1884 he was appointed Vakil with the Agent to the Governor-General at Abu.

(9) **Lala Ganda Mal**, a *Jagirdar* of the Punjab, son of Diwan Ranpat Rai of Sohdra, became a Tahsildar in the Punjab in the year 1890 and was on the recommendation of His Honour the Lieutenant-Governor appointed Sadr Nazim in Bikanir on the 7th April 1891.

* On the death of Mahta Mangal Chand, Maharao Sawai Singh was appointed a member of the Council of Regency. He took his seat in March 1894.

(10) **Lala Narain Das** was employed on settlement work in the Punjab from June 1863 to September 1885 and was finally a Deputy Superintendent of Settlement. He officiated as a Superintendent on two occasions. His services were lent to the Bikanir State in September 1885, when he was appointed Nazim of Suratgarh. Since that time he has held various appointments as Nazim and is now posted at Reni.*

(11) **Babu Gulab Singh** was employed as Second Clerk in the Alwar Political Agency from 1870 to 1875 and as Head Clerk till 1879, when he became Kamdar of Nimrana. After holding this appointment for eight years he took service in the Bikanir State, where he was appointed Nazim of Sujangarh. He is now Nazim of Suratgarh.

KISHANGARH.

The Chief.

The Chief of the Kishangarh State is **His Highness Maharaj Adhiraj Maharaja Sir Sardul Singh Bahadur, G.C.I.E.** The Maharaja is a Rahtor Rajput and a descendant of the conqueror of the State and the founder of the city of Kishangarh, Kishen Singh, the second son of Maharaja Udai Singh (1583—1594) of Jodhpur. The State was confirmed to Kishen Singh by the Emperor Akbar in 1594. The present Chief who was born on the 10th December 1857 succeeded his father, the late Maharaja Prithwi Singh, on the 10th January 1880. The Maharaja is by religion a Hindu of the Ballabhkul Vaishnav sect. He married in 1870 the eldest daughter of Rao Ummed Singh of Sirohi and has one son, the heir-apparent **Maharaj Kunwar Madan Singh,** born on the 2nd November 1884. His Highness has two brothers, **Maharaj Jawani Singh** and **Maharaj Raghunath Singh,** and no other near relations. The Thakurs of Fathgarh and Ralaota are distant relatives, being descended from former Chiefs of the State.

The Chiefships allied to Kishangarh by consanguinity are Jodhpur, Bikanir, Ratlam, Jhabua, Sailana, Sitamau, and Idar. Marriages have taken place between the Kishangarh family and the Sesodia houses of Udaipur and Partabgarh, the Kachhwaha houses of Jaipur and Alwar, the Hara houses of Bundi and Kotah, the Bhatis of Jaisalmer, the Jhalas, and the Shaikhawats. The Maharaja's grandmother, widow of Maharaja Mohkam Singh, was daughter of Maharaj Kunwar Amar Singh of Udaipur, and his eldest sister was married to the late Maharana Sajan Singh. The second sister was married to the late Maharaja Mangal Singh of Alwar, the third sister is the wife of the present Maharaja of Jaipur, and the husband of the fourth is the Maharaj Rana of Jhalawar. The Maharaj Kunwar of Kishangarh is betrothed to the fourth daughter of the present Chief of Udaipur, and a niece of the Maharaja is betrothed to the younger brother of the Maharao Raja of Bundi. Maharaja Sardul Singh's mother was a daughter of the late Raja Dhiraj Madho Singh of Shahpura.

* The services of this officer have recently been replaced at the disposal of the Government of the Punjab.

The following table shows the Chiefs of the Kishangarh family from its commencement:—

MAHARAJA KISHEN SINGH (1597—1615).

- **Maharaja Sahasmal** (1615-18).
  - **Maharaja Jagmal Singh** (1618-28).
  - **Maharaja Hari Singh** (1628-43).
    - **Maharaja Rup Singh** (1643-58).
      - **Maharaja Man Singh** (1658—1706).
        - **Maharaja Raj Singh** (1706-48).
          - **Maharaja Sawant Singh** (1748-64).
            - **Maharaja Sardar Singh** (1764-66).
              - **Maharaja Birad Singh** (1766-88).
                - **Maharaja Partap Singh** (1788-97).
                  - **Maharaja Kalyan Singh** (1797—1838).
                    - **Maharaja Mohkam Singh** (1838-40).
                      - **Maharaja Prithwi Singh** (1841-79) (adopted from the Fathgarh family).
                        - **Maharaja Sardul Singh,** the present Chief (succeeded 1880).
          - Bahadur Singh (1764-81).
            - Birad Singh (adopted by **Maharaja Sardar Singh**).
          - Bir Singh (Ralaota family).
- Bharmal.
  - Rup Singh (adopted by **Maharaja Hari Singh**).

The first treaty with the British Government was made in the year 1818 by Maharaja Kalyan Singh.

Leading men.

The leading men of the State fall into three divisions—(1) the **Rajwis** and hereditary nobles, (2) the hereditary office-bearers, and (3) the non-hereditary officials.

Hereditary nobles.

Of the first division the principal are the **Rajwis**, the descendants respectively of Maharaja Prithwi Singh (the brothers of the ruling Chief), of Maharaja Bahadur Singh (the Fathgarh family), and of Maharaja Raj Singh (the Ralaota family). After the Rajwis come a number of families of which the following are the chief:—

(1) Bhuptots * and (2) Sakatsinghots,† descended from Bhupat and Sakat Singh, brothers of Maharaja Kishen Singh; (3) Jagannathots,‡ descended from the family of Parbatsar in Marwar; (4) and (5) Govindasots § and Ratnots, || descended from grandsons of Maharaja Udai Singh of Jodhpur; (6) Karmsots, ¶ descended from a son of Rao Jodha of Jodhpur; and (7) Chandawats.**

Among these the Rajwis take the first place and after them nine nobles known as the **nau**, *viz.*, the Thakurs of Naraina, Chosla, Kotri, Bhambolao, Pandarwara, Gothiana, the senior Thakur of Sinodia, and the Thakurs of Khatoli and Raghunathpura. With the exception of the Rajwis, none of the nobles hold large estates or are men of much note.

In the case of all the noble families succession is by primogeniture, suitable provision being made for the maintenance of the younger sons. Service is rendered to the Darbar by the **Jagirdars** who generally pay no other revenue.

The following are the leading nobles of Kishangarh:—

Karkheri.

(1) **Maharaj Jawani Singh of Karkheri,** own brother to His Highness the Maharaja, holds an estate of eight villages, of which two are alienated, with an estimated income of R30,000. The estate was conferred on him by his father Maharaja Prithwi Singh in 1878. Maharaj Jawani Singh is thirty-two years of age, has received a good education, and is the author of several vernacular poems. He has no son and his nearest relatives are his brothers.

Dhasuk.

(2) **Maharaj Raghunath Singh of Dhasuk,** the Chief's second brother, holds an estate of six villages, with an estimated income of R20,000, of which, however, R8,500 are enjoyed by the Thakurani and subordinate *Jagirdars*. The Thakur, who is nineteen years of age, has received a fair vernacular education. He has no sons.

Fathgarh.

(3) **Maharaj Man Singh of Fathgarh,** a descendant of Maharaja Bahadur Singh (1748—1781), is one of the most important nobles of the State. He holds eighteen villages, with an annual income of R50,000, of which more than half is alienated. The Maharaj is nineteen years of age and succeeded his adoptive father, Maharaj Govardhan Singh, his second cousin by blood, in 1883. He was educated at the Mayo College and has no sons or other relatives nearer than the Rajwis of Dhos, Zorawarpura and Kucholia who are descended from his great-great-great-grandfather.

Ralaota.

(4) **Raja Samrat Singh of Ralaota** who is descended from a younger son of Maharaja Raj Singh (1706—1748) holds two villages of the estimated value of R10,000. The Raja is now thirty-two years of age. He succeeded his father Raja Durjan Sal on the latter's death

* Thakurs of Naraina, Pandarwara, Bhadun, and Kherian.

† Thakurs of Raghunathpura and Nalu.

‡ Thakurs of Chosal, Gothiana, Narwar, and Manduwaria.

§ Thakur of Titiari.

|| Thakur of Hingtara.

¶ Thakurs of Kotri, Bhambolao, Khatoli, Patu, Jharol, Sapranda, Hingolia, and Nalu.

** Thakurs of Sinodia and Kathoda.

in 1880. He has three sons, Nand Singh, aged thirteen years, Lala, aged nine years, and an infant, aged two years, and has no other relatives nearer than his second cousin Raja Zorawar Singh. One branch of the Ralaota family holds the revenue-free *jagir* of Gangwana, in the Ajmer district (page 113).

Bhambolao.

(5) **Thakur Jet Singh of Bhambolao,** a Rahtor Rajput of the Karmsot sub-clan, holds the first seat in Darbar among the *nine* leading nobles of Kishangarh. He has a service *jagir*, with an estimated income of R5,000. He is thirty years of age, and succeeded his father Thakur Bagh Singh in 1883. He has two sons, Bahadur Singh and Nahar Singh, aged six and three years respectively, and one brother Govind Singh. He has no other relatives nearer than third cousins.

Naraina.

(6) **Thakur Sawai Singh of Naraina,** a descendant of Bhupat Singh, brother to Maharaja Kishan Singh, holds a service *jagir*, with an estimated income of R5,000. He is forty-five years of age and succeeded his father Thakur Ranjit Singh in 1886. He has one son, Gopal Singh, aged seven years, and a younger brother Biradh Singh who has two young sons. After these the Thakur's nearest relatives are distant cousins.

Sinodia.

(7) **Thakur Govind Singh of Sinodia,** a Mertia Rahtor, is entitled to the first seat on the left in Darbar and holds a *jagir* of the estimated value of R2,000. Thakur Govind Singh was adopted by his cousin, the late Thakur, in 1885 and is now twenty-one years of age. He has no near relatives.

Chosla.

(8) **Thakur Bairi Sal of Chosla** is a descendant of the Parbatsar family in Marwar, and holds a *jagir* of the value of R2,000. The Thakur who is now forty years of age succeeded his father Thakur Padam Singh in 1869. He has no sons. His only brother Sheodan Singh has been adopted into the family of the *Jagirdar* of Bhogadit.

Kotri.

(9) **Thakur Megh Singh of Kotri,** a Karamsot descendant of Rao Jodha of Marwar, holds a *jagir* of the value of R4,000. He is seventy-two years of age, and was a member of the Council of Regency during the minority of Maharaja Prithwi Singh. His daughter is the mother of the present Chief of Shahpura. The Thakur, who succeeded his father in the year 1848, had two sons who are now dead. By the elder he has two grandsons, Bherun Singh, aged twenty, and Kalyan Singh, aged fifteen years, and by the younger one son who has been adopted into another family.

Pandarwara.

(10) **Thakur Ram Singh of Pandarwara,** a descendant of Bhupat Singh, brother to Maharaja Kishan Singh, holds a *jagir* of the estimated value of R1,700. He is twenty years of age and succeeded his father Thakur Madho Singh on the death of the latter ten years ago. This family which was the most influential in the State held Dhasuk in *jagir* till about eighty years ago, when the estate was confiscated owing to their refractory conduct. Eventually Pandarwara was given instead of Dhasuk. The Thakur's nearest relatives are his third cousins.

Khatauli.

(11) **Thakur Sheonath Singh of Khatauli,** a Karamsot descendant of Rao Jodha, holds a *jagir* of the value of R1,500. The Thakur who is forty years of age succeeded by adoption to his brother Thakur Kesri Singh. He has two sons, Sardar Singh and Ujain Singh, aged twenty-four and twelve years, respectively, two uncles, Bhim Singh and Dungar Singh, and four first cousins, Devi Singh, Sawai Singh, Gulab Singh, and Sultan Singh.

Raghunathpura.

(12) **Thakur Bharat Singh of Raghunathpura,** a descendant of Maharaja Kishan Singh's brother Sakat Singh, holds a *jagir* of the value of R4,000. Thakur Bharat Singh, who is a member of the Council, is now forty-three years of age. He succeeded his father Thakur Gopal Singh in 1869. Thakur Gopal Singh, who was originally a petty *jagirdar* and

attendant on the late Maharaja Prithwi Singh, rendered useful service to the State during that Chief's minority, and by the construction of embankments and irrigation works did much to increase the revenue of the State. He became a member of the Council and was invested with the *jagir* of Rághunathpura and the rank of a *nau* noble. He has no son, but has adopted his brother and only near relative Jawahir Singh.

Gothiana.

(13) **Thakur Govind Singh of Gothiana,** a Jaganathot descendant of the Parbatsar family, holds a *jagir* with an income of R3,000. He is fifty years of age, and succeeded his father Thakur Kishan Singh in 1853. He has one son, Zorawar Singh, aged twenty-five years; one grandson, Bhanwar Lal Singh, aged five years; one brother, Nonad Singh, and two nephews. After these his nearest relatives are first cousins once removed.

The above Thakurs are all entitled to the honour of the *tazim* and belong to the *nau* class.

Hereditary office-bearers.

Of the hereditary office-bearers of the State, the most important are the following:—

(1) **Mahta Sobhag Singh,** an Oswal by caste, son of the late Diwan Kishan Singh, is a member of the Council and head of the Land Revenue Department. He succeeded his father in the latter capacity in 1862 and enjoys a *jagir* and the *tazim.*

(2) **Purohit Mukund Das,** a member of a family of Pushkarna Brahmans which has been in the service of the State since its foundation, is forty-eight years of age, and holds the appointment of *Amir Bakhshi.* He enjoys a grant of lands in several villages.

(3) **Munshi Bihari Das,** a Kayastha, is the representative of the Mir Munshi family which came from Delhi in the time of Maharaja Bahadur Singh. He holds the appointment of Judge of the Appellate Court and keeper of the State records. He is a good Persian scholar, and is celebrated for his skill in writing *kharitas* (complimentary letters).

(4) **Bhatt Madan Mohan,** a Srimali Brahman, is in charge of the Treasury, an appointment which has been held by his family for four generations. He is twenty-nine years of age, and holds a small grant of lands.

(5) **Lala Ichchha Dayal,** the *Peshkar* and Secretary to the Council, belongs to a family which came into the State with Maharaja Kishan Singh. He was educated at the Ajmer College, and before he obtained his present post was Vakil in attendance on the Agent to the Governor-General, and subsequently Judge of the Sadr Criminal Court.

Besides these there are a number of hereditary officials of less note, of whom only the names and appointments need be given.

(6) **Mohnot Chhagan Singh,** Oswal, Kamdar to the Dowager Maharani Ranawatji.

(7) **Mohnot Sahaskarn,** Oswal, Hákim of Rupnagar.

(8) **Purohit Srinath Das,** Pushkarna Brahman, Head of the Audit and Account Department.

(9) **Mahta Ranjit Singh,** Oswal, Joint Treasury Officer and Judge of the Appellate Court.

(10) **Munshi Faiz Ali Khan,** Pathan, Vakil in attendance on the Agent to the Governor-General at Abu.

(11) **Purohit Magni Ram,** Pushkarna Brahman, Civil Judge of Kishangarh.

(12) **Purohit Bishan Das,** Pushkarna Brahman, Kamdar of the villages attached to the Raj temples.

(13) **Mohnot Sujan Singh,** Oswal, formerly Joint Civil Judge.

(14) **Pancholi Mathura Das Nag,** Kayastha, Kamdar to Maharaj Raghunath Singh.

(15) **Lala Kesri Singh,** Kayastha, Fauj Bakhshi.

(16) **Khoja Nand Lal,** Kayastha, Superintendent of the Zanana Deorhi, formerly English tutor to His Highness the late Maharaja Prithwi Singh.

(17) **Lala Kesri Lal,** Kayastha, Assistant Amir Bakshi.

(18) **Mohnot Girdhar Singh,** Oswal, formerly Kamdar to Maharaj Jawani Singh.

The more important of the new or non-hereditary officials are—

Non-hereditary officials.

(1) **Babu Syam Sundar Lal, B.A.,** Mahesri, a native of Etawa, who was educated at the Agra College. He was teacher of Mathematics at the Ajmer Government College till 1883, when he became Private Secretary to His Highness the Maharaj Rana of Jhalawar. In 1886 he was transferred as a member of Council to Kishangarh. He is now thirty-seven years of age.

(2) **Pandit Govardhan,** a Parikh Brahman, has been a member of the Council since 1884. He is a native of Palri and received a good English education at the Ajmer College. In 1869 he became Private Secretary to His Highness the late Maharaja. Subsequently he was tutor to the present Chief, and for several years was Judge of the Appellate Court.

(3) **Lala Ram Nath,** a Mair Sunar, is a native of Ajmer where he was educated at the Government College. He was formerly an Inspector of Police in Ajmer from which appointment he retired on pension. He has been for five years Superintendent of Raj *Girai* (Police).

(4) **Mir Akbar Ali, Saiyid,** a pensioned Sub-Inspector of Police in the Ajmere District, was formerly Judge of the Criminal Courts at Kishangarh and is now Vakil at the Western Rajputana States Residency. He is a native of Ajmer and was educated at the Government College there.

Other persons of position.

Besides the nobles and officials there are a few persons whose positions call for special mention :—

(1) **Sakal Mahant Saromani Swamiji Maharaj Sri Ghanshyam Saran Devaji Sriji Maharaj of Salimabad,** the High Priest (**Acharyya**) of the Nimbarak division of the Vaishnav sect. Maharaj Ghanshyam, who lives at Salimabad, is the highest ecclesiastical authority of his sect and is held in very great respect by the ruling Chiefs and nobles of Rajputana and other parts of India. He has an estate of the estimated value of about R15,000 a year, consisting of revenue-free grants in Kishangarh, Marwar, Bundi, and other States. In Marwar he receives a cess of a rupee a village. He is the disciple and successor of the late Sriji Maharaj Sri Gopeswar Sarandeva who had once great influence in Jaipur where he held large endowments which he relinquished owing to religious differences with the late Maharaja Ram Singh. The Sriji Maharaj is thirty-six years of age and a fair Sanskrit scholar. He is also noted for his piety. He succeeded the late Sriji Maharaj in 1871, the latter having selected him and obtained approval of his choice from the Darbar. The Sriji Maharaj, who comes from the Gaur Brahman family, has chosen as his successor a disciple, Balkrishna Das, from the same family.

(2) **Barait Chandi Dan,** the head of the Charans and a Hindi poet, holds small estates in Kishengarh and Mewar.

(3) **Rao Chatar Singh;** a Bhat, and (4) **Kavishwar Jay Lal,** a Brahman, are also influential poets who hold small charitable grants. The latter is a descendant of the poet Brinda, author of the "*Brind Satsai*" and "*Bharpancharika,*" who was brought to Kishangarh from Delhi by Maharaja Raj Singh.

(5) **Misir Janki Das,** Court Vaidik Physician, a Moghya Brahman by caste, is descended from Sheoram Das, who came from Delhi one hundred and fifty years ago. He is sixty-six years of age and holds small grants of land.

(6) **Joshi Hari Datta** and (7) **Vyasa Krishna Gopal** are leading ecclesiastical authorities, and (8) **Joshi Govardhan** is Court artist.

CHAPTER III.

SESODIA STATES.

[*Udaipur—Dungarpur—Banswara—Partabgarh.*]

Notice of the clan.

The Sesodia clan of Rajputs claims to be descended from Rama, the legendary king of Oudh, whose son Loh is said to have emigrated in A. D. 145 from the Punjab to Gujarat, where his descendants reigned till their capital Balabhi, near the present city of Bhaunagar, was destroyed by an invasion of foreigners in A. D. 524. In the course of the flight of the family a prince was born near Mount Abu, who afterwards reigned at Idar which was held by his descendants for eight generations, when the Bhils rose and killed their ruler. His son Bapa was preserved and removed to Nagindra, ten miles to the north of the modern Udaipur. Eventually he sought refuge with the Mori Chief of Chitor, then the ruling lord of Malwa. Later on, he led the Chitor forces against the Muhammadans from Sind, defeated them, and ultimately he made himself master of Chitor and founded the kingdom of Mewar.

For the next four centuries little is known, till in 1193 Lomarsi, the Chief, was killed near the banks of the Ghagar when fighting in defence of his brother-in-law Prithwi Raj, the last Chauhan king of Delhi, against Shahabu-d-din. Lomarsi's grandson Mahap was driven from Chitor by his brother-in-law, the Chief of Jhalor, and rather than fight to regain his inheritance, he retired to the hills and founded the State of Dungarpur. He retained the sept name of Aharya which the family had substituted for the original term Gehlot on their migration to Nagindra. In 1201 Mahap's uncle Bharat recovered Chitor and placed his son Rahap on the throne. Rahap changed the title of the sept from Aharya to Sesodia and his own style from Rawal to Rana. In 1290 Chitor was sacked by Alau-d-din Khilji, when the *johur*, or sacrifice of the women, was for the first time performed preparatory to the last sortie of the besieged host. Lakhansi, the Chief, was killed and his son became a fugitive. The latter on his death in 1301 nominated Hamir, his nephew, as his successor. Hamir retook Chitor, which was held by his father-in-law Maldeo, Chief of Jhalor, for the Muhammadans. Hamir was regarded as the leading prince of Central India until his death. In the reign of Lakha, who succeeded to the *gadi* in 1373, the Chieftainship passed from the elder to the younger branch or the family, the Rana having taken to wife a princess of Marwar with the promise that any son born of the marriage should succeed to Mewar, to the exclusion of the elder son Chanda. A child, Mokul, being born, Chanda resigned his rights in his favour, reserving to himself the first place in the Council of the State and stipulating that his symbol, the lance, should be superadded to that of the prince in all grants. Chanda became the ancestor of the Raos of Salumbar and the other Chandawat families. Mokul's grandson, Udai, succeeded to the *gadi* after assassinating his father, and brought dishonour on the State in various ways—by the cession of Ajmer and Sambhar to Jodhpur, by making the Deora prince dependent on Abu, and by offering his daughter in marriage to the Emperor of Delhi. This marriage did not take place. He left three sons, of whom Raimal succeeded him in 1474, after a conflict, in which one of his brothers was killed and the other was forced to retire to Deolia, where he founded the State of Partabgarh. Under Raimal's son and successor, Sanga, Mewar reached its highest prosperity. The following reigns of Ratna, Bikramjit, and Ude Singh were marked by severe struggles with Bahadur Shah, king of Gujarat, and subsequently with the Emperor Akbar, in both of which the *johur* sacrifice was performed. On the last occasion Chitor was captured after terrible slaughter and demolished. Ude Singh subsequently founded Udaipur, which has since been the capital of Mewar. Ude Singh's successor, Partap, was a gallant warrior who after severe struggles with the Muhammadans, in the course of which his life was on one occasion only saved by the Chieftain of Sadri raising the royal insignia over his own head and sacrificing himself for his sovereign,* succeeded in recovering Chitor and the whole of Mewar. Ultimately when Jahangir took the field in person, Umra, son of Partap, yielded and soon afterwards abdicated

* In memory of this event, the descendants of the Sadri house are privileged to use the royal insignia to this day.

in favour of his son Kurzasi. Rana Umra, who succeeded to the *gadi* in 1700, made a tripartite alliance for mutual defence with Jaipur and Jodhpur, stipulating as a condition on which the latter houses should again be admitted to the honour of marriage with Mewar, a privilege which they had lost by giving their daughters in marriage to the Mughal Emperors, that sons of princesses of the Udaipur house should in all cases succeed to the throne in preference to the elder sons by other mothers. This stipulation led to constant quarrels and eventually to the disastrous result of the Mahrattas being called in as arbiters in the affairs of Rajputana. For nearly a century Mewar was harried by Sindia and Holkar and afterwards by Amir Khan, the Pindari, till in 1817 Maharana Bhim Singh made a treaty with the British Government, by which the latter agreed to protect the territory of Udaipur, and to use its best exertions for the restoration of the territories it had lost, when this could be done with propriety. This Chief died in 1828, and was succeeded by his son Jawan Singh, who reigned till his death in 1838. In default of male issue, the succession went by adoption to Sardar Singh, the Chief of Bagor. Maharana Sardar Singh died in 1842 and was succeeded by his younger brother and adopted son Maharana Sarup Singh, who distinguished himself by his loyal service during the Mutiny. Maharana Sarup Singh died in 1861, and was succeeded by Maharana Shimbhu Singh, who was, on his death in 1874, succeeded by Maharana Sajan Singh. That Chief having died without issue in 1884, the unanimous choice of the family and nobles fell on the present Chief, Maharana Fath Singh.

UDAIPUR.

The present Chief.

His Highness Maharana Dhiraj Fath Singh Bahadur, G.C.S.I., was born in 1850. His Highness is the third son of the late *jagirdar* of Seorati, Maharaj Dal Singh, and had been adopted by his brother Maharaj Gaj Singh. On the death, however, of Maharana Sajan Singh in December 1884 without natural or adopted heirs, the unanimous choice of the family and leading men of the State fell on Fath Singh, whose succession as Maharana was approved by the Government of India. The Maharana has married (1) in 1867 the daughter of the late Thakur of Khod in Marwar, who died in 1877 and (2) in 1878 the daughter of Chanda Kol Singh of Barsoda (Warsora) in Mahi Kantha, Gujarat. The only surviving son is Kunwar Bhupal Singh who was born on the 22nd February 1884. The Maharana's nearest relative is his predecessor's uncle Maharaj Sohan Singh. He has also two brothers of his own (Seorati) family, Maharaj Gaj Singh and Maharaj Surat Singh. The latter of these has four sons. His Highness has also four daughters, of whom the first is married to His Highness the Maharao of Kotah, and the second and fourth have respectively been betrothed to His Highness the Maharaja of Bikanir and the Maharaj Kunwar of Kishangarh. The ruling families closely connected with Mewar are Dungarpur, Sirohi, and Partapgarh, which are offshoots of the Sesodia clan, and Kishangarh, Idar, and Rewa, with which marriages have taken place.

Marriages.

Leading men.

The nobles of Mewar are a numerous and powerful body, whose estates comprise about one-third of the territory of the State. In the Gazetteer of Mewar, Colonel Walter wrote regarding them: "The Chiefs of Mewar enjoy rights and privileges which do not obtain in any other part of Rajputana. The Court maintained at their own estates is almost an exact counterpart of that of their prince, and they exhibit few of the marks of vassalage observable at other Courts; and only on particular festivals and solemnities do they join the prince's cavalcade. In Darbar they take rank above the heir-apparent—a custom unprecedented in India, and granted in consequence of the heir-apparent having attended the Emperor's court. When a Chief enters the presence, the entire court rises and the ceremonial is most intricate."

In the reign of Maharana Umra Singh II (1700—1716), the nobles were arranged into (1) sixteen of the first rank, known as the **Solah**; besides the heir-apparent and the Maharana's nearest relatives, who sit below the sixteen; (2) thirty-two of the second rank, known as the **Battis**; and (3) the mass or **Gol** consisting of the rest, to whom no special precedence is assigned. The first class, though still termed the sixteen, consists now of twenty nobles besides the near relatives of the Chiefs who are seven in number. Of the whole twenty-seven, eighteen are Sesodias, and nine belong to other clans. The families of the Sesodia clan are divided into five classes. To the first of these belong eight—Salumbar, Deogarh, Begun, Amet,

Mehja, Bhainsrorgarh, Korabar, and Asin, descendants of the Chanda who in 1398 resigned his right to the Chiefship to his younger brother Mokul. In the second class there is one family, that of Kanor, descended from Sarangdeo, a son of Aja and grandson of Lakha, the father of Chanda and Mokul. The third class comprises the families of Bhindar and Bansi, descended from Sakat Singh, a son of Maharana Ude Singh (1541—1572). Two of the nobles hold the independent title of Raja—the Rajas of Shahpura and Banera. Of these, the former is descended from Maharana Amar Singh, and the latter from Maharana Raj Singh. The descendants of Maharana Sangram Singh II (1716—34) constitute the five **hawelis** or houses of Karoi, Banlas, Bagor, Karjali, and Seorati.

The following pedigrees, compiled by Colonel Walter, show the descent of the chief and the principal Sesodia families of Mewar :—

GENEALOGICAL TABLE No. I.

Showing the main line of the Udaipur family from Sangram Singh II downwards and adoption from Bagor branch.

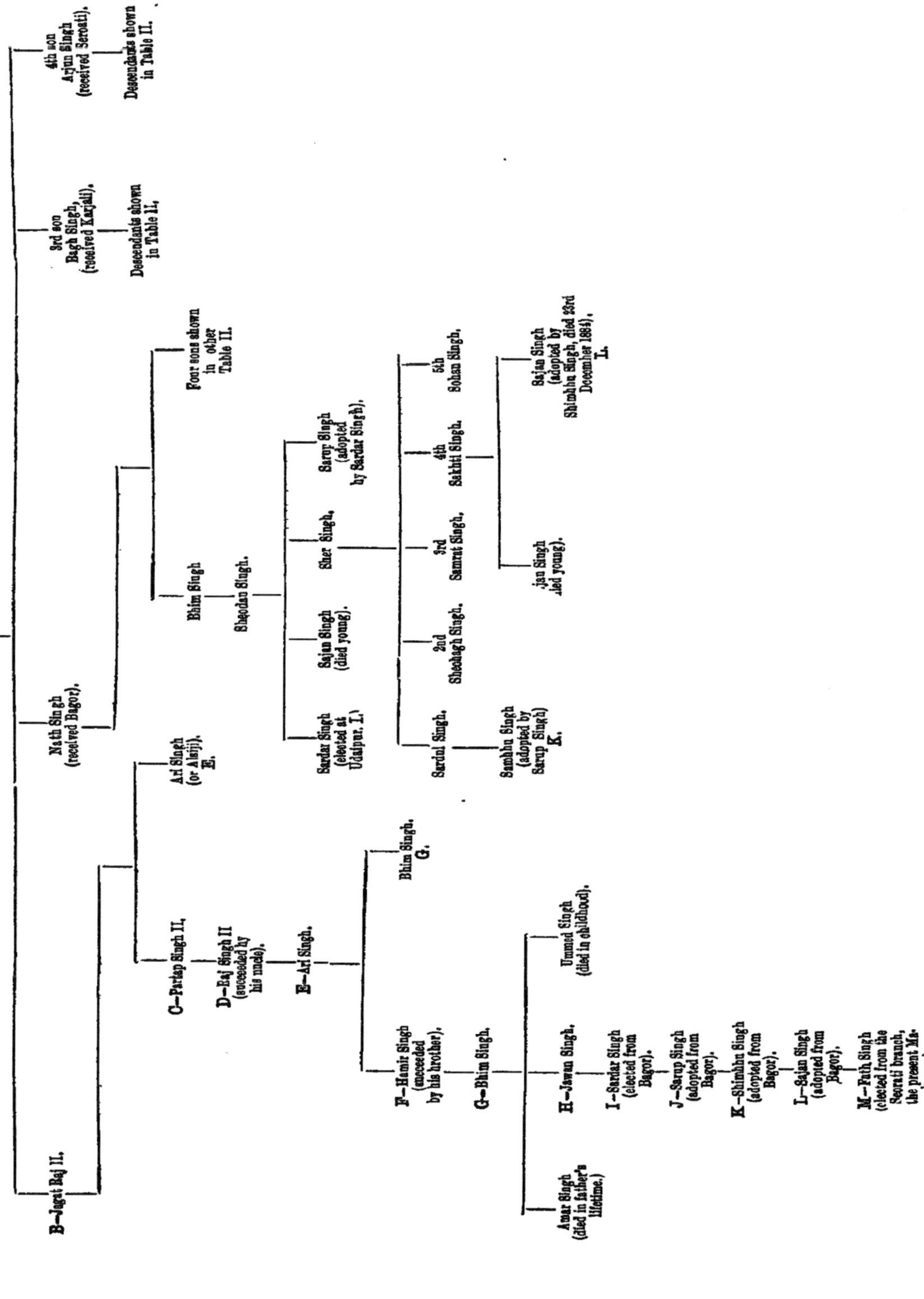

NOTE.—The capital letters indicate the sequence of the Maharanas.

GENEALOGICAL TABLE No. II.

Showing the three Hawelis *(collateral branches) of the Udaipur family descended from Sangram Singh the Second.*

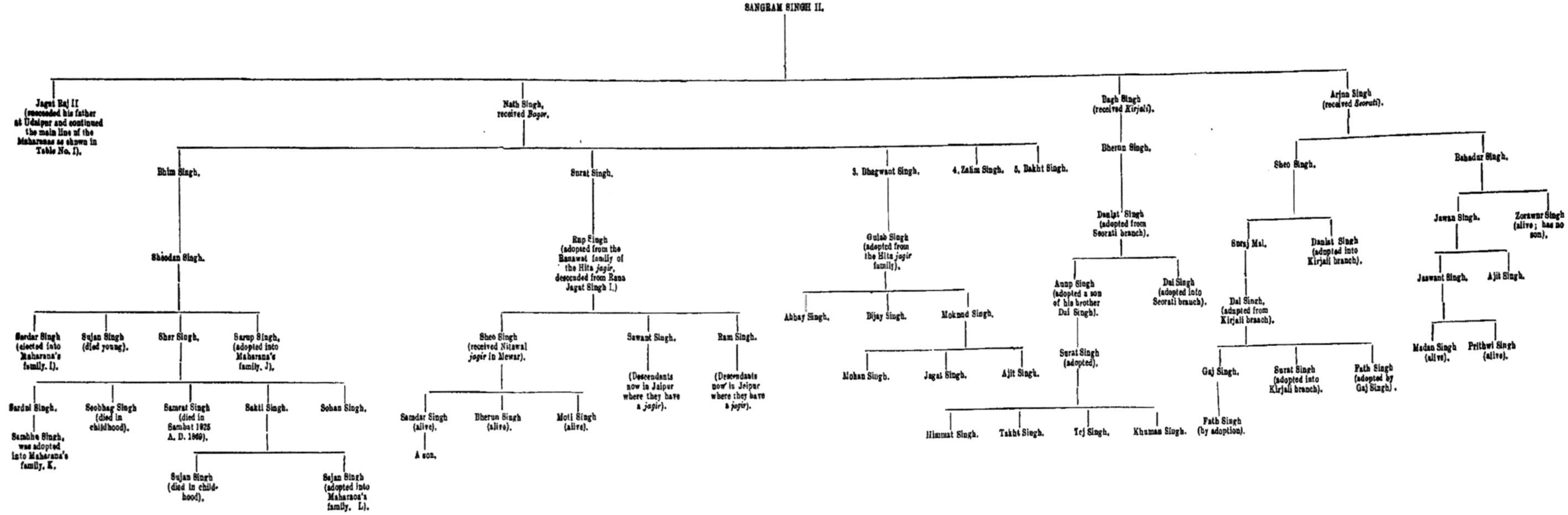

Of the nine nobles not belonging to the Sesodia clan, three—Sadri, Dilwara, and Gogunda—are Jhalas, and three—Bedla, Kotaria, and Parsoli—are Chauhans. The remainder—Bijoli, Bednor, and Sardargarh—are Puar (Pramar), Rahtor, and Dudhiya respectively. The precedence of the **Solah** among themselves is as liberal as the composition of the group. The first place is held by a Jhala; Chauhans occupy the second and third places. The fourth place belongs to a Sesodia noble, the Rawat of Salumbar, who, as the head of the senior and most numerous branch of the family, the Chandawats, is the most prominent Chief of Mewar. The same liberality is observable in the composition of the Mahand Raj Sabha, which is the highest tribunal in the State, and is a Council of reference and revision. The Maharana sits as president of the body, in which are associated with him eleven nobles and eight officials. Of the nobles five only are Sesodias. Of the officials three belong to Mewar, and the rest are outsiders.

Leading nobles.

Karjali.

(1) **Maharaj Surat Singh,** the elder brother of the Maharana, holds the estate of Karjali situated 55 miles to the east of Udaipur, and consisting of twenty-two villages of the annual value of R22,000.* The Maharaj succeeded to the estate by adoption in 1857. He is now forty-six years of age and is married to daughters of the Thakurs of Raipur and Khad in Marwar, by whom he has four sons, Himmat Singh, Sukh Singh, Tej Singh, and Khuman Singh.

Seorati.

(2) **Maharaj Gaj Singh,** the adoptive father of His Highness the Maharana, holds the estate of Seorati, 60 miles to the north-east of Udaipur, comprising eighteen villages of the annual value of R45,000. The Maharaj, who is fifty-eight years of age, is a member of the Mahand Raj Sabha. He succeeded his father Dal Singh in 1867 and has no issue. He married the daughter of the Thakur of Baroda in Gujarat. Both the estates of Korabar and Seorati which are held revenue-free from the Darbar were conferred upon the founders of the present families by Maharana Sangram Singh II (1716—1734).

Shahpura.†

(3) **Raja Dhiraj Nahar Singh of Shahpura,** who is a descendant of Suraj Mal, younger son of Maharana Amar Singh I (1597—1621), holds the estate of Shahpura comprising eighty-nine villages of the annual value of R75,000 and paying a tribute of R2,002 to the Mewar Darbar. The Raja Dhiraj succeeded to his Chiefship in 1869 in accordance with the wishes of the Thakurs of the State on the death of Raja Lachhman Singh. The succession was unsuccessfully disputed by Thakur Ram Singh of Beshnia. The Raja Dhiraj, who is twenty-eight years of age, is married to a daughter of the Thakur of Baghera in Jaipur, and has two sons, Ummed Singh and Sardar Singh, who are both being educated at the Mayo College. He is a member of the Mahand Raj Sabha. The Chief of Shahpura, besides his estates in Udaipur, holds the *patta* of Phulia from the British Government. This estate was granted to the son of Suraj Mal, the founder of the house, by the Emperor Shah Jahan. In respect of Shahpura the Raja Dhiraj is not subject to any British Court, but he was required by the terms of his *sanad* to report all heinous crimes involving the punishment of death or imprisonment for life to a British Officer—formerly the Commissioner of Ajmer and now the Political Agent in Haraoti and Tonk to whom the political control of Shahpura has been transferred.

Banera.

(4) **Raja Govind Singh of Banera** is descended from the brother of Rana Jay Singh of Mewar. He holds an estate consisting of one hundred and fourteen villages situated about 90 miles east of Udaipur. The estimated income of the estate is R1,10,000. A tribute of R6,124 is paid to the Darbar. Raja Govind Singh, who is now fifty-eight years of age, has two sons, Akhay Singh and Ram Singh, aged twenty-five and twenty-one years respectively. The Raja of Banera enjoys certain privileges not possessed by the other nobles of Mewar. Of these, the chief is the right on succession to the *gadi* to have a sword sent to him with all honour to Banera, instead of having to attend at Udaipur for investiture. On receipt of the sword, he proceeds to Udaipur for installation. On the death of the late Raja, Sangram Singh, the present Chief was placed in possession of his estates by the inhabitants of Banera without the consent of the Darbar. In 1855 the British Government interposed to support the authority of the Maharana, but the submission of the people obviated the necessity for

* The value of all estates in Mewar is given in Udaipur rupees, which are worth about 12 annas 6 pies in British currency.

† See also page 47.

sending a force to Banera. As a penalty for his contumacy Raja Govind Singh was compelled to proceed to Udaipur without receiving the sword of honour and to ask pardon, which was granted on payment of a fine and on execution of a written promise that no succession to Banera should be considered valid without the previous consent of the Darbar.

Bari Sadri.

(5) **Raj Rana Rai Singh of Bari Sadri,** a Jhala Rajput, holds the first place among the Solah nobles. His estate, which is valued at R60,000 a year, consists of eighty-nine villages and pays a tribute of R1,024 to the Darbar. The Raj of Sadri, who is now thirty-two years of age, succeeded his uncle and adoptive father in 1883. He has no son. His nearest relatives belong to the family of Dilwara. Marriages have taken place between the house of Sadri and princesses of the ruling family of Mewar. As already noticed (page 27), the Chiefs of Sadri hold their present rank in Darbar in recognition of the gallantry displayed by their ancestor Mana who at the battle of Haldighat in 1576 saved the life of Rana Partap by assuming the insignia of royalty and drawing the brunt of the battle on himself. The fief of Sadri was conferred at the same time with the title of Raj and the Chief was allowed the privilege of bearing the royal insignia of Mewar and of beating his kettle-drums up to the gate of the palace. These honours are still enjoyed by his successors.

Bedla.

(6) **Rao Karn Singh of Bedla,** a Chauhan Rajput, holds an estate of one hundred and fifteen villages of the annual income of R80,000, situated partly near the capital and partly in the neighbourhood of Chitor. The Rao, who is twenty-nine years of age, is married to a daughter of the Thakur of Bhadrajan in Marwar and has no issue. He has three brothers, Raj Singh and Rup Singh, aged twenty-two years, and Gobind Singh, aged thirteen years. He succeeded his father Rao Bahadur Takht Singh in June 1892. Rao Takht Singh, who was a member of the Mahand Raj Sabha, received the title of Rao Bahadur from the British Government in 1887. Rao Bakht Singh, C.I.E., the father of Rao Takht Singh, was noted for his ability and honesty and for his loyalty alike to his own Chief and to the Supreme Government. He received a sword of honour after the Mutiny in recognition of the services rendered by him by order of Maharana Sarup Singh in bringing from Dungla to Udaipur the European families from Nimach. At the Imperial Assemblage of 1877 the title of Rao Bahadur was conferred on Thakur Bakht Singh and in the following year he was appointed a Companion of the Indian Empire. The Bedla family, like that of Kotharia, claims descent from Prithwi Raj, the last Hindu king of Delhi, their ancestors having taken refuge at Chitor after the conquest of Delhi by Shahabu-d-din in 1193.

Kotharia.

(7) **Rawat Jawani Singh of Kotharia,** also a Chauhan descendant of Raja Prithwi Raj of Delhi, holds an estate of seventy villages of the estimated value of R40,000 on the banks of the Banas, about 30 miles north-west of Udaipur. It pays a tribute of R1,502 to the Darbar. The present Rawat, who is only six years of age, succeeded Rawat Kesri Singh in 1888 by adoption. The estate is at present under the management of the Darbar.

Salumbar.

(8) **Rawat Jodh Singh of Salumbar** who holds the fourth place in Darbar, is a Sesodia Rajput and is perhaps the most important of the Mewar nobles. His estate consists of one hundred and seventy-five villages of the annual value of one lakh of rupees. It pays no revenue to the Darbar. The Rawat, who is now sixty years of age and blind, succeeded his predecessor and adoptive father Rawat Kesri Singh in 1863. The adoption was not in accordance with custom, Jodh Singh being a member of the family of Bambora which was more distantly connected with that of Salumbar than was the family of Bhadesar. The present Rao, who has no children, has adopted Tej Singh, a son of the Rawat of Bhadesar. As noticed above (page 27), the family of Salumbar is descended from Rawat Chanda, who yielded his right to the Mewar succession in favour of his young brother Mokul, the offspring of a Marwar princess. Chanda retained for himself and his descendants the right to advise in all important matters of State, and to the first place in the State Councils. The Rawat claims the office of chief hereditary councillor, and an unsuccessful attempt was made to have this claim recognized in the treaty of 1818.

The fifth place in Darbar is kept vacant, having formerly belonged to the Rahtor Thakur of Ganerau who has been transferred to Marwar.

(9) **Rao Sawai Gobind Singh of Bijoli,** a Puar (Pramar) Rajput, holds an estate of ninety villages, with an income of R72,000, on the eastern frontier of Udaipur, about 100 miles from the capital. The Rao, who is now about sixty-five years of age, has one son, Kishan Singh, aged twenty-five years. Rao Govind Singh succeeded his grandfather Rao Kesho Singh in 1856. His father, Sheo Singh, died during Kesho Singh's life-time, leaving three sons. Of these the eldest died soon afterwards and Rao Kesho Singh passed over the second, Nathji, in favour of Govind Singh whom he nominated as his successor. The family of Bijoli is related to that of Dhar. It came into Mewar in the time of Umra Singh early in the seventeenth century, the Rana having married a daughter of Rao Asoka of Jagnair near Biana to whom he assigned an estate valued at five lakhs of rupees.

Bijoli.

(10) **Rawat Kishan Singh of Deogarh,** a Sesodia Rajput, descended from Chandaji, holds an estate of two hundred and sixteen villages near the borders of the Merwara district, with a revenue of one and a half lakhs of rupees. An annual tribute of R7,142 is paid to the Darbar. The Rawat, who is forty-six years of age, succeeded his father, Rawat Ranjit Singh, in 1869. He has no children, and no successor has yet been nominated. His son, Jaswant Singh, married a daughter of the Thakur of Bednor and, together with his wife, was poisoned by the Kamdar of Deogarh in January 1886. The Kamdar was convicted of the crime and sentenced to imprisonment for life. The family of Deogarh is descended from Sanga or Sangram Singh, a younger son of Singhji, the founder of the Amet family, who was the grandson of Chanda through his younger son Kandhal.

Deogarh.

(11) **Rawat Sawai Megh Singh of Begun,** a Chandawat Sesodia Rajput, holds an estate of one hundred and sixty-five villages, about 70 miles east of Udaipur. The estate, which yields an income of R60,000, pays R6,532 as tribute to the Darbar. The Rawat, who is thirty-six years of age and succeeded his uncle Maha Singh in 1861, has one son, Anup Singh. Rawat Maha Singh in 1824 gave up his estate to his son Kishor Singh and became a religious mendicant at the shrines of Nath Dwara and Kankroli. Fifteen years later Kishor Singh was for some unknown reason murdered in cold blood by a Brahman, and Maha Singh resumed the management of his estate. He nominated as his successor his younger brother Madho Singh, who, however, predeceased him, and on his death Megh Singh, Madho Singh's brother, succeeded to the estate.

Begun.

(12) **Raj Rana Zalim Singh of Dilwara** is a Jhala Rajput. The estate consists of eighty-one villages with an income of R90,000 and pays a tribute of R6,124 to the Darbar. The Raj, who has no sons, is now about thirty years of age. He succeeded his father, Raj Fath Singh, in 1891. The latter received the title of Rao Bahadur from the British Government.

Dilwara.

(13) **Rawat Sheonath Singh of Amet** is another descendant of the Chandawat family of the Sesodia clan. Amet, which lies about 50 miles to the north of Udaipur, consists of forty-six villages, with an income of R35,000, paying a tribute of R3,415 to the Darbar. Rawat Sheonath Singh, who was educated at the Mayo College, is now about twenty-four years of age. He succeeded his father Rawat Chatar Singh in 1874 and has no male issue.

Amet.

The Amet family is the elder branch of the descendants of Singhji, of which the younger branch is represented by the family of Deogarh.

(14) **Rawat Amar Singh of Mehja** is also a Chandawat Sesodia. He holds an estate of fifteen villages in the centre of Mewar. The annual income is R32,000 and the tribute payable to the Darbar is R3,121. The estate is of recent creation. On the death without issue of Rawat Prithwi Singh, Zalim Singh of Bemali, the father of Rawat Amar Singh, claimed Amet for his son. This Maharana Sarup Singh refused to grant, but on the Maharana's death his successor, Maharana Shimbhu Singh, permitted Amar Singh to occupy the Rawat of Amet's seat in Darbar and conferred upon him the title of Rawat. In the next year he gave him the Mehja estate. The Rawat has one son, Raj Singh, aged about eighteen years. The Jiloli and Bemali families are closely connected with Amet and Mehja.

Mehja.

Gogunda.

(15) **Raj Ajay Singh of Gogunda,** a Jhala Rajput, holds an estate of eighteen villages, with an annual income of R30,000, situated at a distance of about 20 miles from Udaipur. The Raj is fifty-two years of age and has no sons. His three brothers, Jhujhar Singh, Govind Singh and Prithwi Singh, are aged forty-five, thirty-seven, and thirty-five years, respectively. Raj Ajay Singh succeeded his father Man Singh in 1891. This family is connected with those of Bari Sadri and Dilwara, being descended from the ninth Raj of Bari Sadri.

Kanor.

(16) **Rawat Nahar Singh of Kanor,** a Sesodia Rajput of the Sarangdevot sub-clan, owns an estate of seventy-eight villages yielding an annual income of R40,000 and paying R3,166 as tribute to the Darbar. The Rawat, who succeeded his father Ummed Singh in 1884, is thirty-four years of age and has no male issue. The family is descended from Maharana Lakhaji of Mewar.

Bhindar.

(17) **Maharaj Kesri Singh of Bhindar** is a Sesodia Rajput of the Bhanawat division of the Sakhtawat clan. The estate, which is situated 30 miles to the south-east of Udaipur, consists of a hundred villages, with an income of R60,000 and pays a revenue of R4,002 to the Darbar. The present Maharaj succeeded his adoptive father Maharaj Madan Singh in 1887. He is eighteen years of age and is now being educated at the Mayo College. The family is descended from Maharaj Sakht Singh, son of Maharana Udai Singh.

Bednor.

(18) **Thakur Govind Singh of Bednor,** a Rahtor Rajput of the Mertia branch, holds an estate of one hundred and fifty-eight villages of the annual value of R90,000 on the Merwara border. The tribute payable to the Darbar is R4,084. Thakur Govind Singh succeeded his grandfather Thakur Kesri Singh in 1889. His younger brother has been adopted into the family of Rampur. The Thakurs of Bednor are descended from Rao Duda, a younger son of Rao Jodha of Jodhpur, who was the founder of Merta and the Mertia family. The Mewar branch of the family emigrated to Mewar in the time of Thakur Jaymal, who fought on the side of Mewar against the Delhi troops under Ranbe Khan. A *talwar* belonging to the Imperial General, a shield of elephant hide and a kettle-drum which were captured on this occasion are kept as heirlooms in the family.

Bansi.

(19) **Rawat Sakht Singh of Bansi,** a Sesodia of the Sakhtawat sub-clan, holds an estate 18 miles to the south of Udaipur, comprising forty-one villages of the annual value of R30,000. The tribute payable to the Darbar is R202. The Rawat who succeeded his father Thakur Man Singh in 1887, is now thirteen years of age. He is betrothed to the daughter of the Thakur of Chandawal in Marwar. The family is descended from Achal Das, the younger son of Maharaj Sakat Singh, the founder of the Bhindar estate.

Bhainsrorgarh.

(20) **Rawat Pratap Singh of Bhainsrorgarh,** a Sesodia of the Chandawat clan, holds an estate of one hundred and nineteen villages of the annual value of a lakh of rupees. The estate which pays a tribute of R7,502 is situated at the confluence of the rivers Bamni and Chambal. The place is said by Colonel Tod to take its name from a merchant named Bhainsa and Rora, a Banjara or carrier, and to have been built to protect caravans. It commands the trade route from Mewar into Haraoti. The present Rawat, who succeeded his brother Bhim Singh in 1881, is thirty-nine years of age. He has no male issue. The Bhainsrorgarh family is descended from Lal Singh, the younger son of Rawat Kesri Singh of Salumbar, on whom the separate estate and title were conferred by Maharana Jagat Singh II in 1741.

Parsoli.

(21) **Rao Ratn Singh of Parsoli** is a Chauhan Rajput. His estate is situated 28 miles to the north-east of Chitor, and comprises forty-six villages yielding an annual income of R25,000 and paying R926 as tribute to the Darbar. The present Rao succeeded his father Rao Lakshman Singh in 1880. He is forty-five years of age and has three sons, Devi Singh, Madho Singh, and Abhay Singh, aged eighteen, fifteen, and eleven years, respectively. He is a member of the Mahand Raj Sabha. The founder of the family of Parsoli was Kesri Singh, the younger son of Rao Ram Chandra of Bedla, on whom the estate was bestowed by Maharana Raj Singh.

(22) **Rawat Jet Singh of Korabar,** a Sesodia Rajput of the Chandawat sub-clan, holds an estate of sixty-five villages, situated 30 miles to the south-east of Udaipur. The estate, which yields an annual income of R50,000, pays no tribute to the Darbar. Rawat Jait Singh succeeded his father Ratn Singh in 1880. He is now about thirty-five years of age, and has three sons, Kishor Singh, aged fourteen years, and Sangram Singh and Ranjit Singh, aged twelve and ten years, respectively. Korabar was bestowed as an independent estate by Maharana Jagat Singh II in 1747 on Arjun Singh, the younger son of Rawat Kesri Singh of Salumbar.

Korabar.

(23) **Rawat Arjun Singh of Asin** holds a large estate of seventy-five villages of the annual value of a lakh of rupees, situated about 80 miles to the north-east of Udaipur near the Merwara border. Rupees 1,300 are paid as tribute to the Darbar. Rawat Arjun Singh succeeded his father Rawat Khuman Singh in 1873. He is forty-one years old and has no issue. He is a member of the Mahand Raj Sabha. The founder of the family was Ajit Singh, the fourth son of Arjun Singh, the founder of the Korabar family. He received a grant of the Gorkhya estate of fourteen villages from Maharana Bhim Singh, on whose behalf he signed the treaty of 1818 with the British Government. He was succeeded by his adopted son Dule Singh of Satola who previous to his adoption had received the title of Rawat and several villages, including Asin, from Amar Singh, son of Maharana Bhim Singh. Dule Singh was then raised to the position of a first-class Sardar with the twentieth place among the **Solah.**

Asin.

(24) **Thakur Manohar Singh of Sardargarh** is a Rajput of the Indrabhanot division of the Dudhiya clan. His estate, which is situated 56 miles to the north-east of Udaipur on the right bank of the Chandra-Bhaga river, consists of twenty-two villages which yield an income of R33,000 and pay a tribute of R1,740 to the Darbar. Thakur Manohar Singh, who succeeded his father Thakur Zorawar Singh in 1859, is sixty-three years of age. He had two sons, both of whom are dead. He is a member of the Mahand Raj Sabha and resides at the capital. The Thakur has the hereditary privilege of guarding the Maharana's person in time of war. The Sardargarh family is among the oldest of the Raj servants of Mewar and received from Maharana Sajan Singh a place among the nobles of the first class.

Sardargarh.

One of the most important personages in Mewar is the guardian of the Nathdwara temple. **Sriman Tikait Goswami Maharaj Sri Govardhan Lalji** is the head of the Vallabhacharyya sect of Brahmans. He succeeded his father Maharaj Girdhariji in 1876 on the deposition of the latter for contumacious conduct. He is about thirty years of age, and is a well-educated gentleman, who has done much to promote the welfare of his people. The Maharaj, besides his estates in Mewar, holds *jagirs* in Kotah, Jhalawar, Bikanir, Bhartpur, Karauli, Gwalior, Indore, Partabgarh, Baroda and elsewhere, of the annual value of about two and a quarter lakhs of rupees. The offerings received by him yearly are estimated at between four and five lakhs. One village, Bhawanikhera, of the value of R1,500, is held by the temple in the Ajmer district. The grant was originally made by Maharaja Daulat Rao Sindia. The origin of Nathdwara is thus described in the Gazetteer of Mewar: "The shrine owes its celebrity to the image of Krishna, said to be the same that was worshipped at Mathura ever since his deification between eleven and twelve centuries before Christ, and it is consequently one of the most frequented places of pilgrimage. Krishna was proscribed by the Emperor Aurangzeb, and the god was subsequently conducted by Rana Raj Singh of Mewar, about 1671, from Mathura to Mewar. An omen decided the spot of his future residence: as he journeyed towards the capital the chariot-wheel sank deep into the earth and defied extraction, upon which the augur interpreted it as the desire of the god to dwell there. This incident occurred at an inconsiderable village called Siarh in the fief of Dilwara, one of the sixteen nobles of Mewar. The Chief hastened to make a perpetual gift of the village and its lands, which was speedily confirmed by the patent of the Rana. Nathji was removed from his car and in due time a temple was erected for his reception, when the hamlet of Siarh became the town of Nathdwara which now contains many thousand inhabitants. The territory contains abundant space for the town, the temple, and the establishments of the priests, as well as for the

Other influential personages.

numerous resident worshippers, and the constant influx of votaries from distant regions. Within its bounds is the sanctuary of Kanya, where the criminal is free from pursuit and no blood can be spilt. The guardians of the shrine belong to the Vallabhacharyya sect, and the image is one of the seven famous images possessed by this division of the votaries of Krishna."

Officials.

Of the officials of the State two only call for special notice—

(1) **Rai Mahta Panna Lal, C.I.E.,** an Oswal Mahajan by caste. The family is descended from Bar Singh Bachawat, one of the officials who accompanied Rao Bika from Jodhpur at the foundation of the Bikanir State (see page 16). The family did good service till the time of Karm Chand who was Diwan of Bikanir under Raja Rai Singh in the days of Akbar. Karm Chand conspired against his master and, the plot being discovered, fled to Delhi, where he remained till the death of Rai Singh, enjoying the favour of the Emperor.* Rai Singh before his death is said to have laid on his son Sur Singh the injunction to entice the Bachawats to Bikanir and destroy them. Sur Singh on succeeding to the *gadi* went to do homage at Delhi, visited Karm Chand's sons and, having guaranteed their safety, induced them to return to Bikanir. This they did and for a time were treated with distinction. At the end of two months, however, their house was surrounded by Raj troops, and after a hard fight the family was exterminated to a man, with the exception of one boy who was absent with his mother's family in Udaipur. From this boy Mahta Panna Lal is descended. The family has held many high positions in Mewar, no less than three members of the elder branch, Devi Chand, Sher Singh, and Gokul Chand, having held the office of *Pardhan* or Chief Minister. Rai Panna Lal who is a member of the younger branch has for many years exercised the chief ministerial authority in the State, though the title of *Pardhan* has never been formally conferred on him. He possesses much influence with all classes, both on account of his family and of his personal ability. This influence has been uniformly employed in the best interests of the Darbar and people. He is now forty-nine years of age, and has one son, Fath Lal. The title of Rai was bestowed on Mahta Panna Lal at the Delhi Assemblage of 1877, and ten years later he was nominated a Companion of the Indian Empire. He possesses a *jagir* of six villages valued at R10,000 a year.

(2) **Kaviraj Syamal Das, Mahamahopadhya,**† a Charan of a family which originally came to Mewar in the days of Maharana Sangram Singh I, who in 1519 conferred a *jagir* on the then representative, is the chief historian of Mewar and has recently written a complete history of the country, which is now being printed. He is fifty-nine years of age and a member of the Mahand Raj Sabha. Some of the State equipage departments are under his care, and he is now and then deputed by the Maharana on special duty. The Kaviraj has one son, Jaskarn, aged thirteen years. The title of Mahamahopadhyaya was conferred on him in January 1888. The *jagir* held by the family now consists of seven villages of the value of R4,000.

DUNGARPUR.

The founder of the Dungarpur house, as already mentioned (page 27), was Mahap, son of Karna and grandson of Rawal Lomarsi of Mewar who was driven from Chitor, the then capital of Mewar, by his brother-in-law the Chief of Jhalor. The possessions of Dungarpur were divided early in the sixteenth century, one portion becoming the independent Raj of Banswara. Dungarpur, of which the early history calls for no special notice, entered into relations with the Mughals and, after the fall of the Empire, became tributary to the Mahrattas, the tribute being taken after some dispute with Sindia and Holkar by the State of Dhar. Dungarpur was subsequently harried by Pindari and other freebooters, till in 1818 an agreement was entered into with the British by which the tribute was assigned to them and the State was guaranteed against external aggression.

Present Chief.

The present Chief, **His Highness Maharawal Ude Singh Bahadur,** is a Sesodia Rajput of the house of Mewar. His Highness was the son of Maharaj Jaswant Singh of Sabli and succeeded Maharawal Jaswant Singh of Dungarpur in 1846. Maharawal Jaswant Singh had been deposed in 1825 for his incompetency, and his adopted son Dalpat Singh, son of the Partabgarh Chief, was made Regent. On Dalpat Singh's succession to Partabgarh in

* Another version of this story is that Karm Chand, who was a good chess-player attracted by his skill the notice of the Emperor, who would often cause him to sit down and play while his master and other Rajas stood by in humble attendance. This was naturally most galling to Rai Singh, who conceived a hatred towards his servant who after his return home, sought to kill him—a fate which Karm Chand only escaped by flight to Delhi. (*Powlett, Gazetteer of Bikanir, page 26*).

† Kaviraj Syamal Das has died since this notice was written.

1844 it was decided that he could not hold both States, and he was, therefore, permitted to adopt the present Chief. The Maharawal married in 1855 the daughter of the Maharao of Sirohi. He has one son, Khuman Singh, aged thirty-five years, and through him one grandson, Bijay Singh, aged five years. His Highness has also three nephews, Shimbhu Singh, Parbat Singh, and Ummed Singh. The next nearest relatives are the *Jagirdars* of Nandli, Sabli, and Oara. The Dungarpur family is related by blood to those of Udaipur, Banswara, and Partabgarh.

Only one succession, that of the present Chief, has taken place since the time of Jaswant Singh, who seventy-four years ago entered into the first alliance with the British Government.

Leading personages.

The leading men of Dungarpur are the **nobles**, including the Hawelis or relatives of the Maharawal, and hereditary office-bearers, the nobles being again subdividod on the same plan as those of Mewar into **solah** and **battis**, though neither number is strictly observed.

Hawelis.

The **Hawelis** are the Thakurs of Nandli, Sabli, and Oara. These are all Sesodia Rajputs.

Nandli.

(1) **Thakur Ummed Singh of Nandli** is descended from Rawal Jaswant Singh through his grandson Bakht Singh and Prithwi Singh, the second son of the latter. The Thakur, who is forty years of age, succeeded to the estate on his father's death. He has five sons, Gopal Singh, Amar Singh, Khuman Singh, Takht Singh, and Bhopal Singh; one brother, Zorawar Singh, and two uncles, Bijay Singh and Ram Singh. The estate consists of the whole or part of five villages with an income of R1,800.

Sabli.

(2) **Thakur Shimbhu Singh of Sabli** is descended from Maharawal Girdhari of Dungarpur. The Thakur, who is eight years of age, succeeded his nephew. His nearest relatives are his cousins Parbat Singh, Thakur of Oara, and Ummed Singh, Thakur of Mandwa. The present Maharawal is, as noticed above, by birth a member of the Sabli family. The Sabli estate consists of five villages with an income of about R1,200.

Oara.

(3) **Maharaj Parbat Singh, Thakur of Oara,** is a descendant of Rawal Jaswant Singh. He is a boy of fourteen years of age. He succeeded to the estate, which consists of three villages with an income of about R1,200, on the death of his uncle. His nearest relatives are the Thakur of Sabli, Mandwa and Sesod, and His Highness the Maharawal.

Tazimi nobles.

The **tazimi** nobles comprised in the **solah** are eleven in number, exclusive of the Hawelis—the Thakurs of Bankora, Peit, Mandor, Thakurda, Chitri, Lodawal, Bamasa, Bichiwara, Sulaj, Kua, and Ramgarh. Of these two are Chandawat Sesodias, one is a Rahtor, and the remaining eight are Chauhans.

Bankora.

(1) **Thakur Dalpat Singh of Bankora,** a descendant of the Chauhan Raja Prithwi Raj of Delhi, is the chief noble of Dungarpur. He holds an estate consisting of the whole or part of thirty-eight villages, which yields an income of R23,000 and pays a tribute of R3,602 to the Darbar. The Thakur, who is twenty-eight years of age, succeeded his uncle, Kesri Singh, in 1885. He has no children, and his nearest relatives are his uncle, Gopal Singh, and his first cousins, Parbat Singh, Kishan Singh, and Basant Singh.

Peit.

(2) **Thakur Zorawar Singh of Peit** is also a Prithwi Rajot Chauhan. His estate, which yields an income of R5,600 and pays R1,547 as tribute to the Darbar, consists of fifty villages. The Thakur, who is twenty-six years of age and has no male children, succeeded his father in 1885. He has no near relatives.

Bichiwara.

(3) **Thakur Dhirat Singh of Bichiwara,** a Prithwi Rajot Chauhan, holds an estate of nine villages, which yields an income of R4,000 and pays R1,408 as tribute to the Raj. He is now twenty-eight years of age and succeeded his uncle Bakht Singh. His nearest relative is the son of his uncle Kodarji.

Mandor.

(4) **Thakur Suraj Mal of Mandor,** a Prithwi Rajot Chauhan, holds an estate consisting of the whole or part of seventeen villages. The annual income is ₹6,600 and the tribute payable to the Darbar is ₹1,275. He succeeded his elder brother, and is now thirty-one years of age. He has no sons. His nearest relatives are his elder brother Jawan Singh and his nephews Dalpat Singh and Bahadur Singh.

Thakurda.

(5) **Thakur Ude Singh of Thakurda,** a Prithwi Rajot Chauhan, holds an estate of seventeen villages yielding an income of ₹77,000 and paying ₹1,408 as tribute to the Darbar. The Thakur, who is forty-three years of age, succeeded to the estate on the death of his father. He has four sons, Kishor Singh, Hanwant Singh, Sangram Singh, and Madan Singh. Of these Sangram Singh has been adopted into the Garhi family of Banswara. Other near relatives are the Thakur's cousins, Prithwi Singh, Amar Singh, Dalpat Singh, and Chatar Singh.

Sulaj.

(6) **Thakur Pahar Singh of Sulaj** is a Chandawat Sesodia of the family of the Thakur of Salumbar in Mewar (*q. v.*). His estate consists of eleven villages, with an income of ₹4,000, and pays a tribute of ₹296 to the Darbar. The Thakur is twenty-six years of age and succeeded his father, Thakur Muhabbat Singh. He has no sons and his nearest relative is his cousin Raj Singh of Pardla.

Kua.

(7) **Thakur Ram Singh of Kua,** a Rahtor Rajput of the Mertia family, holds an estate of thirty-six villages with an income of ₹4,500. The tribute payable to the Darbar is ₹902. The Thakur, who is sixteen years of age, succeeded his cousin the late Thakur Fath Singh. He has no children and his nearest relations are his uncle Amar Singh and his cousin Zorawar Singh.

Lodawal.

(8) **Thakur Kishor Singh of Lodawal** is a Chauhan Rajput of the Prithwi Rajot clan. The estate of Lodawal consists of five villages yielding an income of ₹1,800 and paying a tribute to the Darbar. The Thakur succeeded on the death of his uncle. He is now forty-two years of age and has no son. His nearest relatives are his nephews Bhawani Singh and Sher Singh and his cousin Anup Singh.

Bamasa.

(9) **Thakur Fath Singh of Bamasa,** a Prithwi Rajot Chauhan, holds an estate consisting of the whole or part of three villages with an income of ₹1,500, which pays a tribute of ₹252. The Thakur, who succeeded his uncle, is fifteen years of age and has no sons. His nearest relatives are his uncle Kishor Singh and his cousin Lal Singh.

BANSWARA.

The origin of the Banswara family, which is an offshoot from that of Dungarpur, is thus given in the Gazetteer, the author of which has taken his facts from a local chronicle: "The Rawals of Banswara are a junior branch of that family of the Sesodia clan of Rajputs which is now ruling in Dungarpur, from which they separated about the year 1530. At that period, and for many years previously, the whole country, which now comprises the two States of Banswara and Dungarpur, was known as Bagar, and was under the dominion of the family of the Sesodias which still holds Dungarpur, though the Chief's control over the lawless Bhils inhabiting the wilder part of his territory was merely nominal. Udai Singh, who came to power in A. D. 1509, had two sons, the elder named Prithwi Raj and the younger Jagmal. He himself marched under his kinsman, Rana Sanga of Chitor, against the Emperor Babar, and was killed at the great battle of Kanwa in 1528. After his death his territory was divided between his two sons, and the descendants of the two families are the present Chiefs of Dungarpur and Banswara. Whether this division was made amicably or by force is not clear. There is a tradition that Ude Singh ordered it to be made before he died. There is another legend that Jagmal Singh, his son, was left for dead on the battle-field, but recovered, and on returning to his country was disowned as an impostor. Thereupon he took refuge in the hills to the north of the present site of Banswara, and having collected a body of followers began to make incursions into his father's territory. This asylum is still known as Jagmer. It is related that Jagmal's first acquisition of territory came about in this wise. In those days there resided to the east of the Mahi river a powerful nobleman, who hardly deigned to acknowledge the authority of the ruler of Dungarpur. His estate was known as that of Kuanya. With him Jagmal speedily came into collision and a protracted feud ensued. After harassing each other for a number of years, they at length became reconciled, and on the death of the old Thakur of Kuanya, Jagmal gained possession of his estate without opposition. Having thus obtained a firm foothold, he turned his arms against the Bhils, who held nearly the whole of the country now constituting Banswara. Where the town of Banswara now stands there was a large Bhil *pal* or colony under a powerful chieftain named Wasna, and against him Jagmal directed his principal attack. Wasna was killed during the storming of his *pal*, his followers were routed, and his lands passed into the hands of his Rajput conquerors. The name Banswara is by tradition said to be a corruption of Wasnawara.

"Jagmal now transferred his residence to Banswara, whence he continued his forays against Dungarpur and the Bhils. In Dungarpur, Ude Singh had been succeeded by his elder son, Prithwi Raj, and the two brothers, finding their continual border war intolerable, agreed to abide by the arbitration of the Raja of Dhar as to the partition of their lands. Accordingly in 1529, the river Mahi was fixed as the boundary between the two States of Dungarpur and Banswara, which since that date have remained perfectly distinct and independent of one another.

"Other records relate that the Chief of Bagar, Udai Singh, divided his territory at his death between his two sons, Prithwi Raj and Jagmal."

There is little of note to be found in the history of Banswara till in 1812, nearly three centuries after its foundation, the then Chief, anxious to get rid of the supremacy of the Mahrattas, offered to become tributary to the British Government. In 1818 a definite treaty was made, and soon afterwards the tribute formerly paid to the Mahratta Chief of Dhar was transferred to the British Government.

The Chief.

His Highness Rai-Rayan Maharawal Sri Lachhman Singh, Bahadur, the present Chief of Banswara, was born in the year 1839, and is a Rajput of the Aharya Gehlot subdivision of the Sesodia clan. His Highness, whose natural father was Bakhtawar Singh, second son of Thakur Khushhal Singh of Surpur in Banswara, was adopted by the late Maharawal Bahadur Singh. The fourteenth Chief of Banswara, Maharawal Prithwi Singh, died in the year 1786, leaving five sons. Of these, the eldest, Bijay Singh, succeeded his father, the second, Bakhtawar Singh, received the *jagir* of Khandu, and the third, Khushhal Singh, that of Surpur. Maharawal Bijay Singh was succeeded by his son Ummed Singh, and subsequently by his grandson Bhawani Singh who died in 1839, leaving no son or brother. The nearest relative according to the rule of primogeniture was thus the eldest descendant of Bakhtawar Singh of Khandu, his grandson Man Singh. The Chauhans, who were then the most influential personages in the State, fearing the rivalry of the Khandu family, placed Bahadur Singh, the second son of Bakhtawar Singh and uncle to Man Singh, on the *gadi* before Man Singh was aware of what was going on. Bahadur Singh, who was old, was persuaded to adopt Lachhman Singh, the infant grandson of Thakur Khushhal Singh of Surpur. Five years later, Maharawal Bahadur Singh died and Lachhman Singh succeeded him. Maharawal Lachhman Singh has been married twelve times, namely, to the daughters of (1) the Raj of Pal in Idar, (2) Maharaj Sheo Singh of Sirohi, (3) Thakur Bakht Singh of Namli in Ratlam, (4) Thakur Jiwan Singh of Bordera in Gujarat, (5) Thakur Zorawar Singh of Sarwan in Ratlam, (6) Thakur Parbat Singh of Posina in Idar, (7) Thakur Kodarji of Pithapur in Mahikanta, (8) Thakur Sher Singh of Bordera in Gujarat, (9) Thakur Kodar Singh of Pithapur, (10) and (11) Thakur Sardar Singh of Molan in Banswara, and (12) Thakur Gulab Singh of Bordera in Gujarat. He has three sons living, one by each of the ladies of the Bordera family, the eldest, Shimbhu Singh, who is now twenty-three years of age, being the heir-apparent. The other sons are Surya Singh, aged seventeen years, and a boy aged three years. Kunwar Shimbhu Singh has a son aged four years. Outside his own family the Chief has no very near relatives. The family most closely connected with His Highness's house is that of Bakhtawar Singh of Khandu, of which the present representative, the fifth in descent from the founder, is Raghunath Singh aged eight years.

The descent of the Banswara house through that of Dungarpur from the ruling family of Mewar has already been noticed.

The Maharawal is related by marriage with the Chiefs of Bundi (Hara), Kishangarh, Sailana, and Idar (Rahtor), and Sirohi (Deora).

The following table shows the principal rulers of Banswara:—

- MAHARAWAL UDAI SINGH of Dungarpur (died 1540).
  - **Maharawal Prithwi Singh** of Dungarpur (ancestor of the Chiefs of Dungarpur).
  - **Maharawal Jagmal Singh** of Banswara (died 1540).
    - **Maharawal Jay Singh.**
    - **Maharawal Pratap Singh.**
    - **Maharawal Kandede Singh.**
    - **Maharawal Kalyan Singh.**
    - **Maharawal Agar Singh.**
    - **Maharawal Ude Singh.**
    - **Maharawal Saman Singh** (said to have wrested a portion of Partabgarh territory from the Maharawat of that State).
    - **Maharawal Khushhal Singh** (founder of Kushalgarh and Kushalpura, who subjugated the Bhils).
    - **Maharawal Ajab Singh.**
    - **Maharawal Bhim Singh** (died 1713).
    - **Maharawal Bishan Singh** (died 1737).
      - **Maharawal Udai Singh** (died 1747).
      - **Maharawal Prithwi Singh** (died 1786).
        - **Maharawal Bijay Singh** (died 1816).
          - **Maharawal Ummed Singh** (died 1819). (This Chief made the first treaty with the British Government in 1818, after which the tribute formerly payable to Dhar was transferred to the British Government. The Gwalior troops were driven out of Banswara in this reign by Thakur Arjun Singh of Garhi).
          - **Maharawal Bhawani Singh** (died 1839).
        - Thakur Bakhtawar Singh of Khandu.
          - Sardar Singh of Khandu (killed in 1817 by Maharawal Ummed Singh).
            - Man Singh.
            - Fath Singh (died 1890).
            - Jaswant Singh (died 1885).
            - Raghunath Singh (alive, aged eight years).
          - **Maharawal Bahadur Singh** (died 1844).
            - (by adoption) **Maharawal Lachhman Singh** (the present Chief).
        - Khushhal Singh of Surpur.
          - Hamir Singh.
            - Madho Singh (died without issue.)
          - Bakhtawar Singh.
            - **Lachhman Singh** (present Chief, adopted by Maharawal Bahadur Singh).
              - Shimbhu Singh.
              - Surya Singh (adopted by Madho Singh of Surpur).
              - An infant.

Leading men.

The leading men of Banswara are the hereditary nobles, the Kamdar, and a few office-bearers. The latter are only hereditary in the sense that they hold *jagirs* from the Darbar. They do not necessarily succeed to any particular office. The Kamdar is generally a foreigner.

As in Mewar, there seem originally to have been sixteen nobles of the first class (Solah), of whom eight, Chauhans and Sesodias, sit to the right of the Chief in Darbar. On the left sat formerly eight Rahtors, but the number has now dwindled down to three. In the second class come a number of nobles, chiefly the descendants of the younger sons of former Chiefs, to whom no special place is allotted.

The following are the principal nobles :—

Chauhans.—(1) Thakur Madan Singh of Mola.
(2) Thakur Balwant Singh of Metwala.
(3) Thakur Fath Singh of Arthuna.
(4) Rao Sangram Singh of Garhi.
(5) Thakur Dule Singh of Ganora.

Sesodias.—(6) Bhai Raghunath Singh of Khandu.
(7) Bhai Surya Singh of Surpur.
(8) Thakur Balwant Singh of Kushalpura.

Chauhans.—(9) Thakur Dalpat Singh of Bankura.
(10) Thakur Udai Singh of Thakurda.
(11) Thakur Suraj Mal of Mandwa.
} These nobles belong to Dungarpur, but hold estates in Banswara.

Rahtors.—(12) Rao Udai Singh of Kushalgarh.
(13) Thakur Bakhtawar Singh of Tilwara.
(14) Thakur Anup Singh of Orwara.

The *Jagirdars* of Khandu and Surpur, who have the title of Bhai, are descended from Maharawal Prithwi Raj, as mentioned in the notice of the Chief. The Bhai of Surpur is by birth the younger son of the present Maharawal, who was adopted by Thakur Madho Singh. The Bhai of Kushalpura is a Sesodia of the Sakhtawat branch of the Mewar family. The Chauhan families all claim descent from Raja Prithwi Raj of Delhi and are said to have migrated from the neighbourhood of Sambhar when defeated by the Muhammadans. The Rahtor nobles are all connected with the ruling family of Marwar. All the *Solah* nobles have the *tazim*, which is not enjoyed by any of the others. The Rao of Kushalgarh pays a tribute to the Banswara Darbar of R1,100 a year and attends when marriages take place in the ruling family, but is in other respects independent of his nominal Chief, the boundary between whose territories and his own has been defined by a British officer. The Rao of Garhi holds a very large estate, but is in no way independent. Of the *Solah* nobles, only the Rao of Garhi, the Thakur of Kushalpura, and the *Jagirdars* of Khandu and Surpur received their estates from the present ruling family. The estates of all the rest date from before the foundation of the separate State. Succession is in all cases by primogeniture, provision being made for the younger sons. All the nobles have to render feudal service when required, in person if the Chief himself leads the troops of the State, in other cases by deputy. Tribute is paid by all, save the Rao of Kushalgarh. The custom of levying it apparently originated in the forced contributions taken from the nobles in aid of the blackmail paid by the Chiefs to Sindhia and other Mahrattas and to Pindaris at the beginning of the present century. Until recent years most of the offices in the State were held by descendants of Mina Baniyas settled in Banswara, who accompanied the first Chief from Dungarpur. These now carry on their private trade only, having been superseded by Nagar Brahmans and Oswals entertained by subsequent rulers. The latter still hold minor posts. The only official of importance is the Kamdar, who has for some time been a foreigner. Each occupant of the post has generally secured as many as possible of the posts subordinate to him for his relatives and dependants. The Kamdar supervises all public departments and disposes of the public revenues after consultation with the Chief, with whose private revenues he has no concern.

The following nobles alone call for separate notice :—

Individual nobles.

Kushalgarh.

(1) **Rao Udai Singh of Kushalgarh** is a Rahtor of the Ramawat sub-clan. He is nominally subordinate to the Chief to whom he pays tribute, but in consequence of frequent attempts on the part of the Darbar to claim rights over the estate to which it was not entitled, Kushalgarh was finally decided by the British Government to be practically independent for all purposes other than the payment of tribute and personal attendance at marriages in the Chief's family. The Rao corresponds directly in all matters with the Assistant Political Agent. The estate, which is populated almost entirely by Bhils, consists of sixty villages situated to the south of Banswara. The annual income is estimated at R60,000. In addition to the tribute of R1,100 a year paid to Banswara, R1,200 are paid annually to Ratlam on account of the *jagir* of Khera comprising sixty villages granted by that State in 1782. The Kushalgarh family is descended from Rao Jodha of Marwar, whose great-grandson, Askarn, obtained a grant of Kushalgarh from the Emperor Aurangzeb. The distinctive name of Ramawat, by which the sub-clan is known, is derived from Ram Singh, the sixth in descent from Rao Jodha. Ram Singh was killed about 1631 in a war between the Chauhans of Banswara and the Rahtors regarding the succession to the *gadi* of Banswara, which was disputed between the son of a Chauhan and the son of a Rahtor Rani. The latter eventually gained the day. Kushalgarh itself was founded by Akhay Raj in 1670. The title of Rao was conferred on Thakur Zalim Singh by Maharana Bhim Singh of Mewar. The present Rao is the great-grandson of Rao Zalim Singh. He succeeded his father Rao Zorawar Singh in 1891 and is now thirty-four years of age. He has one son, Ranjit Singh, aged ten years, a brother, Jaswant Singh, aged thirty years, and three nephews. The family of the Rao is closely connected with that of the Rahtor Raja of Jhabua. On the accession of a new Rao to the Kushalgarh estate, the ceremony of *talwar-bandi* (investiture by buckling on a sword) is performed by the Raja, who attends at Kushalgarh for this purpose.

Garhi.

(2) **Rao Sangram Singh of Garhi** is a Chauhan Rajput. The family of Garhi, which has for some time been the most powerful and influential in Banswara, is of comparatively recent origin in the State. The first of the line, Agar Singh, came from Thakurda in Dungarpur towards the middle of the eighteenth century and received from Maharawal Udai Singh the *jagir* of Wasi. Agar Singh was killed in an attempt to reduce to subjection certain mutinous members of the Maharawal's family, but his son, Udai Singh, brought the enterprise to a successful conclusion and received as his reward the *jagirs* of Nawagama, taken from the rebels, and of Garhi. Other villages were added later. For services rendered to the Maharawal of Dungarpur in expelling the Mahrattas, Thakur Arjun Singh subsequently received a grant of villages in that State. Arjun Singh's successor, Thakur Ratn Singh, who was the prime mover in the substitution in the Chiefship of the Surpur line for that of Khandu, received the title of Rao from his son-in-law the Maharana of Udaipur.

The estate consists of one hundred and fifty villages, of which the majority are situated to the west of Banswara, yields a revenue of about R80,000 and pays a tribute of R3,500 to the Darbar. Of the whole estate, one hundred and twenty-five villages, comprised in the district of Chilkari, were conquered by Banswara troops from the neighbouring State of Sonth Rampur in Mahikantha and were subsequently bestowed free of tribute on Thakur Agar Singh, the leader of the force. The estate held in Dungarpur is worth about R1,200 a year. The present Rao, who is a younger son of the Thakur of Thakurda in Dungarpur, succeeded the late Rao, Gambhir Singh, by adoption in 1890. He is nineteen years of age, and his estate, which is much involved, is temporarily under the supervision of the Darbar. Rao Sangram Singh, who married the daughter of the Rahtor Thakur of Semlia in Sailana, has no son. His nearest relatives are his natural father, the Thakur of Thakurda, and his brother, the latter's eldest son. For the last three generations, the successor to the estate has on failure of natural issue been adopted from Thakurda.

Khandu.

(3) **Maharaj Raghunath Singh of Khandu,** owing to his kinship with the ruling Chief called the Bhai of Khandu, is a Sesodia Rajput descended from Maharawal Prithwi Singh (1747—1786). An account of the origin and descent of the family has been given in the sketch of the Chief. The estate, which is situated to the east of Banswara, comprises thirty villages,

with an annual income of R30,000. In consideration of the succession to the Chiefship of a junior branch of the family the tribute was reduced to the nominal sum of R400. Maharaj Raghunath Singh is eight years of age and succeeded his grandfather Fath Singh in 1890. He has no brothers, uncles, or cousins. During the minority of the Maharaj, the estate is under the management of the Darbar.

Molan.

(4) **Thakur Madan Singh of Molan** is a Chauhan Rajput of the Dungariya clan, and is in point of descent the leading noble of Banswara, his ancestors having held an important *jagir* on the east side of the Mahi river under the Dungarpur Darbar before the separation of the two States. Until the days of Maharawal Prithwi Singh, by whom a considerable portion of the estate was confiscated and transferred to Garhi, Molan was the most important estate in Banswara, being worth about a lakh of rupees. The present value of the seven villages to which it has been reduced is only R8,000. Rupees 551 are payable as tribute to the Darbar. Thakur Madan Singh, who is now twenty-nine years of age, succeeded his father in 1880. He is a personal friend of His Highness the Maharawal, to whom two of his sisters are married. He has no children. The Thakurs of Metwala and Arthuna are the heads of junior branches of the Molan family.

PARTABGARH.

The Partabgarh family according to local accounts is descended from Khim Singh, second son of Rana Mokul and younger brother of Rana Kumbhu, who held the throne of Mewar from 1419 to 1474. Khim Singh's second son, Suraj Mal, possessed himself of the Sadri and Dhariawad districts. In 1535, when Chitor was invested by Bahadur Shah of Gujarat, Bhag Singh, the eldest son of Suraj Mal, headed the defence, and sacrificed his life for the safety of Udai Singh, the infant son of Rana Sanga. Bhag Singh was succeeded at Sadri by his son Rai Singh. In 1553, Rai Singh's son Bikaji is said to have left Mewar and, after residing for some years at Giaspur near Deolia, finally defeated and killed a powerful Bhil chieftain named Devi and founded the town of Deogarh or Deolia in 1561. Bika may, therefore, be considered the real founder of the Partabgarh State, though it was not known by that name till some generations later. Bhawa, the grandson of Bika, is said to have afforded shelter to Muhabbat Khan after the defeat of the latter by the Emperor Jahangir. Afterwards when restored to favour Muhabbat Khan remembered the kindness received and furthered the cause of Hari Singh, Bhawa's grandson, at the Court of Delhi. Bhawa was killed in battle fighting for the Governor of Mandisor against the Rana of Udaipur in 1604. His nephew, Jaswant Singh, who succeeded to the *gadi* in 1623, being considered dangerously powerful, was invited to Udaipur and, together with his eldest son, was treacherously killed by Rana Jagat Singh. Kanthal was occupied by Mewar troops. Nine years later, Jaswant Singh's second son, Hari Singh, being taken to Delhi by the Thakur of Damotar, succeeded, partly by the interest of Muhabbat Khan and partly by his own skill and address, in getting himself recognized as an independent Chief by the Emperor Shah Jahan, who bestowed on him the district of Kanthal of which the value is said to have then been nine lakhs of rupees. On his return the Mewar troops were withdrawn and Hari Singh established himself at Deolia, built a palace and gradually brought into subjection the whole tract now known as Partabgarh. His tribute to the Emperor of Delhi was fixed at R15,000, and he was granted the title of Maharaj Dhiraj Maharawat. Hari Singh was succeeded in 1674 by his son Partap Singh, the founder of the town of Partabgarh, from which the State now takes its name. An attempt made in this reign by the Maharana of Udaipur to recover Kanthal was unsuccessful and ended in the death of Ram Singh, the heir-apparent of Mewar. Prithwi Singh, who succeeded his father in 1708, was received with much courtesy at Delhi and was granted the right to coin money, which was renewed fifty years later to his grandson Salim Singh. The Salim Shahi rupee is the principal coin of Partabgarh and the adjoining districts to this day. In the next reign, that of Sanwant Singh (1775—1824), the country was overrun by the Mahrattas, and the Maharawat only saved his State from destruction by agreeing to pay to Holkar a tribute of Salim Shahi R72,000 * instead of the tribute formerly paid to Delhi. Holkar's tribute is still levied by the British Government and paid over to Indore.

* British R56,887-12.

The first connection of the State with the British Government took place in 1804, when a treaty was entered into which was dissolved by Lord Cornwallis a little later. In 1818 a fresh treaty was made which is still in force. Maharawat Sanwant Singh died in 1844, his son Dip Singh and the latter's eldest son Kesri Singh having predeceased him. In the meantime Dalpat Singh, Dip Singh's second son, had been adopted by Maharawal Jaswant Singh of Dungarpur and had succeeded to that State in 1825. It was decided by the British Government that Dalpat Singh who, on Maharawat Sanwant Singh's death, had become the nearest heir to Partabgarh, could not be allowed to succeed to both Chiefships. He therefore relinquished Dungarpur in favour of his adopted son Ude Singh, son of the Thakur of Sabli, and was installed as Maharawat of Partabgarh. On his death, he was succeeded by his son Ude Singh, the late Chief.

The following is an abstract genealogical tree of the Partabgarh Chief's family ;—

MAHARANA MOKULJI OF MEWAR, died 1419.

Khim Singh.

Rawat Suraj Mal (established himself at Sadri and Dhariawad).

Rawat Bhag Singh, 1531 (killed when commanding Mewar troops at the siege of Chitor by Bahadur Shah, 1538). | Sais Mal (ancestor of the Damotor family). | Rau Mal (ancestor of the Kalyanpura family).

Maharawat Rai Singh, 1533. | Ancestor of the Thakur of Ambirama.

Maharawat Bikaji, 1553 (left Mewar and established himself at Kanthal ; founded Deolia, 1561).

Maharawat Tej Singh, 1579. | Kishan Das (ancestor of the Thakur of Barlia). | Surjan Das (ancestor of the Thakur of Raipur).

Maharawat Bhanaji, 1594 (killed fighting against Mewar). | **Maharawat Sendhaji, 1604.**

Maharawat Jaswant Singh, 1623 (killed at Udaipur by Maharana Jagat Singh).

Maharawat Hari Singh, 1634 (made Chief of Kanthal by the Mughal Emperor). | Udai Singh (ancestor of the Jhantla family).

Maharawat Partap Singh, 1674 (founded Partabgarh, 1698). | Amar Singh (received the *jagir* of Salimgarh). | Madho Singh (ancestor of the Achlaoda family).

Maharawat Prithwi Singh, 1708 (granted the right to coin money).

Pahar Singh. | **Maharawat Ummed Singh, 1718.** | Gopal Singh, 1723.

Maharawat Ram Singh, 1717. (son of Pahar Singh) | **Maharawat Salim Singh, 1758** (granted the right to coin rupees). (son of Gopal Singh)

Maharawat Sanwant Singh, 1775 (paid tribute to Mahrattas. First treaty with British Government, 1818). | Lal Singh (ancestor of Arnod family).

Dip Singh, died 1834. | **Maharawat Raghunath Singh** (present Chief, adopted by Maharawat Udai Singh's widow).

Maharawat Dalpat Singh, 1844 (originally adopted to Dungarpur).

Maharawat Udai Singh, 1864.

Maharawat Raghunath Singh (by adoption).

The Chief.

The present Chief is **His Highness Maharawat Raghunath Singh Bahadur,** who was born in the year 1859. His Highness, as has been shown above, is a Sesodia Rajput, descended from the ruling house of Mewar. His natural father was Maharaj Khushhal Singh of Arnod, third in descent from Lal Singh, younger brother of Maharawat Sawant Singh (1774—1824). The late Chief Maharawat Udai Singh having died in February 1889 without a legitimate successor, either natural or adopted, his widow adopted Raghunath Singh, the nearest relative.

His Highness has been twice married, first to the daughter of the Thakur of Khawasa in Mewar and second to the daughter of the Maharaj of Semlia in Sailana. By the senior of these Ranis who died in 1891 His Highness has one son, Man Singh, aged seven years, and one daughter. He has no near relatives on the male side, the closest connection being Thakur Khushhal Singh of Salimgarh, whose family is descended directly from Amar Singh, third son of Maharawat Hari Singh, who succeeded to the Partabgarh *gadi* in 1634. The present Chief and the Thakur of Salimgarh are ninth in descent from a common ancestor.

The Chief's natural mother was a daughter of the Chauhan Rao of Asin in Mewar. His adoptive mother, the widow of the late Maharawat, was a daughter of the Rahtor Thakur of Namli in Mewar.

Leading men.

The leading men of the State consist of hereditary nobles, hereditary office-bearers, non-hereditary officials, hereditary bards, priests, etc.

The hereditary nobles are all Rajputs and are fifty in number, nearly all of them being descended from some member of the ruling family. They possess altogether one hundred and sixteen villages with an annual income of about two and a half lakhs of rupees, and pay R32,296 as tribute to the Darbar.

Of the nobles only nine, who are considered to belong to the first class, are entitled to the *tazim*. They are all Sesodias and take rank as follows:—

1. The Thakur of Damotar.			5. The Thakur of Jhantla.		
2.	Do.	Kalyanpura.	6.	Do.	Barlia.
3.	Do.	Ambirama.	7.	Do.	Salimgarh.
4.	Do.	Raipur.	8.	Do.	Achlaoda.

9. The Thakur of Arnod.

Their estates were presented to the ancestors of the present holders directly by the Chief, in some cases as a reward for special service, in others as maintenance for younger sons and brothers. Succession is always by primogeniture, adoption in case of failure of issue being generally permitted and recognized by the Darbar. Besides the annual tribute, the nobles are expected to render military and police service in accordance with their means, to report to the Darbar all heinous offences committed within their estates, and to be present at the capital at certain annual festivals and other special occasions, when summoned.

The hereditary office-bearers are mostly Bagria* mahajans, who hold *jagirs* for services rendered by their ancestors and receive small salaries according to the actual appointment which they hold. A few Nagar Brahmans, Muhammadans, and Kayasthas hold office as occasion requires, but are not hereditary *jagirdars*. The family priests of the Chief (*Purohits*) are Amaitha Brahmans, and the State priests (*Karmantris*) are Tarwari Mewar Brahmans. These hold *jagirs*, as do the *Dasunds* or family bards (*Bhats*), of whom the present representative is Dasund Chandan Singh, and the Charans, of whom the Raos of Sanchair and of Isardar are the heads.

Individual persons of note.

The following personages call for individual notice :—

Damotar.

(1) **Thakur Kesri Singh of Damotar,** a Sesodia Rajput, is the senior noble of the State and sits first on the right hand of the Chief in Darbar. On the demise of a Chief, the Thakur of Damotar takes temporary charge of affairs, and after consultation with the widows of the late Chief and any influential nobles who may be present at the time, instals the new ruler

* See page 38. The tract comprised in the Banswara, Dungarpur and Partabgarh States is known as *Bagar*. The same name is applied to the local dialect.

No accession without his intervention would be recognized as valid. The family is descended from Sahis Mal, younger brother of Bhag Singh, who after the latter's death at Chitor settled at Nimbahera. Some seventy years later, in 1571, Kamalji, Sahismal's son, received a *jagir* in Kanthal. Kamalji was killed at Haldighat in 1575 fighting for the Maharana of Mewar against the Emperor Akbar. The estate, which comprises eleven villages of the estimated value of ₨60,000 and pays an annual tribute of ₨6,000, is situated to the north of Partabgarh. The Thakur is closely related to the Jodhpur family, and his frequent absences at Marwar interfered until recently with the good management of the estate. The present Thakur succeeded his uncle, Thakur Hamir Singh, by adoption in 1866. His grandfather, Thakur Ror Singh, had three sons and two daughters. One of the latter married Maharaja Takht Singh, then Chief of Ahmadnagar and afterwards ruler of Marwar, who bestowed the *jagir* of Jhalawand on Gambhir Singh, Ror Singh's second son. On Ror Singh's death in 1848, his eldest son Thakur Hamir Singh succeeded him, and subsequently, having no male issue, adopted Thakur Kesri Singh, the second son of his brother Gambhir Singh. Thakur Kesri Singh has two sons, Hardeo Singh and Prithwi Singh, aged respectively twenty-two and fourteen years. He has also one elder brother, Zorawar Singh, now Thakur of Jhalawand, and two younger brothers, Madan Singh and Sajan Singh, of whom the former lives with him and assists in the management of the estate.

Raipur.

(2) **Thakur Ratn Singh of Raipur** is a Sesodia Rajput of the Rama-wat sub-clan, so called from Ram Das, the first Thakur. He occupies the first seat in Darbar on the left of the Chief. The estate, which is situated 20 miles to the south of Partabgarh, consists of eight villages with an annual rental of ₨38,000. The tribute payable to the Darbar is ₨4,362. The estate was bestowed on Ram Das, son of Surjan Das, third son of Maharawat Bikaji (1553—1579) as a reward for subduing the Bhil tribes. The Raipur Thakur in addition to the revenue from his own villages receives tribute from the Thakurs of Manpura and Kangarh and the produce of a small estate in Gwalior. The Thakurs of Manpura and Kangarh are descended from Man Singh and Kan Singh, the second and third sons of Thakur Ram Das. In 1789, during the time of Dal Singh the eighth Thakur, the Ramawats were driven from their estates by the Parawat family, but with the aid of the Darbar, recovered them six years later when the Parawats were expelled to Dhar.

Kalyanpura.

(3) **Thakur Takht Singh of Kalyanpura** is a descendant of Ran Mal, third son of Suraj Mal, a brother of Bhag Singh. He holds the second place on the right in Darbar. The estate of Kalyanpura comprises two villages with a revenue of ₨8,000 and pays a tribute of ₨2,195 to the Darbar. Ran Mal, the founder of the house, was killed in the service of Mewar in a boundary dispute with Bundi in 1541. His son Sultan Singh, who commanded the Mewar troops against Muhabbat Khan, received as a reward for his success the *jagir* of Bhairwi in Udaipur, together with the *Sanad* (grant) *of Kurba* (the insignia of royalty) and was raised to the rank of a first-class noble. When Bikaji established himself in Deolia in 1561, Sultan Singh accompanied him and received a *jagir*. Kalyan Singh, who succeeded to the estate in 1614, received a grant of a village in Mandisor from the Subah of that place for his services in repressing the Grasias. This estate is still held by the descendants of his younger brother Madho Singh. Thakur Ranchor Das successfully led an army to repel an attack from the Subah of Mandisor.

Barlia.

(4) **Thakur Lal Singh of Barlia** is descended from Kishan Das, second son of Maharawat Bikaji. Of the nine sons of Kishan Das, the eldest, Jeth Singh, succeeded to the Chiefship of Salumbar by adoption. The remainder accompanied him to Mewar. In 1678 Maharawat Pratap Singh, on his return from a visit to Salumbar, brought with him Manohar Das son of Janiji the ninth son of Kishan Das, and bestowed on him the *jagir* of Barlia. The estate, which is situated to the north of Partabgarh on the Gwalior border, comprises two villages with a revenue of ₨8,000 paying a tribute of ₨1,322. Thakur Lal Singh, who succeeded his father Thakur Chiman Singh in 1861, has three sons, Sawant Singh, Fauj Singh, and Unkar Singh, aged twenty-seven, tweny-four, and ten years, respectively.

Achlaoda.

(5) **Thakur Madho Singh of Achlaoda** is a descendant of Thakur Madho Singh, third son of Maharawat Hari Singh (1634—1674). The estate, which is situated nine miles to the south of Partabgarh, comprises seven villages with a revenue of R8,000 and pays a tribute of R1,833. The present Thakur, who is now twenty-seven years of age, succeeded his father Thakur Ratn Singh in 1869. He has no sons living.

Jhantla.

(6) **Thakur Takht Singh of Jhantla** is a descendant of Kesri Singh, third son of Maharawat Jaswant Singh, who was killed at Udaipur in 1634. The estate is situated fifteen miles north of Partabgarh. It comprises five villages with an annual rental of R12,000 and pays a tribute of R1,416 to the Darbar. Thakur Takht Singh succeeded his father Thakur Lal Singh in 1861. He is now sixty-three years of age and has three sons, the eldest of whom is named Pratap Singh.

SHAHPURA.* (See also page 31).

The founder of this Chiefship was Sujan Singh, son of Suraj Mal, the third son of Maharana Amar Singh of Udaipur, who received from the Emperor of Delhi in A. D. 1629 a grant in *jagir* of the Phulia *pargana* and the title of "Commander of two thousand troops." Sujan Singh was succeeded in 1664 by his son Daulat Singh. In 1685 Daulat Singh wa succeeded by his son Bharat Singh, who received from the Emperor the titles of Raja and of "Commander of three thousand five hundred troops." He died in 1729 and was succeeded by his son Ummed Singh who was killed at Ujain when fighting for Maharana Arsi of Udaipur against Madho Rao Sindia. Ummed Singh's grandson Ram Singh succeeded to the *gadi* in 1768 and received from the Maharana of Udaipur the *pargana* of Kachola as blood-money. His son Bhim Singh succeeded him in 1774 and was followed in 1796 by his son Amar Singh, who received from Udaipur the title of Raja Dhiraj. The *pargana* of Jahezpur and Anguncha, Kotri and other villages were resumed at the same time. In 1827 Amar Singh was succeeded by his son Bhim Singh. The latter's son Jagat Singh, who had succeeded in 1845, received from the British Government in 1848 a *sanad* continuing to him the grant of the Phulia *pargana* and a *khilat*. Jagat Singh, who died in 1853, was succeeded by his adopted son, Lachhman Singh, who received in 1862 a *sanad* guaranteeing to him the right of adoption. On his death in 1870 the present Chief, Raja Dhiraj Nahar Singh, came to the *gadi*.

The Chief.

Raja Dhiraj Nahar Singh, the Chief of Shahpura, is the son of Thakur Dhirat Singh of Dhanop, of the family of Ummed Singh, as shown in the following table :—

ZALIM SINGH.

(Second son of Ummed Singh.)

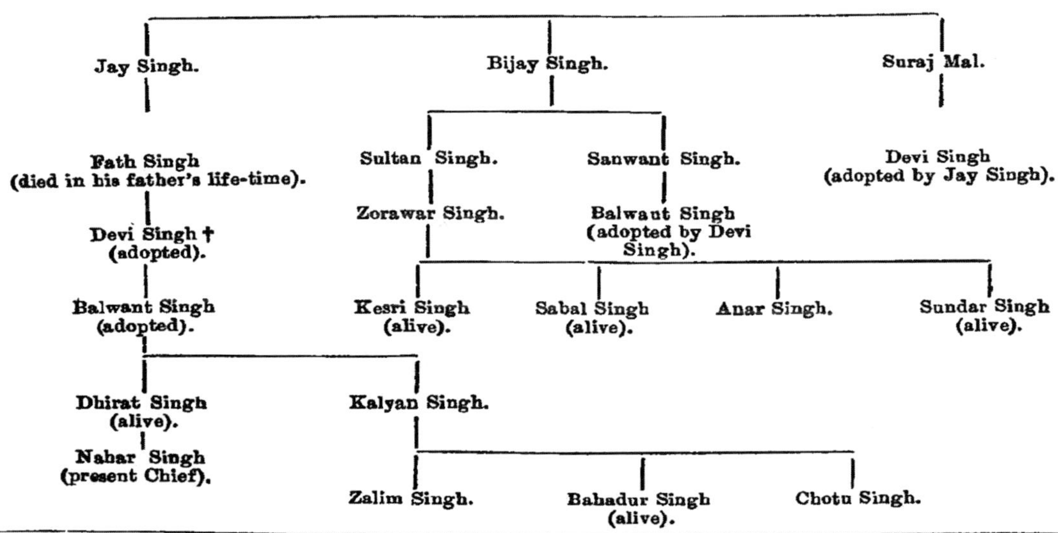

* This account has been compiled by the Chiefship *ex parte* and contains much controversial matter which would be strenuously contested by the *jagirdars* if given a hearing.

† On the death of Jay Singh, Bijay Singh assumed the succession without the permission of the Darbar. He was deposed and went to Udaipur, Devi Singh being adopted into Jay Singh's family.

The Chief, who is a Sesodia Rajput of the Ranawat sub-clan and an Arya Vaidik by religion, was recognized by the British Government in 1870 as successor to Raja Dhiraj Lachhman Singh, and received the usual *khilat* from Government as well as the customary presents of horses and elephants from Native States. He married first, on the 19th August 1870, the daughter of Thakur Ram Singh, a Jodha Rajput of Baghera in Ajmer; second, on the 16th May 1874, the daughter of Chatur Sal, the Khichi Rajput Chief of Maksudangarh in Central India; third, on the 7th July 1889, the daughter of Hari Singh, brother to Man Singh, the Chief of Dharangdara in Kathiawar of the Jhala clan; and fourth, on the 4th March 1893, the sister of the Maharawal of Chhota Udaipur in Rewa Kantha. Of these four Ranis the second and third are dead. By the second the Chief has two sons, Ummed Singh, aged sixteen years, and Sardar Singh, aged twelve years, and two daughters. The Chief has no uncles or other near relations of the ruling family. His nearest relatives belong to his own family of Dhanop whose names are given in the pedigree. After these his nearest relations in succession are the descendants of Bhabhut Singh, Daulat Singh, and Sujan Singh. The Raja Dhiraj is related to the Chief of Udaipur, being descended from Maharana Amar Singh of Mewar, but otherwise has no clan or family relationship with other Chiefs in Rajputana. His mother by adoption is the daughter of Lachhman Singh, *Jagirdar* of Poroli in Mewar, a Chauhan Rajput, and his own mother is the daughter of Thakur Megh Singh, *Jagirdar* of Kotri in Kishangarh, a Rahtor Rajput.

Leading men.

Only three nobles are recognized as such by the grant of the title of Omrao. Of these the Thakur of Khamor, who holds the oldest and richest *jagir* in the chiefship, claims to hold his *jagir* under a grant anterior to that of the Chiefship, but though this is admitted by the Chief, no documents concerning the original grant are in existence. The other two nobles are the *Jagirdars* of Birdaul and Thinnal, situated respectively in the Kachola and Phulia *parganas*.

There are also a number of smaller *jagirdars*. Succession to all *jagir* estates is by primogeniture, suitable provision being made for younger sons. In default of legitimate male issue succession is by adoption, subject to the approval of the Chief, but the right to succeed by adoption is limited to cousins distant by not more than four generations from the adopter. Persons who are of unsound mind or who have committed any act by which their claim is forfeited are excluded from the succession. These rules apply also to the Chiefship. Cousins to the third generation are looked on as brothers to the Chief, after which they sink to the rank of *jagirdars*. The service to be rendered by *jagirdars* has after much dispute been settled by *sanads* granted in 1889, according to which the *jagirdars* are now required to furnish a certain number of horsemen for two months in each year at Shahpura, and to do such service as can properly be demanded of them. They are bound also to attend on the Chief with their following at the Dasehra, Holi, and other festivals, and to accompany him and serve him as directed in accordance with ancient usage on all customary occasions both in and out of Shahpura. All periods of occasional service beyond the limits of the Chiefship exceeding twenty days are reckoned as equivalent to an equal period of the two months' fixed annual service abovementioned, but if such period of foreign service shall unavoidably exceed two months in any one year, no further deductions are to be made in subsequent years. The amount of tribute payable to the Chief is fixed in the case of the older *jagirs* by an assessment made in 1848 A.D., in that of the newer by *sanad*.

There are five hereditary office-bearers of note, all of whom hold revenue-free villages for performing religious duties on the Chief's accession and at marriages and funerals, and for instructing the Chief and his sons in subjects of a scientific nature. Their ancestors came to the Chiefship in the time of Rajas Bharat Singh (1685), Ummed Singh (1729), and Bhim Singh (1774). There are also four hereditary officials whose ancestors came to the Chiefship in the time of Rajas Surjan Singh and Bharat Singh and received land in *muafi* and *jagir*. Of these all four receive monthly salaries and two hold lands and receive in addition fixed dues for special occasions and duties. Their duties are to keep the accounts and records of the Chiefship, to prepare *kharitas* and *sanads* and to act when required as *motamids* and *vakils*. Of the new and non-hereditary officials two only deserve special mention, the kamdar and the Judicial Officer. The *kamdar*, Munshi Bholanath Kayasth, was appointed in 1891 after having served for thirteen years as *vakil* at the Deoli Political Agency. He is a *zamindar* of the Meerut district in the North-Western Provinces, has passed the Entrance Examination of the Calcutta University, and draws a salary of R180 a month.

The Judicial Officer, Maulvi Karimu-d-din Khan, who enjoys the title of Khan Bahadur is also a resident of the Meerut district. He was appointed to his present post in 1892 on a salary of R150 a month and is in receipt of a pension from the British Government.

The only other leading men are the Mahant of Ramdwara and Bakhtawar Singh, the latter of whom holds no office. Their ancestors came into the Chiefship in the time of Rajas Bharat Singh and Ram Singh respectively. The Mahant resides at Shahpura and has followers in various Native States, one of whom is with the approval of the Chief and citizens of Shahpura selected to succeed on the occurrence of a vacancy. Bakhtawar Singh holds lands and is in receipt of a monthly cash allowance. He is at present engaged in compiling an historical account of the Chiefship.

Leading individuals.

Khamor.

(1) Of the three Umraos, **Thakur Zorawar Singh of Khamor** ranks highest, his title having been conferred by Raja Bharat Singh. The Thakur, who is a Rahtor Chandrawat Rajput related to the *Jagirdar* of Belonda in Mewar, is forty years of age. He has two sons, Jaswant Singh and Karn Singh, aged fourteen and eight years respectively, and two brothers, Mor Singh and Devi Singh, of whom the former has two sons. The Khamor estate consists of a village of which the annual income is about R12,000, of which R110 are paid to the Chief as tribute and R351 on account of partial commutation of service.

Birdaul.

(2) **Thakur Nahar Singh of Birdaul,** the second of the Umraos, is a Rajawat Rajput related to the Rajputs of Panwora in Jaipur. He holds one village in the Mewar portion of the Kachola pargana which yields about R5,000 a year, and pays to the Chief a tribute of uncertain amount. The Thakur, who is forty-two years of age, has three sons, Kalyan Singh, aged twenty years, Kesri Singh, aged eighteen years, and Bhim Singh, aged eight years. He has also one uncle, Nahar Singh.

Thynal.

(3) **Thakur Jawahir Singh of Thainal,** the third Umrao, is a Sesodia Ranawat Rajput descended from Jagmalji, son of Rana Udai Singh of Mewar. He holds a village which yields about R8,000 a year and pays an annual tribute of about R500. He also renders certain fixed service. The Thakur, who recently succeeded by adoption to his brother the late Thakur Bhabut Singh, has no sons. He has two brothers, Ratn Singh and Kalyan Singh, of whom the last named has male issue.

CHAPTER IV.

CHAUHAN STATES.

[*Bundi—Kotah—Sirohi.*]

The Chauhan tribe, which is represented in Rajputana by the Haras of Bundi and Kotah and the Deoras of Sirohi, claims descent from a legendary hero named Anhil. Anhil's descendant, Bisaldeo, who lived about the beginning of the eleventh century and was the progenitor of the Chauhan kings of Delhi, became, through his grandson Ishtpal, the founder of the Hara family. About one hundred and fifty years after the time of Ishtpal, Sohi Rao, a near connection of the celebrated Raja Prithwi Raj of Delhi, established his capital at Nadol in Marwar, whence his tribe gradually overspread the territory which borders on Sirohi. The sixth in succession from Sohi Rao built the fort of Jalor in Marwar, and his grandson, Deoraj, became the ancestor of the ruling family of Sirohi, which took from him the name of Deora, by which it is now known.

BUNDI AND KOTAH.

The Hara branch of the Chauhans has been settled for many centuries in the tract now occupied by Bundi and Kotah, to which it has given the name of Haraoti. Regarding its earlier history, the following account is given in the Gazetteer of Rajputana:—"All that can be distinctly collected from the records is that the Haras went through the ordinary course of incessant fighting with rival clans for lands and dominions; that they drove out or extirpated the non-Rajput tribes whom they found in possession (a massacre of the Minas in the fourteenth century is particularly mentioned, which cleared the country round Bundi itself); that they built strong places and gradually acquired predominance in the eastern districts, which they still hold. The Chiefs appear to have admitted the supremacy of the Sesodia Chiefs at Chitor, whenever the latter were strong enough to enforce it; and to have enlarged their borders at the expense or in defiance of the Sesodia Chief at Chitor whenever he was weakened by foreign invasions. Alau-d-din's sack of Chitor gave them an opportunity of this sort, the Hara country being protected by a range of hills and wilds from easy invasion out of the Mewar plains. There are numerous accounts of feuds and battles between Bundi and Chitor, two capitals distant about 60 miles; but the most dangerous enemy of the Haras in the fifteenth century was the powerful Muhammadan dynasty of Malwa. . . . . We may conclude generally that the Eastern Chiefs of Mewar and Bundi were hard pressed by the Muhammadans from the open south-west country, until Rana Sanga restored the power of the Rajputs and retook from the Muhammadans their most important fortresses in this quarter; but this brief period of brilliant revival ended with the great defeat of the Rana at Fathpur Sikri; and Bahadur Shah of Gujarat soon afterwards took Chitor, when Rao Arjun of Bundi with his Haras was slain in the storm. Sher Shah, the Afghan, also marched down into this country and again took Chitor; though, after his death, the Haras got possession of the great fort of Rantambor on their eastern border, which had long been an imperial outpost. This they held as feudatories of the Sesodia Chief; but when Akbar undertook the pacification of Rajputana, he induced Rai Surjan, the Hara Chief, to transfer his allegiance to the Emperor of Delhi, and the fortress yielded after a short siege. Rai Surjan and his sons entered the service of Akbar, receiving rank and pay. From this time forward ceased the supremacy of the Sesodias, and began the connection of the Haras of Bundi with the Mughal Emperors. Several of their Chiefs took service with the Emperors, obtained high rank at the Delhi Court, and received large grants of lands which were alternately resumed and restored as the Chief lost or gained favour, or took the wrong or right side in the dynastic struggles for the throne of Delhi. The bravery of the Hara Chiefs in the field is constantly recorded; they accompanied the Emperor upon distant expeditions and took leading parts in the political revolutions of the time. One of them fell fighting for Dara in the decisive battle near Agra (1658 A. D.), and of course his family became the object of Aurangzeb's revenge; who, however, pardoned the Haras after a vain attempt to ruin them. Another Chief had better luck in the battle for

Aurangzeb's vacant throne, for he took the winning side of Bahadur Shah, while his kinsman of Kotah was killed on the losing side, whereby the Bundi family secured predominance for the time. Soon after, however, a furious feud broke out between the Bundi Chief and the powerful Jay Singh of Amber (now Jaipur), when the Bundi Chief was driven out of his land and died in exile; while the Kotah and Amber Chiefs annexed large portions of his territory. The successor appealed to Malhar Rao Holkar, who forced the Amber Raja to disgorge and replaced the Bundi Chief, keeping Patan as payment for his services. After this time the most important incident chronicled is the death of Rana Ursi of Udaipur, who was killed by the Rao of Bundi during a hunting party, whence arose a feud between the two great houses which is not yet forgotten. From the time of the appearance of the Mahrattas in these parts the Rajput States were constantly exposed to plundering excursions and heavy contributions with occasional loss of territory, and Bundi was among the greatest sufferers. In 1804 the Chief of Bundi assisted Colonel Monson's expedition against Holkar through his country, and gave friendly aid when Monson was forced to retreat. From that time up to 1817, the Mahrattas and Pindaris constantly ravaged the State, exacting tribute and assuming supremacy. The territory of Bundi was so situated as to be of great importance in 1817 in cutting off the flight of the Pindaris. Maharao Bishan Singh early accepted the British alliance, and a treaty was concluded with him on the 10th February 1818. Although his forces were inconsiderable, he co-operated heartily with the British Government. It was this connection with the British Government that raised Bundi from the lamentable condition to which it was reduced by the Mahrattas." Maharao Raja Bishan Singh was succeeded in 1821 by Maharao Raja Ram Singh, G.C.S.I., C.I.E., who died in 1888 after a reign of sixty-seven years. He was succeeded by Maharao Raja Raghubir Singh, the present Chief.

The Kotah State, which formerly formed an integral part of Bundi, was bestowed in 1579 by the Emperor Jahangir upon Madho Singh, the second son of Rao Ratn of Bundi. Of Rao Madho Singh's six successors, three were killed fighting for the Delhi Emperors, and a fourth perished fighting for Prince Azim against Prince Muazzam in the war of the succession. Ummed Singh I. succeeded to the *gadi* in 1771 and co-operated with Colonel Monson against Holkar, aiding with supplies and men. Through the instrumentality of his able Minister Raj Rana Zalim Singh (see Chapter VII) he was the first Rajput Chief to conclude a treaty with the British Government. This took place in 1817. He died in November 1819, and was succeeded by Kishor Singh II. as titular Chief. The administration was vested by a supplementary article to the treaty of 1817 in Zalim Singh and his heirs. On Kishor Singh II.'s death in 1828, his nephew Ram Singh came to the *gadi*, the administration being vested in Madho Singh, son of Zalim Singh. Disputes arose between the nominal and actual ruler in 1834, and on the 18th April 1838, with the consent of the Kotah Chief, seventeen *parganas*, yielding a revenue of twelve lakhs of rupees, were made over to Madan Singh and his heirs as a separate provision for the descendants of Zalim Singh. These districts now form the Jhalawar State. In 1857 the Kotah troops and the Kotah Contingent mutinied, murdering Captain Burton, the Political Agent, and his two sons. The Maharao made no attempt to offer assistance to the Political Agent and as a mark of the displeasure of the British Government his salute was reduced from seventeen to thirteen guns. Maharao Ram Singh, who died in 1866, was succeeded by his son Bhim Singh, who on his accession took the name of Chatar Sal II. In recognizing his succession, the British Government restored to him the full salute of seventeen guns. This Chief's incapacity having led to misrule and oppression, the administration of the State was at his request taken over by the British Government in 1874 and placed in the hands of the Political Agent and a Council of Regency. Maharao Chatar Sal II. died on the 11th June 1889, and was succeeded by his adopted son Udai Singh, the present Chief, who assumed the name of Ummed Singh.

SIROHI.

During the reigns which followed that of Deoraj the Chauhans were engaged in constant struggles with the Pramars or Puars who held Sirohi, and eventually vanquished them. Sirohi itself was founded in 1425 by Rao Sains Mal. Little more is known of the history of the country till the latter portion of the eighteenth century, when Rao Udai Bhan, the then Chief, was engaged in frequent struggles with Jodhpur. Rao Udai Bhan was deposed in 1816 in favour of his younger brother Rao Sheo Singh, who ruled first as Regent and subsequently as Chief. The first relations between Sirohi and the British Government took place in 1817, Sheo Singh having asked assistance in consequence of an invasion from Jodhpur, which had for its object the reinstatement of Rao Udai Bhan. In 1823 a treaty was made, whereby the Rao accepted British supremacy and bound himself to govern by the advice of the British Agent, to introduce an efficient administration, and to pay a tribute not exceeding three-eighths of his revenue, receiving in return a guarantee of protection. In 1843 a further treaty was made, whereby land at Abu was ceded for the establishment of a sanitarium. In 1854 the Rao, at his urgent request, received from the British Government a loan of two lakhs of rupees and the direct management of the State was transferred to the Government for a period of eight years which, in accordance with the terms of the agreement, was subsequently extended to eleven years. During this time many improvements were effected, though as little interference as possible was exercised in internal affairs. In 1861, in consequence of the incapacity of the Rao, the management of the State was made over to his eldest surviving son, Ummed Singh, who on his father's death in the following year succeeded to the *gadi*. Rao Sheo Singh did good service in the Mutiny, in consideration of which the tribute of R15,000 payable by him was reduced by one-half. On the removal of Sheo Singh from all active share in the administration, his four younger sons, Hamir Singh, Jet Singh, Jawani Singh, and Jamat Singh, declined the provision made for them, and went into rebellion. On the death, however, of their father in December 1862 they submitted, and received villages for maintenance. Rao Ummed Singh received full powers in 1865, but, though well meaning, proved a weak and unsuccessful ruler. During his time Sirohi was harassed by famine, by a struggle with the outlawed Thakur Nathu Singh of Bhatana, and by frequent incursions of Bhils from Marwar. These events led to the transfer of the political control of the State from an Assistant to the Agent to the Governor-General to the Commandant of the Erinpura Irregular Force. "The measures adopted by the Political Superintendent for the extermination of brigandage on the Sirohi, Mewar, and Marwar frontier were eminently successful, and the few outlaws who had not been captured were induced to forsake their occupation by the offer of land on which they might settle down to habits of industrial life."—(*Aitchison's Treaties, Vol. III, page 237.*)

Rao Ummed Singh died in November 1875, leaving one son, the present Chief, Rao Kesri Singh.

BUNDI.

The Chief.

His Highness Maharao Raja Raghubir Singh is the eldest son of the late Maharao Raja Ram Singh, G.C.S.I., C.I.E., and was born on the 21st September 1869. His Highness succeeded his father in 1888, and was vested with full powers in April 1889. The Chief has been married three times, twice to sisters of the Maharaja of Jodhpur, by the former of which ladies he has one son, Raghu Indar Singh, aged three years, and lastly to a daughter of the Maharaja of Jhabua in Central India. All the Maharanis are of the Rahtor Rajput clan. His Highness has two real brothers, Rangraj Singh and Raghuraj Singh, and is closely connected with the families of the *Jagirdars* of Dugari and Kapren. He is also connected with the Shaikhawat family of Jhunjhnu in Jaipur and the Parihar family of Nagod. The late Chief took two wives from the latter family, one of whom is the mother of the present Maharao Raja. As noticed above, the Kotah ruling family is an offshoot from that of Bundi, from which it was separated during the reign of Rao Raja Ratn Singh (1607—1614).

Notable personages.

According to the account* supplied by the Bundi Darbar "the nobles and *jagirdars* of the Bundi State are not hereditary. They are in receipt of cash allowances and have been granted *jagirs* in lieu of service performed by them. The granting of *jagirs* to persons deserving of the same or resuming them in consequence of any fault depends entirely on the will and pleasure of the Chief. There are altogether twenty-three nobles, of whom seventeen, being Hara Chauhans, sit in Darbar on the right of the Chief. The remaining six sit on the left. Of these, six are Rajputs, one is a Rahtor, three are Solankhyas, one is a Parihar, and one a Shaikhawat (Kachhwaha)." Succession is by primogeniture and is subject to the sanction of the Darbar. Adoption is not permitted.

* This account represents the view of the Darbar and would probably not be accepted by the nobles and *jagirdars* as accurately representing their position.

The following nobles deserve individual notice :—

Bamangaon.

(1) **Maharaja Rangraj Singh of Bamangaon,** the elder of the Chief's brothers, is twenty-two years of age; knows Sanskrit and Hindi. He occupies no official position and has no son. The *jagir,* which is valued at R20,000 a year and is well managed, was conferred on the Maharaj in 1884. It pays no tribute, but renders service to the Darbar.

Bansi.

(2) **Maharaj Raghuraj Singh of Bansi,** the younger of the Chief's brothers, is eighteen years of age, and, like the elder, is acquainted with Sanskrit and Hindi. He also is childless. The *jagir,* which was conferred in 1884, is of the same value and is held on the same terms as that of Bamangaon.

Dugari.

(3) **Maharaja Unkar Singh of Dugari,** a descendant of the younger son of Maharaja Ummed Singh (1748—1770), holds an estate of the annual value of R20,000. The *Jagirdar,* who is twenty-five years of age, knows Sanskrit, Hindi, and Urdu. The estate, which was conferred on the present holder in Sambat 1933, had previously been administered by the Darbar owing to mismanagement, and is still in debt. It is liable for service, but pays no tribute. Maharaja Unkar Singh has a son, Sheo Singh, aged ten years, an uncle, Sheodan Singh, and a cousin, Sheoraj Singh.

Gudha.

(4) **Maharaja Arjun Singh of Gudha,** aged sixty-two years, is a natural son of the late Chief. He knows Sanskrit and Hindi. He has one son, Ranbir Singh, aged eleven years. The *jagir* of Gudha, which was conferred in Sambat 1943 (1856 A. D.), is valued at R10,000 a year and is in debt. It is liable for service, but pays no tribute.

Nimana.

(5) **Maharaja Gordhan Singh of Nimana,** aged fifty-eight years, is also a natural son of the late Chief. He is acquainted with Sanskrit.

Matonda.

(6) **Maharaja Jagannath Singh of Matonda** is the third and youngest of the late Chief's illegitimate sons. He is forty-three years of age and knows Hindi. This estate, like that of Nimana, is of the same value as the *jagir* of Gudha. The former was conferred in Sambat 1913 and the latter in Sambat 1945. Both estates are liable for service, but neither pays tribute. Maharaja Jagannath Singh has two sons, Harnath Singh, aged twenty-one, and Randhir Singh, aged eleven years.

Khera Raidhan.

(7) **Maharaja Indar Sal of Khera Raidhan** is a descendant of Rao Raja Gopinath (1614—1631) through his third son, Bairi Sal. The Maharaja who is sixty years of age succeeded to the estate by adoption. The *jagir* which was granted, in Sambat 1815 (1759 A. D.) yields an annual income of R10,550 and pays R540 as tribute to the Raj. It is also liable to render service with twenty-five horsemen.

Maghana.

(8) **Maharaja Hanwant Singh of Maghana** is also descended from Rao Raja Gopinath through the latter's son Mohkam Singh. The estate which was granted in Sambat 1880 (1824 A. D.) yields an annual income of R5,251-6-0, pays R255-2-9 as tribute to the Raj and supplies six horsemen for service. The Maharaja who is fifty-seven years of age succeeded to the late *Jagirdar,* Balwant Singh, by adoption. He is a member of the Council of the State and holds the office of *Kiladar* (Castellan) of Nainwa. He has one son, Kalyan Singh, aged twenty-five years.

Pagara.

(9) **Thakur Indur Sal of Pagara,** a Solankhya Rajput, holds an estate of the annual value of R3,801, which was granted in Sambat 1815 (1759 A. D.). It is liable to a payment of R172 as tribute, and to service with nine horses. The Thakur, who is sixty years of age and knows Sanskrit and Hindi, has three sons, Samar Sal, Ari Sal, and Sangram Singh, aged thirty-eight, thirty, and thirteen years, respectively.

Dharra.

(10) **Maharaja Mor Singh of Dharra,** a Hara Rajput, descended from Rao Raja Gopinath, holds an estate of the annual value of R8,999-15. The estate which was granted in Sambat 1804 (1748 A. D.) is bound to supply twenty-two horsemen for the service of the Darbar, and pays R974-6-9 as tribute. It is in debt. The Maharaja is thirty-two years of age and childless. He succeeded the late *Jagirdar,* Balwant Singh, by adoption.

Lilera.

(11) **Thakur Ram Singh of Lilera,** a Parihar Rajput, holds an estate of the annual value of R2,285-6, which was conferred upon him in Sambat 1927 (1871 A. D.). He renders personal service and ays no tribute. The Thakur is fifty years of age and childless.

Datonda.

(12) **Rawat Lal Singh of Datonda,** a Solankhya Rajput, holds a *jagir* of the annual value of R1,250 which was conferred in Sambat 1880 (1824 A. D.). The **Jagirdar** performs service with three horses and pays no tribute. The Rawat has one son, Mukund Singh, aged twenty-seven years.

Jalodi.

(13) **Maharaja Nand Singh of Jalodi,** a descendant of Rao Raja Gopinath through his second son Indar Sal, holds a *jagir* of the annual value of R1,500, which was conferred on his ancestor in Sambat 1888 (1832 A. D.). The Maharaja, who succeeded by adoption, is a member of the Council and the Chief Military Officer of the State, and receives a cash allowance of R829-11-0 yearly. He knows Hindi and Urdu. As he performs personal service, he pays no tribute. The Maharaja has two sons, of whom the elder is Ranjit Singh, aged eighteen years.

Jitgarh.

(14) **Maharaja Nath Singh of Jitgarh** is another descendant of Rao Raja Gopinath through his son Mohan Singh. The village of Jitgarh which was conferred in Sambat 1898 (1842 A. D.), yields an annual revenue of R3,300, renders service with six *sawars* and pays a tribute of R650. The Thakur has one son, Harnath Singh, aged twenty years.

KOTAH.

The Chief.

His Highness Maharao Ummed Singh, Bahadur, the present Chief, was born on the 15th September 1873, and succeeded to the *gadi* by adoption on the 11th June 1889, on the death of the late Maharao Chatar Sal. His Highness, whose name till his accession was Ude Singh, is by birth the second son of Maharaja Chhagan Singh of Kotra. Maharao Ummed Singh was educated at the Mayo College, was married on the 21st November 1892 to the eldest daughter of His Highness the Maharana of Udaipur, and was vested with ruling powers in his State on the 21st December 1892. During the minority the State was administered by the Political Agent and a Council of Regency. The Maharao's nearest relatives are his father Maharaja Chhagan Singh, his elder brother Maharaja Jay Singh of Bamulia and his uncle Maharaja Dhirat Singh of Amli. Other relatives are Maharaja Chatur Bhuj Singh of Kherli, and Maharajas Durjan Sal and Madho Singh of Mundli. Next in relationship to the Kishor Singhot family to which the Maharao belongs is the Mohan Singhot family, of which the head is Apji Amar Singh of Palaitha. The Chief's adoptive mother, the widow of the late Maharao Chatar Sal, is a daughter of His Highness the Maharaja of Karauli.

Nobles.

The **Tazimi Jagirdars** of Kotah are thirty-two in number, of whom the majority belong to the Hara division of the Chauhan clan. Of the *jagirs* eight—Indargarh, Balwan, Khatoli, Gainta, Karwar, Pipalda, Phasud, and Antarda—are held in sovereignty by the Kotah State, subject to the payment to Jaipur of an annual tribute of R14,396-13-0. These fiefs, known as **kotris,** were originally assigned by and subject to Bundi, to which State also belonged the fortress of Rantambor. When Rantambor was made over to the Emperor of Delhi, he exacted annual payments from the holders of the fiefs for the protection afforded to them by the fort. In 1760 Rantambor was made over in trust to Jaipur and that State claimed a continuance of the payments. In 1823, Raj Rana Zalim Singh arranged with the

British Government for transfer of the *kotris'* allegiance to Kotah. The position of these sub-Chiefships is therefore peculiar. No succession or adoption can take place without the consent of the Maharao, and, except in the cases of Indargarh and Khatoli, *nazarana* or a fine on succession is levied.

Individuals of distinction.

The following nobles call for individual notice :—

Indargarh.

(1) **Maharaja Sher Singh of Indargarh,** a Hara Rajput, descended from Indar Sal, a son of Kunwar Gopinath of Bundi, holds an estate consisting of ninety-two villages with a population of 26,208 persons, which yields an annual revenue of about R1,20,000 and pays a tribute of R17,506-12-0 to the Kotah Darbar, of which R6,969 are paid by the latter to Jaipur. Indargarh, which is situated about 45 miles to the north of Kotah, was founded by Indar Sal, the ancestor of the present holder. The Maharaja, who is a student at the Mayo College, is nineteen years of age. He is by birth a son of Maharaja Durjan Sal of Chapol and succeeded to Indargarh by adoption in November 1879. His nearest relatives are his father the Maharaja of Chapol and his two younger brothers.

Balwan.

(2) **Maharaja Chhagan Sal of Balwan,** another descendant of Kunwar Gopinath of Bundi, through the latter's son Bairi Sal, holds an estate of twenty villages to the north-east of Kotah which yield a revenue of R8,000 and pay a tribute to the Kotah Darbar of R1,728-6-0, of which R1,128-6-0 are paid by Kotah to Jaipur. The estate is heavily in debt and five of the villages are held under management by the Darbar as security for payment of the tribute and of money owed to the State. The Maharaja, who is forty-five years of age, succeeded his uncle Maharaja Gopal Singh. in July 1881. He has two sons, aged eight and five years respectively, and a cousin, Thakur Madho Singh, the son of Gobind Singh, the youngest brother of the late *Jagirdar*.

Khatoli.

(3) **Maharaja Partap Singh of Khatoli** holds an estate of thirty villages, 50 miles to the north-east of Kotah. The ancestor of the house was Amar Singh, second son of Maharaja Gaj Singh of Indargarh, who served with distinction under Maharao Raja Budh Singh of Bundi (1671—1695) in one of Aurangzeb's campaigns in the Dakhan. Amar Singh in 1673 captured Khatoli, the seat of the family on the left bank of the Parbati river, from Daulat Khan. The estate comprises, besides the villages on the left bank of the river, seven villages on the right bank in Gwalior territory, which were acquired in 1750 from the Raja of Sheopur whose possessions have now passed into the hands of Maharaja Sindia. The estate, of which the revenue is valued at R50,000, pays R7,632-8-0 as tribute to Kotah, of which R3,982-8-0 are payable by the Darbar to Jaipur. The estate, though well managed, is in debt. The present Maharaja, who is forty-four years of age, succeeded his elder brother Maharaja Bhupal Singh in 1890. His nearest relative is his half-brother Syam Singh, who has three sons.

The estates of Karwar, Gainta, Phasud, and Pipalda are known as the **Hardawat Kotris,** from the fact that the *pargana* of Phasud, of which they form subdivisions, was bestowed by the Emperor Shah Jahan in 1649 upon Khushhal Singh, a descendant of Harda Narain, the second son of Rao Raja Bhoj (1588—1607) of Bundi. Khushhal Singh divided the fief into four equal portions between himself (Karwar) and his cousins Amar Singh (Gainta), Jagat Singh (Phasud), and Daulat Singh (Pipalda). The town of Pipalda was retained as the common undivided property of the cousins and remains so to this day—a cause of perpetual quarrels.

Gainta.

(4) **Maharaja Madho Singh of Gainta** holds, besides the seven villages which form his ancestral inheritance, eight villages granted to him in *jagir* by the Kotah Darbar. The estate, which is situated 40 miles to the north-east of Kotah on the right bank of the Chambal, yields an annual rental of R32,000, and, though well managed, is in debt. It pays R1,908-4-6 as tribute to Kotah, of which R193-9-0 are payable by the Darbar to Jaipur. It also supplies nine *sawars* for the service of the Raj. The Maharaja, who is by birth the son of Thakur Bairi Sal, a junior member of the family, is twenty-two years of age and was educated at the Mayo College. He succeeded the late Maharaja Indar Sal by adoption in 1881. His near relatives are an infant son and an elder brother, Syam Singh, who is blind. Of the Maharaja's

ancestors, Natbji, the third in descent from Amar Singh, distinguished himself in the victory gained at Bhatwara in 1761 by Kotah over Jaipur. Nathji's son, Sheodan Singh, was one of the Kotah representatives who helped to negotiate the treaty with the British Government in 1817. He was rewarded by Government for his services by the gift of an elephant, a horse, a robe of honour, and a sword, of which the two latter are still kept as heirlooms in the family.

Karwar.

(5) **Thakur Subhag Singh of Karwar** holds a small estate of seven villages to the north-east of Kotah which yields an annual income of R12,500 and pays R1,002-14-0 as tribute, of which R331-14-0 go to Jaipur. The estate is well managed, but in debt. The Thakur, who is forty years of age, succeeded his father Thakur Sangram Singh in 1869. He has three sons, Sardul Singh, Kesar Singh, and Durga Das, aged eighteen, fifteen, and twelve years, respectively. He has also a cousin, Thakur Bhur Singh.

Phasud.

(6) **Thakur Bakhtawar Singh of Phasud** holds an estate of six villages, 40 miles to the east of Kotah, yielding a revenue of R10,000 and paying R1,002 as tribute to the Darbar, of which R332 are paid to Jaipur. The estate, though well managed, is in debt. The Thakur, who succeeded by adoption to the estate on the death in 1886 of Thakur Ranjit Singh, is by birth the son of Thakur Sarup Singh of a junior branch of the family, and is forty years of age. He has one infant son, and two brothers, Achal Singh and Baldeo Singh.

Pipalda.

(7) **Thakur Guman Singh of Pipalda** holds an estate, 40 miles east of Kotah, consisting of eleven villages and yielding an annual revenue of R16,000. It pays R1,006-1-6 as tribute, of which R331-12-3 is paid to Jaipur. The estate is slightly in debt. The Thakur, who is twenty-three years of age, was educated at the Mayo College. He was by birth the son of Thakur Lachhman Singh of a junior branch of the family, and succeeded to Pipalda by adoption in 1879, on the death of Thakur Ajit Singh. He has one brother and no children. His nearest relatives belong to the Pipalda family.

Antarda.

(8) **Maharaja Devi Singh of Antarda** holds the town of Antarda with six dependent villages, 32 miles to the north-east of Kotah. The estate yields an annual revenue of R13,000. Of the tribute of R3,828-6-0 payable to Kotah, R1,128-6-0 are paid to Jaipur. Maharaja Devi Singh who succeeded his father Maharaja Sheodan Singh in 1871 is thirty years of age and fairly educated. He has one son, Nand Singh, five years of age, and a half-brother, Prithwi Singh. His nearest relatives are the descendants of his ancestors Sangram Singh and Devi Singh I.

Nimola.

(9) **Maharaja Moti Singh of Nimola**, a Hara Rajput of the Indarsalot sub-clan, is descended from the Indargarh family, to the head of which the estate is subordinate and pays a tribute of R871-14-0 (Madhupuri currency). The Maharaja himself is, by favour of the Kotah Chief, considered independent of Indargarh and holds the rank of a fourth grade Kotah Sardar. The estate, which is well managed and free from debt, consists of one village on the right bank of the Chambal, 50 miles north-east of Kotah. The annual revenue is R12,000, but lands yielding R1,000 are allotted to relatives. The present Maharaja, who is sixty years of age, succeeded his father Maharaja Achal Singh in 1863. He has no son, and his nearest relative is his uncle, Thakur Fath Singh, who has one son, Chatar Sal.

Besides the eight Kotris and Nimola there are twenty-four **Tazimi Jagirdars** in Kotah, of whom thirteen only call for individual notice—

Koela.

*(1) **Apji Gobind Singh of Koela** is a Hara Rajput, descended in the tenth generation from Kani Ram, the fourth son of Rao Madho Singh, the first Chief of Kotah. The Apji, who claims the first seat in Darbar, holds an estate of eight villages on the Parbati river, 40 miles east of Kotah, yielding an annual rental of R27,000. The estate, which owing to former bad management is heavily in debt, is now under the care of Raj Bijay Singh of Kunari. It furnishes ninety *sipahis* to the police of the State, and pays R2,394-3-0 annually to the Darbar. The present *Jagirdar* is five years of age and is the only son of the late

* Owing to the dispute for precedence the Apjis of Koela and Palaitha do not attend Darbars together.

Apji Prithwi Singh who was educated at the Mayo College, and who, after two and a half years' service as a member of the State Council, died on the 9th June 1892. One of his ancestors, Apji Amar Singh, distinguished himself in 1804 at the battle of Garot, where he was wounded while fighting on the side of Colonel Monson. The Apji's nearest relative is Lachhman Singh, the grandson of Apji Sangram Singh.

Palaitha.

*(2) **Rao Bahadur Apji Amar Singh of Palaitha,** who also claims the first seat in Darbar, is a descendant of Mohan Singh, second son of Rao Madho Singh, the first Chief of Kotah, who was killed in 1658 at Fathabad near Ujjain while fighting under Rao Ram Singh for the Emperor Shah Jahan against the latter's son Aurangzeb. Another ancestor of Apji Amar Singh of the same name as himself was killed in 1804 at Garot in Indore while fighting under Colonel Monson against Holkar. The estate, which consists of Palaitha founded by Mohan Singh and four dependant villages yielding an annual rental of R18,000, is situated on the right bank of the Kali Sind river, 26 miles to the east of Kotah. It furnishes twelve *sawars,* and pays R164-2-6 annually to the Darbar; is well managed and free from debt. The present Apji Amar Singh succeeded Apji Fath Singh in 1858 by adoption; he was the son of Apji Agar Singh of Nagda, a junior branch of the Palaitha family. He is forty years of age, and a very able member of the State Council to which he was appointed in 1877. He has one son, Kunwar Unkar Singh, aged twenty, who was educated at the Mayo College. The families most closely related to Palaitha are those of Nagda, Dabri, and Rajgarh.

Kunari.

(3) **Raj Bijay Singh of Kunari,** a Rajput of the Jhala clan, Jaitawat sub-clan, holds an estate consisting of Kunari and eight dependent villages situated on the left bank of the Chambal opposite the city of Kotah. The estate, which is well managed, yields an annual income of R25,000 and pays R2,300 to the Darbar. Raj Bijay Singh, by birth the second son of Raj Fath Singh of Dilwara in Mewar, is twenty-three years of age and was educated at the Mayo College. He succeeded by adoption to Kunari in 1888 on the death of Raj Rup Singh. The Kunari estate was bestowed in 1644 by Rao Mukund Singh, second Chief of Kotah, upon Arjun Singh, the third son of Jeit Singh of Dilwara. Raj Bijay Singh has one infant son. His next nearest relative is his brother Raj Zalim Singh of Dilwara who has also one son, an infant.

Bamulia.

(4) **Maharaja Jay Singh of Bamulia** is a Rajput of the Hara clan, descended from Maharao Kishor Singh, fifth Chief of Kotah. He holds an estate consisting of five villages yielding an annual rental of R11,000, situated 30 miles to the east of Kotah. The estate, which pays R264 to the Darbar, was founded by Suraj Mal, the great-grandson of Maharao Kishor Singh. Maharaja Jay Singh, who succeeded Narsingh Singh the late Maharaja by adoption in June 1888, is by birth the eldest son of Maharaja Chhagan Singh of Kotra and elder brother of His Highness the Maharao of Kotah. He is twenty-one years of age, and was educated at the Mayo College. The Maharaja is married to a daughter of Jagannath Singh, a Jadon Rajput of Karauli.

Sarola.

(5) **Pandit Ganpat Rao of Sarola,** a Dakhan Brahman of the Sarsut clan, Shenwai sub-clan, occupies in Darbar the second seat on the left of the Maharao and holds the township of Sarola and seven dependent villages, 50 miles to the south-east of Kotah. The estate, which yields an annual revenue of R27,000, is held service-free, is very well managed, and is reputed to be the richest and most productive in Kotah. Pandit Ganpat Rao, aged twenty-three and fairly educated, is by birth the son of Pandit Sadashiv Rao and nephew to the late proprietor, Pandit Moti Lal, who was for fourteen years a very able member of the Kotah State Council. Balaji Pandit, the founder of the fortunes of the family, was originally in the service of Baji Rao, one of the Peshwa's Generals, under whom the Mahrattas invaded Upper India in 1739. Passing through Kotah territory, Baji Rao nominated Balaji to negotiate with the Bundi and Kotah Darbars for the payment of *chauth* and later on appointed him to collect this tax in his name from Bundi, Kotah, and Mewar. The Pandit selected Kotah as his head-quarters

* Owing to the dispute for precedence the Apjis of Koela and Palaitha do not attend Darbars together.

and started a banking firm on his own account. Lalaji Pandit, the son and successor of Balaji, while continuing to discharge his father's duties, contracted a friendship with Raj Rana Zalim Singh and afforded valuable assistance to the Regent when Kotah was threatened by Holkar in 1766. For his successful conduct of the negotiations, which led to the withdrawal of the Mahratta troops, Lalaji was substantially rewarded by Maharao Ummed Singh. On the completion of the treaty of 1817, by which the Mahratta tribute became payable to the British Government, Lalaji's office of *Chauth* collector came to an end, and he settled down as a Kotah subject. During his life-time, the Kotah Darbar became indebted to him to the extent of R9,27,364, and in 1771 the Sarola estate was hypothecated to him as security for repayment.

Pandit Ganpat Rao succeeded Pandit Moti Lal in March 1892 as co-heir with a boy named Purshottam who was adopted by Moti Lal on his death-bed. No division of property has yet been made. Pandit Ganpat Rao has no children and his nearest relatives are Pandit Mangesh Rao in Kotah and Pandit Gobind Mahadeo in Konkan.

Kachnaoda.

(6) **Thakur Moti Singh of Kachnaoda,** a Hara Rajput, descended from Rao Surjan Singh of Bundi through the latter's third son, Raimal, holds a service-free *jagir,* consisting of Kachnaoda and two dependent villages situated on the left bank of the Kali Sind river, 21 miles east of Kotah. The estate, which yields an annual rental of R7,377, is considerably in debt. Raimal, the founder of the family, obtained the town and dependency of Palaitha from the Emperor Akbar in recognition of his services in the Dakhan and Gondwana. His grandson, Hari Singh, was ejected from Palaitha. Daulat Singh, son of Hari Singh, received the estate of Sairthal from Maharao Bhim Singh. In 1838, when the partition of Kotah took place, Sairthal was included in Jhalawar and Kachnaoda was bestowed instead of it on the then holder, Thakur Nripat Singh, who was succeeded in 1876 by the present *Jagirdar.* Thakur Moti Singh has an infant son, after whom his nearest relatives are Thakurs Raghunath Singh and Devi Sal.

Rajgarh.

(7) **Apji Kishan Singh of Rajgarh,** a Hara Rajput, is descended from Mohan Singh, second son of Rao Madho Singh of Kotah. Mohan Singh's eighth son, Gordhan Singh, obtained Rajgarh from Rao Kishor Singh and was afterwards killed in one of the Emperor Aurengzeb's wars in the Dakhan. His son, Daulat Singh, was killed in 1720 fighting under Maharao Bhim Singh of Kotah against the Nizam of Hyderabad. Nath Singh, the grandson of Daulat Singh, was killed in 1761 at Bhatwara fighting for Kotah against Jaipur. His grandson, Deo Singh, the grandfather of Apji Kishan Singh, actively assisted Maharao Kishor Singh in 1821 in trying to depose the Regent, Raj Rana Zalim Singh, and was severely wounded at Mangrol. The estate of Rajgarh is held service-free, and consists of one village, 26 miles east of Kotah, which yields R4,000 a year. Apji Kishan Singh, who has been a member of the State Council since its formation in 1877, succeeded his father Apji Hamir Singh in 1871 and is now fifty-nine years of age. He has no children. His brother Gopal Singh has three sons—Madho Singh, Bairi Sal, and Chotaji. The most nearly connected families are those of Palaitha, Dabri, and Nagda.

Ghati.

(8) **Rawat Chatar Sal of Ghati,** a Hara Rajput of the Mewawat sub-clam, holds an estate consisting of Ghati and three dependent villages, 38 miles to the south of Kotah, which yield R2,500 a year. The Rawat is descended from Bir Singh, Chief of Bundi, through the great-grandson of the latter, Meo Singh. One of Meo Singh's descendants, Zorawar Singh, took service in Kotah and was killed in 1736 fighting under Maharao Bhim Singh. His son Khushhal Singh received a *jagir* which was resumed in 1758 owing to the murder of the Kotah Minister by Ajit Singh, the then holder of the estate, who saved his life by fleeing to Udaipur. Ajit Singh's grandson Guman Singh returned to Kotah, and in acknowledgment of his services at the battle of Bhatwara received the *jagir* of Ghati. Guman Singh was an ancestor of the present Rawat. Chatar Sal, who is forty years of age, succeeded his father Zorawar Singh in 1864. He has one son, Durjan Sal, aged twenty, and a brother, Girwar Singh. The latter has three sons—Lachhman Singh, Nathu Singh, and Zorawar Singh.

Kherli.

(9) **Thakur Bhim Singh of Kherli** is a Tanwar Rajput of the Jarola sub-clan, who holds an estate consisting of one village of the annual value of ₹3,000, which pays ₹15 as tribute to Kotah. Thakur Bhim Singh, who is twenty-five years of age, succeeded his father Thakur Khushhal Singh in 1870. He has one son, Ude Singh, the next nearest relations being Thakur Bajrang Singh of Srinal and Thakurs Chatar Singh and Devi Singh.

Srinal.

(10) **Thakur Bajrang Singh of Srinal,** who is descended from Pratap Singh, the founder of the Kherli family, holds a *jagir* consisting of one village of the annual value of ₹1,100, situated 38 miles east of Kotah. Thakur Bajrang Singh, who is thirty-five years of age, succeeded his father Thakur Fath Singh in 1868. He has one son, Jawahir Singh, and a brother, Chatar Singh. His next nearest relative is Thakur Bhim Singh of Kherli.

Dabri.

(11) **Apji Karn Singh of Dabri** is a Hara Rajput, descended from Rao Madho Singh, the first Chief of Kotah, through the latter's second son, Mohan Singh who obtained Palaitha. The Dabri estate consists of one village, 30 miles to the east of Kotah, which produces an annual income of ₹3,000. Apji Karn Singh, who is forty years of age, succeeded by adoption in 1864 to Apji Gordhan Singh. He belongs by birth to a junior branch of the Dabri family. The Apji has an infant son, after whom his nearest relatives are Apji Balbhadar Singh, Mor Singh, and Narain Singh; next come the families of Palaitha, Rajgarh, and Nagda.

Kherli.

(12) **Maharaja Chaturbhuj Singh of Kherli** is a Hara Rajput, descended from Rao Kishor Singh of Kotah. The Kherli branch of the Kishor Singhot family is immediately senior to the Mundli branch, to which the ruling Chief belongs. Bakht Singh, the founder of Kherli, and Chain Singh, the ancestor of the Maharao, being respectively the fourth and fifth sons of Prithwi Singh who was the third son of Maharao Kishor Singh, the fifth Chief. The estate consists of one village, yielding an annual rental of ₹1,500, situated on the left bank of the Kali Sind river, 21 miles north-east of Kotah. Maharaja Chaturbhuj Singh, who is twenty-nine years of age, succeeded his father Maharaja Durjan Sal in 1878. He has one infant son and two cousins, Mor Singh and Arjun Sal. The Bamulia, Kotra, and Mundli families are those most closely connected with Kherli.

Mundli.

(13) **Maharaja Durjan Sal of Mundli,** a Hara Rajput, is descended from Chain Singh, an ancestor of His Highness the Maharao, who was the fifth son of Prithwi Singh, the third son of Rao Kishor Singh. The *jagir* consists of 700 bighas of land yielding a rental of ₹700 a year. Maharaja Durjan Sal is forty-eight years of age, and succeeded his father Maharaja Sher Singh in 1889. He has three sons, Lachhman Singh, Narsingh Singh, and Ranjit Singh, and two brothers, Arjun Singh and Devi Singh.

SIROHI.

The Chief.

The Chief of Sirohi, **His Highness Maharao Kesri Singh Bahadur,** is a Chauhan Rajput of the Deora sub-clan, and was born on the 20th July 1857. He succeeded his father, the late Rao Ummed Singh, on the 24th November 1875. His Highness has been married three times—(1) to a daughter of the Puar (Pramar) Rajput Chief of Danta in Mahi Kantha, Gujarat; (2) to a daughter (now dead) of the Thakur of Barsoda, (Warsora) of the Chaora clan of Rajputs, also in Mahi Kantha; and (3) to a daughter of the late Chief of the Sesodia house of Dharmpur in the Surat Political Agency. He has two sons, one by each surviving Rani. The Maharaj Kunwar Sarup Singh, who is six years old, was borne by the Paru Maharani of Danta, and the second son, Lachhman Singh, is about a year old. The Chief's nearest relations after his son are his uncles Jet Singh and Tej Singh, and his cousins Zorawar Singh, son of Jawan Singh, Achal Singh, son of Jet Singh, Dalpat Singh, and Man Singh, sons of Tej Singh, and Amar Singh son of Zorawar Singh.

The only ruling families of note connected with that of Sirohi are those of Bundi and Kotah. Marriages have taken place in recent times with the Kachhwaha family of Jaipur, the Rahtor families of Jodhpur and Kishangarh, the Jadon Bhati family of Karauli, and the

Sesodia families of Dungarpur and Banswara. The Chief's mother was a daughter of the Baghela Thakur of Posina in Idar.

The following tree gives an abstract of the pedigree of the ruling house of Sirohi :—

RARMAL
(founded old Sirohi in 1347; ancestor of the Chief *jagir* families known as Lakhawat, Dungrawat, Tejawat, and Bajawat).
|
Sobhaji.
|
Sains Mal
(founded new Sirohi in 1425).
|
Lakhaji.
|
Jagmal.
|
Akhaji.
|
Dudaji.
|
Man Singh.
|
Sultan Singh (1565)
(reigned for 51 years and said to have fought in 52 wars)
|
Raj Singh.
|
Akhay Raj.
|
Udai Singh.
|
Durjan Singh.
|
Ummed Singh (1705)
(called also Man Singh).
|
Prithwi Singh (1749).
|
Takht Singh (1772).
|
Jagat Singh (1781).
|
Bhairi Sal (1782).
|
Sheo Singh (1819)
(Udai Bhan succeeded Bhairi Sal, but was deposed in favour of Sher Singh, who entered into the first treaty with the British Government in 1823).

Rao Ummed Singh (1865).	Jet Singh.	Jawan Singh.	Tej Singh.
Maharao Kesri Singh (1875) (present Chief).	Achal Singh.	Zorawar Singh.	Dalpat Singh. / Man Singh.
Maharaj Kunwar Sarup Singh (born 1888).		Amar Singh.	

The leading men of Sirohi consist of the nobles, one hereditary office-bearer and one non-hereditary official. The **nobles** are divided into three classes :—

Leading men.

(1) The immediate relatives of the Maharao, known as **Raj Sahiban.** Their descendants fall into a lower grade;

(2) The **Sarayats,** who are styled Thakuran Raj Sri; and

(3) other **Tazimi** Sardars.

All the nobles are Deora Chauhans and the principal of them are Lakhawat, Dungrawat, Tejawat or Bajawat descendants of Rao Rarmal.

The **Raj Sahiban** are three in number, Jet Singh of Nadia, Tej Singh of Manadar, and Zorawar Singh of Ajari, of whom the first two are uncles and the third is a first cousin to the Chief. These occupy the front seats in Darbar and receive the double *tazim*. Similar honours are enjoyed by Raj Sri Sheonath Singh and Prithwi Raj of Mandar.

The four **Sarayats**, the Thakurs of Padiv and Jawal, Kalandri and Motagaon, sit on the right and left of the Chief. In the absence of the Thakur of Padiv his place in Darbar is taken by the Thakur of Nimaj. The two never attend Darbar together. After them come the Thakurs of Rohna and Bhatana, who also receive the double *tazim*. The Thakurs of Mandwara and Dabani are honoured with the single *tazim* only. Succession in the nobles' estates takes place by primogeniture, provision being made for younger sons. In Manadar and Bhatana this provision is so liberal as almost to amount to a partition of the estate. The payment in tribute to the Darbar varies from four annas in the rupee of the collections among those of high rank to twelve annas among the more insignificant. None hold any *jagir* in British territory.

The only hereditary office-bearer is the Thakur of Padiv, who binds on the Chief's sword and on State occasions sits behind him on his elephant.

The connection of the various families of nobles is shown in the following table :—

RAO RARMAL.

Sobhaji.	Gaja.
Sains Mal.	Dungarji (founder of the Dungrawat families of Padiv, Kalandri, Motagaon, Jawal, and Mandwara).
Lakhaji (founder of the Lakhawat families of Madar, Nimaj, Rohera, and Dabani).	Alam.
Uda.	Uda.
Rahdbir.	Haraj.
Pratap.	Baja (founder of the Bajawat families).
Teja (founder of the Tejawat family of Bhatana).	

Individual notices.

The following personages may be noticed separately :—

Nadia.

(1) **Raj Sahiban Jet Singh of Nadia,** uncle to the present Chief, holds an estate valued at R2,500. He is forty-seven years of age. His son Achal Singh is twenty-seven years old. Both father and son know Hindi.

Manadar.

(2) **Raj Sahiban Tej Singh of Manadar,** who is now forty-five years of age, is an uncle of the present Chief. He holds an estate worth about R4,500 a year. Of his two sons, the elder Dalpat Singh, aged twenty, who was educated at the Mayo College, knows English and has passed the University Entrance Examination. Man Singh, the younger son, is only three years of age. Tej Singh is a man of considerable force of character. He obtained the estate of Manadar some years ago on the death of the Bajawat *Jagirdar* on the pretext that the late Thakur's widow had adopted him. The seizure of this property gave rise to an insurrection and Tej Singh was driven out. Ultimately with the help of the Darbar he recovered the *jagir*, and showed much tenacity and some ability.

Ajari.

(3) **Raj Sahiban Zorawar Singh of Ajari** is the son of the late Jawan Singh, an uncle of the ruling Chief. He possesses an estate worth R3,000 a year. Zorawar Singh, who is twenty-eight years of age, has one son, Amar Singh, aged five years.

Madar.

(4) and (5) **Sheo Nath Singh** and his uncle **Prithwi Raj,** **Lakhawat** Deoras, hold the Madar estate of the annual value of about R2,500. They pay eight annas in the rupee as tribute to the Darbar, and enjoy the title of **Raj Sri.**

Padiv.

(6) **Thakur Raj Sri Mal Singh of Padiv** is the Chief of the **Sarayats** (*vide* page **61**). His estate, which is valued at R500 a year, consists of eight villages and pays six annas in the rupee to the Darbar.

Kalandri.

(7) **Thakuran Raj Sri Prithwi Raj of Kalandri,** a Dungrawat Deora Rajput, holds an estate worth about R3,000, which pays six annas in the rupee to the Darbar. The Thakur is thirty-five years old.

Jawal.

(8) **Thakuran Raj Sri Megh Singh of Jawal** is also a Dungrawat. He is sixteen years of age and was adopted from the Nan family of Sirohi. The estate is worth about R2,000 a year and pays six annas in the rupee to the Darbar.

Motagaon.

(9) **Thakuran Raj Sri Lachman Singh of Motagaon,** a Dungrawat, is twenty-seven years of age and was adopted from the Baldut family of Sirohi. The estate, which is worth R2,500, pays six annas in the rupee to the Darbar.

The three last-named nobles are all **Sarayats.**

Nimaj.

(10) **Thakuran Raj Sri Himmat Singh of Nimaj** belongs to the Lakhawat family of the Deora sub-clan and was adopted from the Dhauli family in Sirohi. The estate consists of eight villages of the value of R7,000, and pays six annas in the rupee to the Darbar. The Thakur, who is thirty years of age, possesses also three villages in the Palanpur State. There is a hereditary feud between the Sirohi Darbar and the Nimaj family.

Rohna.

(11) **Thakuran Raj Sri Ajit Singh of Rohna** is also a Lakhawat. He was adopted from the Jolpur family and is now forty years of age. The estate consists of ten villages of the value of about R2,000 which pay eight annas in the rupee to the Darbar. The Thakur also holds some villages in the Palanpur State.

Bhatana.

(12) **Thakuran Raj Sri Bharat Singh of Bhatana** is a Deora Chauhan of the Tejawat branch. The estate, which pays eight annas in the rupee to the Darbar, is worth about R1,000. The Thakur, who is forty years of age and uneducated, was, when young, in outlawry with his father Nathu Singh who for many years defied pursuit and kept the country disturbed. His successful opposition won for Nathu Singh and his family the admiration of Sirohi and songs are sung in his praise.

Mandwara.

(13) **Thakur Dungar Singh of Mandwara** is a Dungrawat. He is sixteen years of age. The estate, which is worth R2,000 a year, pays to the Darbar half the collections in kind and three-fourths of the collections in cash.

Dabani.

(14) **Thakur Ajit Singh of Dabani** is a Lakhawat. He is eleven years of age, and holds, besides one village in Palanpur, an estate in Sirohi of the value of R600 which pays half its income to the Darbar. The Thakur was adopted from the family of a younger brother.

The only official in Sirohi calling for notice is **Singhiji Jawahir Chand,** a Visa Oswal Mahajan, who after serving as a Tahsildar and as Vakil in attendance on the Resident, was appointed Dewan in June 1892. He enjoys the *tazim,* has a fair knowledge of Urdu, and is a capable official.*

* This officer resigned his post while this work has been in the press and has been succeeded by **Milap Chand,** a Mahajan of Surat, who was previously Diwan of the State from 1887 till 1892 when he resigned. He a painstaking officer with a fair knowledge of English.

CHAPTER V.

JADON STATES.

[*Jaisalmer—Karauli.*]

The Jadon clan, of the early history of which very little is known, claims descent from the Yadu or Jadon kings. These monarchs, who in early days were very powerful, took their name from Yadu, the patronymic of the descendants of Bhuda, the progenitor of the lunar race. The capitals of the Yadus are said to have been Pryag (Allahabad), and subsequently Mathura (Muttra). On the death of Sri Krishna, the deified hero of the house, the tribe was dispersed. According to Jaisalmer accounts, many of them, with two of Sri Krishna's sons, abandoning Hindustan, settled beyond the Indus. One of their descendants was defeated and killed in battle, and the tribe was driven southward into the Punjab, where **Salivahan**, son of Gaj, founded a town and named it after himself, Gajgarh (Ghazni). Salivahan's grandson Bhati was also a great and successful warrior, whose name was adopted by his clansmen as a tribal designation. Shortly after this, the tribe was again driven southward by the king of Ghazni and, crossing the Sutlej, took refuge in the Indian desert, which henceforth became its home. "This traditional account;" says Colonel Walter in the Gazetteer of Jaisalmer, "may represent in outline the early migrations of the Bhati tribe which may be supposed to have entered India from the north-west under heroic leaders now deified as the sons of Krishna, and to have been settled for some time in the Punjab. One of the grand expeditions of Mahmud of Ghazni (1004-5 A. D.) was against the city of Bhatia, also called Bhera, which place is now said to have been on the left bank of the Jhelum, opposite the Salt Range, and there can be little doubt that Bhatia was, or had been, in the dominions of the Bhatia Rajputs. Mr. E. Thomas considers that the four last Hindu kings of Kabul (before the Ghaznavides) may have been Bhatia Rajputs. It may be taken as certain that the Bhatis were driven into the desert by the conquests of the Musalmans on the north and west; that they maintained constant warfare on both borders for many generations with the Muhammadans, and that they gradually subdued and drove out the rival tribes or clans whom they found in the territory which they occupied, of whom one, the Sodas, appear to have been very strong; their head-quarters are now further westward towards Umarkot. Their head-quarters appear to have been placed successively at Tamoli, Deorawal, and Jaisalmer: the two first named places still exist, the last is now the State's capital. Deorawal was founded by Deoraj, a famous prince of the Bhati family. . . . . Deoraj became a great warrior and established the power of the Bhatis firmly in this desert tract; the title of Rawal also commenced with him, and he is counted as the real founder of the Jaisalmer family. The Bhatis gradually extended their possessions southwards and many of them became great free-booters, a character they have continued to bear ever since. In 1156, Jaisal, the sixth in succession from Deoraj, founded the fort and city of Jaisalmer on a low range of sandstone hills and made it his capital, as being more secure than his former residence, Lodorva, which was in the open plain. Subsequent to the founding of Jaisalmer, there was a succession of warlike princes, who were constantly engaged in battles and raids, and whose taste for freebooting proved most disastrous, for on two occasions, *viz.*, in 1294 and shortly afterwards, the Bhatis so enraged the Emperor Alau-d-din that the Imperial army was despatched against them, and conquered and sacked the fort and city of Jaisalmer, so that for some time it remained completely deserted." In the sixteenth century the Bhatis formed an alliance with the Amirs of Sind against the Rahtors. Rawal Sabal Singh, the twenty-fifth prince in succession to Jaisal, was the first to acknowledge the supremacy of the Delhi Empire, and to hold his dominions in subordination to it. The Jaisalmer Chiefs had now arrived at the height of their power. Their territory extended northward to the Sutlej, thus including the whole of the province of Bahawalpur, and westward to the Indus, while to the east and south it comprised many districts, which were subsequently annexed by the Rahtors and incorporated in Marwar and Bikanir. From this time to the accession of Rawal Mulraj in 1762 the fortunes of the State rapidly declined, and most of the outlying provinces were wrested from it. Jaisalmer first entered into relations with the British Government in the reign of Mulraj.

Karauli.

According to the Karauli authorities, Maharaja Bijay Pal, a descendant of Sri Krishna, came from Mathura in 995 to the hill Mani which overlooks the modern town of Biana, and established himself as a powerful monarch. Fifty-one years later the rule of Bijay Pal was brought to an end by the Musalmans of Ghazni under the leadership of Abu Bakr Shah, Kandahari. The Karauli chroniclers say that one of the eighteen sons of Bijay Pal was Gaj Pal, the founder of Gajgarh and of the Jaisalmer dynasty, and another Chatar Pal, who was killed near Ghazni in an invasion of Kabul. Regarding this account, which is irreconcilable with that of the Jaisalmer authorities, Colonel Powlett, the writer of the Karauli Gazetteer, remarks: "Thus it is of little value, except as exhibiting the popular view of Jadon history. The allusion to Gajner and Ghazni evidently has reference to the foundation of Ghazni by the Jadons many years before this period, as told by Colonel Tod in his annals of Jaisalmer." Taman Pal, eldest son of Bijay Pal, established himself about 1052 at Tamangarh, 15 miles south-east of Biana, and eventually possessed himself of the *Dang* or high irregular ground above the Chambal comprising the country round the forts of Utgarh and Mandrel and reaching as far as Dholpur, besides the district in which the present towns of Karauli and Machilpur to the north-east of Karauli are situated. Taman Pal's son, Dharm Pal, was ousted from Tamangarh by his illegitimate half-brother, Har Pal, and built a fort and established himself at Dholdera on the present site of Dholpur. His son Kunwar Pal recovered Tamangarh for his father, but the Muslim Governor of Biana taking the part of Har Pal, the whole territory fell into the hands of the Musalmans. Dharm Pal was killed and Kunwar Pal fled to Rewa. Kunwar Pal's brothers became servants to the Musalmans, and their descendants are still a despised race known as **Gonj**, which is said to be a contraction of *Gonkayar* or time-server. Kunwar Pal's descendant Arjun Singh (1327) managed to gain possession of the fort of Mandrel on the Chambal and to obtain confirmation of his occupation from the Court of Delhi. By degrees he recovered the whole of the territory of Taman Pal, established villages along the Badraoti and built the Thakur Kalyanji's temple on the site of Karauli, a name which is said to be a corruption of Kalyanji. In 1348 he laid the foundations of the city. The first remarkable chief among his successors was Chand Pal (1449) who won great fame as an ascetic, and, according to the chroniclers, by his prayers, and by sending his grandson Gopal Das with an expedition of the Emperor Akbar, contributed greatly to the success of the Emperor's arms in the Dakhan. Gopal Das, who is said to have laid the foundations of Agra Fort at Akbar's request, eventually succeeded his grandfather and enlarged the borders of the State. From Gopal Das are descended two of the most important offshoots of the Karauli house, the **Muktawats** of Sir Mathura, Jhiri, and Sabalgarh, and the **Bahadur ke Jadon** sprung from the Tarsam Bahadur, who obtained Sabalgarh, Bahadurpur, and Bijaypur.

Gopal Das's grandson Mukund Das (1585) was the ancestor of the still numerous family of **Mukund Jadons.** His son Chatar Man (1632) was the ancestor through his son Bhup Pal, of the **Inaiti Rao**, one of the five chief nobles of Karauli, and through another son Shast Pal of the **Manoharpur Kotri.** From Dharm Pal, who succeeded in 1645, are descended the Gareri, Hadoti, and Roantra families. Gopal Singh, who succeeded in 1725, was on good terms with Delhi, whence he received the coveted *Mahi Maratib* or fish insignia. He is looked on as the greatest Chief of Karauli after Gopal Das. In the time of Maharaja Manak Pal (1772) the State was much harassed by the Mahrattas under Sindia and his General, Baptiste, and eventually lost Sabalgarh. In the next reign, that of Har Bakhsh Pal, who succeeded in 1804, Karauli first entered into relations with the British Government. These ended in the treaty of 1817, which rid the State of the Mahrattas. The reign of Maharaja Partap Pal, who succeeded in 1837, was marked by much internal dissension and fighting, which continued notwithstanding the intervention of several British officers till the Maharaja died. Order was restored in the next reign, that of the minor Maharaja Narsingh Pal (1850—1852), by Lieutenant Monck-Mason. On this Chief's death, the well-known Karauli adoption case came before the Government, and it was finally decided that though there was no direct heir, the State should be preserved. Madan Pal was recognized as Chief, and in his reign Karauli rendered loyal service to Government during the Mutiny. On his death in 1869, his nephew Rao Lachhman Pal succeeded him, but died very shortly afterwards, being followed by Maharaja Jay Singh Pal, who died in 1875 and was succeeded by Maharaja Arjun Pal, on whose death in 1886 the present Chief, Maharaja Bhanwar Pal, occupied the *gadi*.

JAISALMER.

The Chief.

The present Chief of Jaisalmer is **His Highness Maharaj Adhiraj Maharawal Salivahan Bahadur,** who was born on the 12th June 1887. His Highness, a Rajput of the Jadon Bhati clan, was the son of Thakur Khushhal Singh of Lathi, and before his accession to the *gadi* was known as Syam Singh. He succeeded the late Maharawal Bairi Sal on the 10th March 1891. The nearest surviving male relatives of the Maharawal are his father Thakur Khushhal Singh of Lathi and his younger brother Dan Singh. He has also two cousins, Sheodan Singh and Salim Singh. The last-named of these has one son, Sultan Singh. A deceased cousin Sardar Singh has left two sons, Jaswant Singh and Jawahir Singh. The adoptive mother of the young Chief was a Sesodia Rajput lady of the ruling house of Dungarpur. The Bhatis of Jaisalmer are also connected by marriage with the Rahtors of Jodhpur, Bikanir and Kishangarh, and with the Hara Chauhans of Kotah.

As already mentioned, the first ruler of Jaisalmer to enter into relations with the British Government was Maharawal Mulraj, who in 1818 concluded a treaty whereby the integrity f the State was guaranteed to the Chief and his posterity, provided the cause of quarrel was not ascribable to Jaisalmer. During the life-time of Mulraj, who died in 1820, the State was virtually governed by his Minister, Salim Singh, who committed the most awful atrocities. He put to death nearly all the relatives of the Chief. The town of Jaisalmer was depopulated by his cruelty, the trade of the country was interrupted, and those relatives of the Maharawal who escaped death, fled from the country. Mulraj was succeeded by his grandson Gaj Singh in whose reign after the conquest of Sind the forts of Shahgarh, Gursia, and Gohtaru, which had been wrested from Jaisalmer, were restored to it. Maharawal Gaj Singh died in 1846, and his widow adopted Maharawal Ranjit Singh, who in 1864 was succeeded by his younger brother Maharawal Bairi Sal, the late Chief, who died in 1891.

Leading personages.

The leading men of the State are the relations of the Chief who are known as **Rajwis,** and the Thakurs. These are all Bhatis and are distinguished as Barsang, Khian, Tejmatot, Prithwirajot, Biharidasot, Dwarkadasot, Sakat Singhot, and Udai Singhot, according to the subdivision of the clan to which they belong. The chief of the nobles are the Raos of Bikampur and Barsalpur and the Thakurs of Jhinjinyali, Baru, Kindha, Girajsar, Gehun, Khuri, Satyaya, and Nawatala, all of whom have the *deorhi* or double *tazim*. Except the first two whose incomes are R5,000 and R8,000, respectively, all are unimportant, being petty Thakurs whose income in no case exceeds R1,700 a year. Primogeniture obtains among the Khian and Barsang Bhatis, the younger sons receiving maintenance only, but among the rest estates are generally equally divided. None of the nobles, except the Thakur of Bikampur, pay tribute or render service, though all present a horse on the accession of the Chief to the *gadi*. The only hereditary office-bearer of note is the Thakur of Chelak, whose position as Raj Pardhan entitles him to a seat behind the Chief on an elephant on State occasions. The official class is composed chiefly of Oswals and Mahesri Mahtas, Purohits, and Byases. The Mahtas generally hold the principal posts.

Among the Rajwis, the following may be mentioned :—

(1) **Thakur Khushhal Singh of Lathi,** the real father of the present Chief. The Thakur, who holds two villages with an annual income of R1,000, is twenty-nine years of age. He has one son, Dan Singh, besides His Highness the Maharawal.

(2) **Thakur Sultan Singh,** son of Kesri Singh of Machna, holds eleven villages with an income of R2,000.

(3) **Thakur Man Singh,** son of Tej Singh of Eta, aged forty-seven years, has one village with an income of R1,000.

(4) **Thakur Jaswant Singh,** son of Sardar Singh, aged fifteen years, and **Thakur Salim Singh,** son of Ummed Singh, aged thirty-three years, own between them one small village.

(6) **Thakur Sheodan Singh**, son of Anar Singh, aged thirty-five years, holds one village of the annual value of R1,000. The Thakur is a man of good education and administrative experience which was acquired in Jhalrapatan, where his father Thakur Anar Singh of Gajwara (see page 88) lives. He does not reside in Jaisalmer, but is in receipt of an allowance from the State.

The principal nobles of the State are mentioned in the following list:—

Name of estate.	Name of Noble.	Father's name.	Age.	Sub-clan.	Number of villages.	Income.	Tazim.	Male issue.
						R		
1. Bikampur	Rao Khetsi	Sheo Singh	45	Barsang	9	5,000	Double	Amar Singh, Abhay Singh.
2. Girajsar	Thakur Amar Singh.	Jetmal	17	Do.	1½	1,700	Do.	...
3. Bikasar	Thakur Bulidan.	Sahibdan	36	Do.	1	1,000	Single.	...
4. Sirran	Thakur Nawal Singh.	Partap Singh	36	Do.	2	1,000	Do.	Three sons.
5. Sirran	Thakur Kan Singh.	Mul Singh	18	Do.		1,000	Do.	...
6. Barsalpur	Rao Dhanji	Ranjit Singh	36	Khian	16	8,000	Double	Moti Singh, Meghji.
7. Jhinjinyali	Thakur Bulidan	Sheoji Singh	41	Udai Singhot	4	1,350	Do.	Four sons.
8. Bhadli	Thakur Lalji	Jaswant Singh	54	Do.	5	1,700	Single	Four sons.
9. Deoran	Thakur Bulidan	Shimbhudan	31	Do.	1	700	Do.	...
10. Rindhan	Thakur Bakhtawar Singh.	Prithwiraj	51	Tejmatot	1	700	Double	Two sons.
11. Modhan	Thakur Ranjit Singh.	Nahar Singh	51	Do.	1	200	Single	Two sons.
12. Baru	Thakur Panji	Muhabbat Singh.	21	Dwarkadasot.	6	1,350	Double	...
13. Baru	Thakur Bakhtawar Singh.	Hirji	36					One son.
14. Satyaya	Thakur Fath Singh.	Bhojraj	26	Sakat Singhot.	1	500	Do.	One son.
15. Nawa Tala	Thakur Pratap Singh.	Bulidan	46	Prithwirajot	1	1,000	Do.	Two sons.
16. Chelak	Thakur Hemji	Prithwiraj	36	Do.	1	400	Single	...
17. Baragaon	Thakur Madho Singh.	Jiwraj	51	Biharidasot.	1	400	Do.	...
18. Dangri	Thakur Lachhman Singh.	Hemji.	26	Do.	1	1,000	Do.	...
19. Dangri	Thakur Satidan	Sahibdan	11	Do.				
20. Rajgarh	Thakur Jodh Singh.	Akhji	66	Do.	1	200	Do.	Two sons.
21. Khuri	Thakur Rai Singh.	Ranjit Singh	36	Sodha Puar (Umarkot).	3	1,500	Double	One son.
22. Lunar	Thakur Anand Singh.	Madho Singh	51	Do.	1	500	Single	Four sons.

Only four of the officials call for mention. Of these one, the Diwan, is a foreigner, and three are natives of Jaisalmer.

Officials.

(1) **Mahta Jagjiwan**, the Diwan, is an inhabitant of Kachh Bhuj, whence he was sent for by the late Chief in 1890. He is fifty-one years of age, by caste a Modh Mahajan, and receives an annual salary of R4,800.

(2) **Mahta Nathmal,** a Mahesri Mahajan of Jaisalmer, aged fifty-four years, was for many years Diwan of the State. He is in receipt of an annual income of R780.

KARAULI.

The Chief.

The present Chief is **His Highness Maharaja Bhanwar Pal Deo Bahadur Yadukul Chandra Bhal, K.C.I.E.** His Highness, who was born on the 24th February 1864 and was the son of Thakur Durjan Pal, succeeded to the *gadi* of Karauli on the 14th August 1886 by adoption to His Highness the late Maharaja Arjun Pal. The Chief, who has no relations nearer than cousins, has been married three times, (1) in 1878 to the daughter of Ajit Singh of Koela in Kotah of the Hara family, (2) in 1880 to the daughter of the Raja of Khandela in Jaipur, and (3) in 1889 to the daughter of Ajit Singh of Mandawa in Jaipur, both of the Shaikhawat family. The first and last of these ladies are still alive. The following table shows the nearest surviving relatives of the Chief:—

BHERUN PAL.

- Mangal Pal.
  - **Maharaja Arjun Pal.**
  - Durjan Pal.
    - **Maharaja Bhanwar Pal** (present Chief); (adopted by Maharaja Arjun Pal).
  - Sujan Pal.
    - Bhum Pal.
    - Moti Pal.
- Padam Pal.
  - Jatu Pal.
    - Surjan Pal.

The ruling family of Karauli is connected by marriage with Bundi, Kotah, and Sirohi. In 1785 a daughter of Maharaja Manak Pal was married to Rao Raja Bishan Singh of Bundi. A daughter of Maharaja Partap Pal (1837-53) married Maharao Chatar Sal of Kotah, and Maharaja Madan Pal (1854-69) married a daughter of the then Rao of Sirohi.

The Karauli family all bear the distinguishing appellation of Pal in token that they, as descendants of Sri Krishna, are protectors (*pal*) of cows, whereas the lion (*singh*) does not respect the sacred animal.

Leading personages.

The leading men of Karauli are the nobles who are divided into Thikanedars, Bapotidars, and others; hereditary office-bearers, and other officials.

The feudal aristocracy of the State consists entirely of the Jadon Thakurs connected with the ruling house. These pay as tribute a fixed sum, which though nominally one-fourth of the produce of the soil, is in reality much less,—in fact less than half the share paid by common land-holders. This tribute is in lieu of constant military service which is not performed in Karauli. In case of military emergencies or State pageants, the Thakurs come in with their retainers, who on these occasions are maintained at the expense of the Darbar. The Thakurs' families (**Kotris**) paying tribute are thirty-seven in number, of which those of Hadoti, Amargarh, Rawantra, Inaiti, Barthun, and Padampura are known as Thikanedars. The remainder are styled Bapotidars. The other families of nobles are of little importance and belong chiefly to the Haridas and Mokund Kotris or to the Pal family. Succession is generally by primogeniture, but by custom a Thakur on succeeding to his estate is bound to assign grants of land for maintenance to his younger brothers. In some cases estates are equally divided among all sons, and in others partition takes place, the eldest son receiving a double share. The nobles, though for the most part illiterate, are a very powerful body in the State, and have till quite recent times frequently defied the authority of the Darbar.

The only hereditary office-bearers of note are **Raja Bahadur Lakhpat Singh** and **Jamadar Fazl Rasul Khan.** The most prominent of the non-hereditary officials are the members of Council, the heads of the Revenue Department, the privy purse (*gumat*), and the wardrobe (*toshakhana*), and the personal Physician and Private Secretary.

CHAPTER VI.

KACHHWAHA STATES.

[*Jaipur—Alwar.*]

JAIPUR.

The accepted legend traces back the lineage of the Kachhwaha tribe to Kash, the second son of Rama who ruled at Ajudhya and who is said to have emigrated thence to Rhotas on the Son river, whence, after several generations, a second migration brought Raja Nal westward across the Jumna to Narwar. At Narwar the family established itself till one Dhola Rao founded the parent city of the present Jaipur State at Amber in A. D. 967. After years of warfare, Dhola-Rao and his Kachhwahas are said to have absorbed or driven out the petty Mina and Rajput Chiefs by whom the neighbouring territory was then held, and to have set up a tribal sovereignty known as Dhundar. The head-quarters of the State were fixed early in the eleventh century at Amber, but it is probable that the Chiefship remained of small importance till in the sixteenth century its head attached himself to the side of the Mughal Emperors. Raja Bihari Lal was presented at Court in the first year of Akbar's reign and subsequently gave his daughter in marriage to Akbar. His immediate successors did good service under that Emperor, and Jay Singh, later on, fought in the Dakhan for Aurangzeb, at whose instigation he was afterwards murdered. The next Chief of note was Jay Singh II., who received the itle of Sawai* from the Emperor and founded the present city of Jaipur in 1728. This Chief, who attained great celebrity as a mathematician and astronomer, availed himself of the confusion prevailing at Delhi considerably to augment his dominions. After his death, however, the Chiefship was much harassed by the attacks of its enemies and internal troubles. The Jats of Bhartpur annexed a portion of its territories. Another portion became the separate Chiefship of Alwar, and later in the century the Mahrattas interfered in the quarrels which arose between Mewar, Jaipur, and Marwar owing to the treaty by which the two last-named houses had bound themselves to disregard the claims of primogeniture in favour of any son who might be born from a princess of Udaipur. In 1803 the Jaipur Chief, Jagat Singh, entered into relations with the British Government, but the treaty then made was dissolved by Lord Cornwallis. A quarrel between Jaipur and Jodhpur for the hand of a Mewar princess, which was only brought to a close by the murder of the lady, reduced both States to the verge of ruin, and Amir Khan took advantage of the prevailing confusion to harry Jaipur with his Pindaris. Jaipur again sought the protection of the English, which was granted by the treaty of 1818, by which the Maharaja, in consideration of payment of a tribute, was admitted to subordinate alliance and was guaranteed against external enemies. Jagat Singh died in 1818 and was succeeded by his posthumous son Maharaja Jay Singh. This Chief was followed by his son Maharaja Ram Singh, who died in 1880, when the present ruler came to the *gadi.*

ALWAR.

The ruling family of Alwar traces its descent from Udai Karn, who succeeded to the Chiefship of Amber in 1367. Udai Karn's eldest son, Bar Singh, was excluded from the succession in favour of Nar Singh, the younger son, and received a grant of eighty-four villages in the neighbourhood of Jaipur. Naru, the grandson of Bar Singh, was the founder of the Naruka house and left five sons, of whom the eldest Lala was the ancestor of the ruling family of Alwar. His great-grandson Rao Kalyan Singh settled in what is now Alwar territory and received from Jaipur the grant of Macheri and other villages of which some were held by his successors till the time of Rao Partap Singh who developed his little estate of two and a half villages into a principality and threw off his allegiance to Jaipur. Partap Singh having rendered great service to Jaipur by defeating the Jats at the battle of Maonda (1766) received permission to build a fort at Rajgarh near Macheri. Shortly afterwards he became practically independent, established other forts, and ultimately, in November 1775 obtained possession of Alwar which till then had been held by the Jats of Bhartpur. From this time Partap Singh was recognized as their Chief by the other Narukas, and towards the

* The literal meaning of *Sawai* is one and a quarter and the title implies that the holder is greater by one-fourth than ordinary rulers.

end of his reign obtained from Delhi the much-coveted fish insignia (*mahi maratib*). Partap Singh died in 1791, having adopted as his successor Bakhtawar Singh, who at the commencement of the Mahratta war entered into an offensive and defensive alliance with the British Government and rendered useful service to Lord Lake at the battle of Laswari. A treaty was made in 1803. In 1811, in consequence of the discovery of certain negotiations between Jaipur and Alwar, the Chief was obliged to bind himself not to enter into political relations with other States. On Bakhtawar Singh's death in 1815 he was succeeded by Maharao Raja Bane Singh, whom he had intended to adopt and who was accepted as their Chief by the Rajputs and the artillery. The succession was claimed on behalf of his illegitimate son Balwant Singh and after much dispute it was settled that Bane Singh should have the title and Balwant Singh the power. Eventually the British Government interfered to secure proper maintenance for Balwant Singh, on whose death in 1845 his possessions reverted to the State. Bane Singh proved his loyalty by his attempt during the Mutiny to assist the beleaguered garrison of Agra. He died in 1857 and was succeeded by his only son Maharao Raja Sheodan Singh, then a boy of twelve. The powers conferred upon the Maharao Raja in 1863 were greatly curtailed six years later owing to the misgovernment of the Chief and a Political Agent was again appointed to Alwar. Sheodan Singh died on the 11th October 1876 and was succeeded by Mangal Singh, a son of the Thakur of Thana, whose selection was approved by the Rajputs of the twelve kotris or houses closely allied to the ruling branch. Maharao Raja Mangal Singh, G.C.S.I., on whom the title of Maharaja was conferred in 1890, died on the 23rd May 1892, and was succeeded by the present Chief, Maharaja Jay Singh.

JAIPUR.

The Chief.

The present Chief of Jaipur, **His Highness Saramad-i-Rajaha-i-Hindustan, Raj Rajindar Sri Maharaj Adhiraj Sawai Sir Madho Singh Bahadur, G.C.S I.**, is a Kachhwaha Rajput. His Highness, whose name till he came to the *gadi* was Kaim Singh, was born in 1860, and is by birth the son of the late Thakur Raghunath Singh of the Rajawat family of Isarda. He succeeded by adoption to the late Maharaja Ram Singh on the 29th September 1880. The Maharaja, who has no children alive, has contracted five marriages—(1) with the daughter of Thakur Budh Singh Pal, a Jadon Rajput of Amargarh in the Etah district of the North-Western Provinces; (2) in 1881 with the daughter, who died on the 25th March 1893, of His Highness the late Maharaja of Kishangarh (see page 21); (3) in 1882 with the daughter of the Raja of Dhrangadra in Kathiawar of the Jhala clan; (4) in 1891 with the daughter of the Rahtor Thakur of Khamor in Shahpura; and (5) in 1892 with the daughter of the Tanwar Thakur Jiwraj Singh of Bikanir. The first of these alliances took place before the Maharaja's accession to the Chiefship, the rest afterwards. By each of the first two Maharanis a daughter was born to the Chief, but both these children have died. His Highness has no near relations on the male side, and there is a dispute as to what family is most closely allied to him. By clan the Maharaja is related to the Kachhwaha houses of Kashmir and Alwar. His adoptive mother the widow of the late Maharaja Ram Singh, is the eldest sister of His Highness Maharaja Jaswant Singh of Jodhpur.

The abstract genealogical tree of the ruling family of Jaipur given on the following pages is said to be correct, but the earlier portion differs from the account given in the Gazetteer.

Abstract Genealogical Table of the Chief of Jaipur.

1. *Sodu* (succeeded to the *gadi* of Narwar in 958 A. D., settled in Dausa 966 A. D., and died 1007 A. D.).
2. *Dula Rai* (generally known as founder of the State, died 1013 A. D.).
3. *Hkodro* (died 1015 A. D.).
4. *Kakilji* (died 1015 A. D., said by Dr. Stratton, formerly Resident at Jaipore, to have founded Amber about 1150).
5. *Hani Rai* (died 1053 A. D.).
6. *Janan Deo* (died 1071 A. D.).
7. *Prajjawan* (said to have married the sister of Pritbwi Raj, Chauhan, King of Ajmer and the last Hindu King of Delhi, died 1095 A. D.).
8. *Malesi* (died 1147 A. D.).
9. *Bijaldeo* (also said to have founded Amber, died 1179 A. D.).
10. *Deoji* (died 1216 A. D.).
11. *Kilandeo* (died 1276 A. D.).
12. *Kuntaldeo* (died 1318 A. D.).
    - **Gogawats** of Duni, etc.
13. *Joshi* (died 1367 A. D.).
    - Kumbhani of Banskbo (one of the 12 *kotris*).
14. *Udai Karn* (died 1388 A. D.).
15. *Narsingh* (died 1413 A. D.).
    - Patal. — Patalpota.
    - Sheobaran. — **Sheobaranpota** (one of the 12 *kotris*).
    - Balu. — Mokal. — Shaikba. — **Shaikhawats.**
    - Barsingh. — Maharaj. — Naru. — **Narukas.**
16. *Banbir* (died 1424 A. D.).
    - **Banbirpota** (one of the 12 *kotris*).
17. *Udai Karn* (died 1453 A. D.)
18. *Chandra Sen* (died 1488).
    - **Kumbhawats** of Mahar (one of the 12 *kotris*.)
19. *Prithwi Raj* (established the 12 *kotris*, died 1528 A. D.).

Sons of Prithwi Raj: 20. *Puran Mal* (died 1534 A. D.). — 21. *Bhim* (died 1537). — 22. *Rata Singh* (died 1548). — 23. *Askaran* (died 1548). — 24. *Bharmal* (died 1574). — Gopal — Natha. — **Nathawats** (Kotri). — **Pichan** (Pichanot *Kotri*). — **Jagma** (Khangarot *Kotri*). — **Sultan** (Sultanot *Kotri*). — **Chaturbhuj** (Chaturbhujot *Kotri*). — **Kalyan** (Kalyanot *Kotri*). — **Balbhadra** (Balbhadrot *Kotri*). — Ram Singh. — Sanga (founded Sanganer). — Partap. — Sahasmal. — Raimal. — Samdasi. — Bhika. — Rupsi. — Tejsi

25. *Bhagwandas* (died 1519 A. D.).
    - Bhagwat Das.
    - Jagannath. — **Jagannathots.**
26. *Man Singh* (a celebrated General of Akbar's time, died 1615 A. D.).
27. *Bhao Singh* (died 1622 A. D.).
    - Jagat Singh.
        - Maha Singh.
        - Jhujhar Singh. — **Rajawats** of Jhilai.
    - Sakat Singh. — **Rajawats** of Kordya.
    - Himmat Singh.
    - Durjan Singh. — **Rajawats** of Gohadi.
    - Kalyan Singh. — **Rajawats** of Chandlot.
28. *Jay Singh I* (a great Military Commander in the time of Aurangzeb from whom he obtained the title of *Mirza Raja* and the *Mansab* of 6,000, died 1668 A. D.).
    - Kirat Singh (settled at Kansa).
29. *Ram Singh* (died 1690 A. D.)
    - Kishan Singh.
30. *Bishan Singh* (died 1700 A. D.).
31. *Jay Singh II* (received the title of *Sawai* from the Emperor, founded the city of Jaipur, and was a great patron of science and arts, died 1744 A. D.).
    - 33. *Madho Singh I* (founded Sawai Madhopur, died 1768 A. D.).
32. *Isri Singh* (died 1751 A. D.).
34. *Pirthi Singh* (died 1779 A. D.).
    - 35. *Partap Singh* (during this reign Partap Singh Naruka, the Rao of Macher (now Alwar) secured his independence, died 1803 A. D.)
36. *Jagat Singh* (concluded the first treaty with the British Government in 1803, died 1818 A. D.).
37. *Jay Singh III* (born after the death of his father, died 1835 A. D.).
38. *Ram Singh II* (succeeded to *gadi* in infancy, died the 18th September 1880, nominating the present Chief as his successor).
39. *Madho Singh II* (succeeded to *gadi* by adoption on the 29th September 1880 A. D.).

Leading men.

The leading men of the Jaipur State are divided into four classes :—

(1) Hereditary nobles.

(2) Hereditary office-bearers.

(3) Non-hereditary office-bearers.

(4) *Udikis* (usually Brahmans or persons belonging to some sacred class).

The nobles generally enjoy hereditary grants of land from the State in reward for services rendered, or by right of descent from the ruling family. Nobles of the Kachhwaha clan descended from the ruling house are known as bhai-betas or kinsmen. There are two classes of nobles, *Tazimi* and *Khass-chcuki*. The members of the former class are received in Darbar by the Chief standing when they present their *nazars*. They are privileged to wear gold anklets. The principal nobles of Jaipur, all of whom will be noticed separately, are Kachhwahas and Rahtors. There are also many Sardars of less importance belonging to these and to the Sesodia, Tunwar, Bhati, and other tribes. The most important of the Muhammadan nobles is the Nawab of Badanpura. The late Pandit Sheodin, who has been succeeded by his eldest son Pandit Bishambar Din, Mumtazu-d-daula Nawab Sir Muhammad Faiz Ali Khan Bahadur K.C.S.I., and Rao Bahadur Kanti Chandra Mukharji, C.I.E., are instances of officials who have been raised to the rank of hereditary nobles.

Gradation of rank among the nobles, though much importance is attached by themselves to kinship with the ruling house, depends less on this qualification than on the position to which the different families have raised themselves. The Rajawats being the nearest connections of the ruling house consider themselves the premier family of Jaipur. Next to them come the so-called twelve kotris, (1) Nathawats, (2) Chaturbhujots, (3) Kangarots, (4) Balbhadrots, (5) Sultanots, (6) Kalyanots, (7) Paranmalots, (8) Pichanots, (9) Kumbhawats, (10) Banpirpotas, (11) Sheobaranpotas, and (12) Kumbhanis.

The following families among others are also known as *Kotris* :—Shaikhawats, Narukas, Bankawats, and Gogawats. The origin of most of the *kotris* and their connection with the ruling family are shown in the genealogical tree given on page 73.

The largest fiefs in Jaipur are those of Sikar and Khetri, the possessors of which enjoy the titles of Rao Raja and Raja respectively and exercise limited judicial powers within their estates.

The *Jagirdars* of Kukas and Talchiri claim descent from Bargujar families which ruled present Jaipur territory before its conquest by the Kachhwahas.

Dhula, Digi, Uniara, Chomu, and Samod held originally small estates which have been enlarged by subsequent grants.

The *Jagirs* of Goner, Kanota, Naila, Raipur, and Karusar are modern grants dating from the reign of Maharaja Ram Singh II.

Succession is generally by primogeniture, the eldest son succeeding to the estate, and the cadets receiving a suitable annuity for maintenance. This rule is, however, not observed in Shaikhawati where an almost equal division of the ancestral estate takes place between the several sons. The appanages thus created are merged again in the parent estate on failure of issue.

All nobles either serve the State with horse and foot or pay tribute in cash, the former being known as *jagirdars* and the latter as *mamla-guzars*. The *Udikis* render no service and pay no tribute.

There are very few hereditary office-bearers of importance, though some families enjoy grants of land as rewards for previous services. There are also some families which have maintained themselves for centuries by State service, one or more members always receiving some kind of employment. In a few cases offices of special importance are held by particular families so long as any member of them is found fit to perform the required duties. The Daroghaship of the Toshakhana and the Palace, and the posts of *Mir Bakhshi* and *Wakia Navis* are instances of offices of this class.

The most important office of the State is the Council, of which His Highness the Maharaja is the President. The Council is divided into three departments :—Military, Foreign, and Miscellaneous, Revenue and Judicial.

Certain Brahmans and other persons of sacred classes who have gained prominence as preceptors or heirs of preceptors of the Chief hold honours and grants.

Individuals of note.

Chomu.

(1) **Rao Bahadur Thakur Gobind Singh Bahadur of Chomu** is one of the most distinguished representatives of the Nathawat branch of the Kachhwaha tribe, which takes its name from Nathaji, the son of Gopalji, and grandson of Raja Prithwi Raj (1488—1528 A.D.). The Chomu estate, which renders service with cavalry and pays no tribute, is situated 20 miles to the north of Jaipur. Of the ancestors of the present Thakur, Thakur Mohan Singh distinguished himself at the battle of Khandela in the reign of Maharaja Sawai Jay Singh II (1700—1744) and Thakur Jodh Singh was killed fighting against the Mahrattas in the reign of Madho Singh I (1751—1768). The late Thakur Lachhman Singh held the offices of *Fauj Musahib* and Prime Minister in the time of Maharaja Ram Singh II (1835—1880).

Thakur Gobind Singh, who is by birth the son of Thakur Sheodan Singh of Ajayrajpura, was born in 1849 and succeeded Thakur Lachhman Singh by adoption in 1862. He has been a member of the State Council since 1881 and his services have been recognized by the bestowal on him as personal distinctions of the titles of Bahadur by the Jaipur Darbar and of Rao Bahadur by the British Government. The latter title was conferred in 1889. The Thakur has no sons and no near relations in the Chomu family. His nearest kinsmen are the Rawal of Samod and the *Jagirdars* of Renwal and Ajayrajpura.

The Chomu family, besides its estate in Jaipur, holds a temple and some lands and buildings at Brindaban in the Muttra district.

Samod.

(2) **Rawal Fath Singh of Samod** also belongs to the Nathawat branch of the Kachhwaha clan. His estate which is situated 24 miles from Jaipur pays no tribute, but renders service with horse. Rawal Fath Singh, who is twenty-two years of age, is by birth the son of Thakur Nathu Singh of Renwal, and succeeded by adoption in 1885 to Rawal Bijay Singh. Of the former Rawals of Samod, Ram Singh was killed in battle against the Mahrattas in the reign of Maharaja Madho Singh I (1751—1768), Rawals Bairi Sal and Sheo Singh were Ministers in the reigns of Maharajas Jay Singh III (1818—1835) and Ram Singh II (1835—1880) and Rawal Bijay Singh was guardian to the present Chief. The present Rawal who holds no official position in the State has no son and no near relations in the family of his adoption. His nearest relatives are the Thakur of Chomu and the *Jagirdars* of Renwal and Ajayrajpura.

Jhalai.

(3) **Thakur Nahar Singh of Jhalai**, a Kachhwaha Rajput, belongs to the Sangram Singhot branch of the Rajawat sub-clan which is descended from Maharaja Jagat Singh (1803—1813). The estate which is exempt from service and tribute is situated 44 miles to the south of Jaipur. Thakur Nahar Singh is fifty-five years of age and is the son of Kunwar Sangram Singh. He succeeded to the *jagir* in 1876 on the death of his eldest brother Thakur Bhawani Singh. Kunwar Sangram Singh and Thakur Bhupal Singh were members of the *Panch Musahibat* (Council) in the last two reigns. The present Thakur has held no office. He has one son Bijay Singh, aged thirty-seven years, and a nephew, Raghunath Singh, who holds a *jagir* in Bikanir. The families of Isarda and Baler are closely related to that of Jhalai.

Uniara.

(4) **Rao Raja Guman Singh of Uniara** is a Kachhwaha Rajput and is the head of the Naruka branch of that family settled in Jaipur. He is a powerful feudatory of the State and holds a *jagir* 70 miles to the north of Jaipur, which pays an annual tribute of R38,335 to the Darbar. None of the family have held any official position in the State, but some of them have rendered important services to the Chief in recognition of which Maharaja Sawai Jay Singh II (1700—1744) conferred the title of Rao and Maharaja Madho Singh I (1751—1768)

that of Raja on Ajit Singh. Thakur Guman Singh who is seven years of age is by birth the son of Thakur Chiman Singh of Bijaygarh and succeeded to Uniara by adoption on the death in 1886 of Rao Raja Sangram Singh. He has no relations in the Uniara family.

Digi

(5) **Thakur Devi Singh of Digi** is the head of the Khangarot sub-clan of the Kachhwaha Rajputs which is descended from Raja Prithwi Raj (1488—1528) through the latter's son Jagmalji. The estate, which lies 40 miles to the west of Jaipur, serves the Darbar with horse. Thakur Devi Singh, who is about twenty-six years of age, is by birth the son of Thakur Bairi Sal of Mundia, and was selected as the fittest claimant to Digi by His Highness the Maharaja on the death without issue of Thakur Pratap Singh in 1892. Thakur Pratap Singh was a member of the State Council from 1881, and his ancestors, Thakurs Megh Singh and Bhim Singh, were members of the *Panch Musahibat*. The present Thakur has held no official position. He has one son, and is nearly related to the families of Mundia and Lambia.

Manoharpur.

(6) **Rao Pratap Singh of Manoharpur** is a Kachhwaha Rajput of the senior branch of the Shaikhawat sub-clan which takes its origin from Raja Udai Karn (1388—1413) through Shaikha, the descendant of his fourth son. The estate which is situated 30 miles to the north of Jaipur renders service with horse and pays R6,300 as tribute to the Darbar on account of the tenure of Bishangarh. Rao Pratap Singh, who is twenty years of age and holds no official position, is by birth the son of Thakur Balwant Singh of Gadh, and succeeded Thakur Sheonath Singh of Manoharpur by adoption in 1881. He has one son, after whom his nearest relatives belong to the Gadh family.

Khandela.

(7) **Rao Hamir Singh of Khandela** is also a Shaikhawat, being descended from Rao Suja of Manoharpur through the latter's son Rai Sal. The estate which lies 60 miles to the north of Jaipur pays an annual tribute of R36,192. On the death of Raja Sanwant Singh, the last holder, the succession was disputed, and Hamir Singh, son of Thakur Dule Singh of Dadia, was selected by the Darbar in 1890 as the rightful claimant. He is twenty-one years of age and holds no official position. He has no son. The Dadia family is the nearest by relationship to that of Khandela.

Sikar.

(8) **Rao Raja Madho Singh Bahadur of Sikar** is a Kachhwaha Rajput of the Shaikhawat sub-clan and belongs to the Raojika family which is descended from Tejmal, son of Raja Rai Sal of Khandela. The estate is situated 72 miles to the north-west of Jaipur and pays a tribute of R42,000 a year. The Sikar family has rendered important services to the Darbar in times of emergency; thus Rao Sheo Singh was severely wounded in battle against the Mahrattas, and Thakur Budh Singh was killed fighting for Jaipur against Jawahir Singh of Bhartpur. The title of Rao Raja was conferred on Lachhman Singh of Sikar by Maharaja Jagat Singh (1803—1818). Rao Raja Madho Singh is thirty-two years of age, and has received as a personal distinction from the Darbar the title of Bahadur. The *panch-ranga** flag was conferred on him by Maharaja Ram Singh in 1877. He belongs by birth to the allied family of Sarwari and succeeded to Sikar by adoption in 1865. He has no son or near relation. The families most closely allied to Sikar are those of Bathnoth, Paluda, and Sarwari.

Khetri.

(9) **Raja Ajit Singh of Khetri** is, like the Rao Raja of Sikar, a Shaikhawat, being descended from Bhojraj, a son of Raja Rai Sal of Khandela. He holds from the Jaipur Darbar the estate of Khetri which lies 90 miles to the north of the capital and pays a tribute of R75,000 a year. From the British Government he holds as a free grant the *pargana* of Kot Putli which was conferred on Thakur Akhay Singh during the reign of Maharaja Jagat Singh (1803—1818). This Chief bestowed the title of Raja on Abhay Singh. Raja Ajit Singh, who is thirty years of age, is by birth the son of Thakur Chatar Singh of Alsisar. He succeeded to Khetri by adoption in 1870 on the death of Raja Fath Singh. He has one

* The striped Rajput standard of five colours.

son and no other near relative. The families of Harina, Alsisar, Aruka, and Badangarh are those most closely connected with Khetri.

Duni.

(10) **Rao Raja Lachhman Singh of Duni,** a Kachhwaha Rajput, is the head of the Gogawat sub-clan which is descended from Raja Kuntal (1274—1318). The estate which serves the Darbar with horse is situated 80 miles south-west of Jaipur. The Rao Raja is twenty-five years of age and is by birth the son of Thakur Biradh Singh of Ajayrajpura. He succeeded by adoption to the late Rao Jiwan Singh who was a Judge of the Appellate Court and subsequently a member of the Jaipur Council. The title of Rao Raja was conferred on Sheonath Singh by Maharaja Prithwi Singh (1768—1779) whom he served first in the capacity of *Fauj Bakhshi* and subsequently in that of Diwan. Another ancestor of the present Rao Raja, Rao Chand Singh, also held the office of Diwan. Rao Raja Lachhman Singh has no sons. The families most nearly allied to Duni are those of Ajayrajpura and Balmukundpura. It is the privilege of the *Jagirdar* of Duni to sit behind the Chief on the same elephant in all State processions and to wave the *chanwar** over him.

Bagru.

(11) **Thakur Sanwant Singh of Bagru** is the head of the Chutarbhujot sub-clan of the Kachhwaha Rajputs which is descended from Chaturbhuj, a son of Raja Prithwi Raj I (1488—1528). The estate, which is situated 18 miles to the west of Jaipur, serves the Raj with horse and pays no tribute. Of the ancestors of the present Thakur one, Thakur Padm Singh, distinguished himself in a battle fought near Agra, and received a robe of honour from Maharaja Jay Singh II (1700—1744); another, Thakur Gulab Singh, was killed in a battle against the Mahrattas in the reign of Maharaja Madho Singh I (1751—1768). Thakur Sur Singh, the late head of the house, was a member of the *Panch Musahibat* and Judge of the Appellate Court in the time of Maharaja Ram Singh II (1835—1880). Thakur Sanwant Singh, who succeeded his father Thakur Sur Singh in 1863 and is now fifty years of age, is a member of the State Council. He had three sons of whom the eldest died leaving a grandson, Jaswant Singh, who is now ten years old. The other two sons, Pratap Singh and Hari Singh, are aged twenty-two and twenty years respectively. The Thakur has no other near relatives.

Achrol.

(12) **Thakur Kesri Singh of Achrol** is the head of the Balbhadrot sub-clan of the Kachhwaha Rajputs, being descended from Raja Prithwi Raj (1488—1528) through the latter's son Balbhadar. Thakur Balbhadar was killed in Gujarat, and his son, Achaldas, quelled a rebellion in Shaikhawati, receiving the office of *Fauj Musahib* in recognition of his services. He and his followers were subsequently killed in the battle of Dhanori. His son Mohan Singh and his grandson, Kan Singh, were also *Fauj Musahibs* in their turn. In the reign of Maharaja Ram Singh II Thakur Ranjit Singh was appointed *Faujdar* (City Magistrate) and subsequently Judge of the Appellate Court. Later on, he became a member of Council. Thakurs Lachhman Singh and Raghunath Singh also held the office of Judge of the Appellate Court. The family estate which is situated eighteen miles to the north of Jaipur serves the Darbar with horse. Thakur Kesri Singh succeeded his father, Thakur Raghunath Singh, in 1891. He has one younger brother, Kishan Singh, aged twelve years, and no son. His next relatives are Thakur Ram Nath Singh and his two brothers.

Banskho.

(13) **Thakur Bairi Sal of Banskho,** a Kachhwaha Rajput, is the head of the Kumbhani sub-clan which is descended from Raja Joshi (1318—1367). His estate, which is situated 24 miles to the east of Jaipur, serves the Darbar with horse. The Thakur who holds no official position is thirty-five years of age, and is by birth the son of Thakur Gulab Singh. He succeeded to the *jagir* in 1877 on the death of his uncle Thakur Amar Singh and has one son, Sheo Singh, aged eighteen years, and a brother Kanh Singh. One of his ancestors, Thakur Chur Singh, held the office of Diwan.

* Yak's tail, used to keep off flies.

Dhula.

(14) **Rawat Bane Singh of Dhula,** a Kachhwaha Rajput, is a Rajawat of the Durjan Singhot family, which traces its origin to Raja Man Singh (1590—1615). The estate which renders military service to the Raj is situated 25 miles to the east of Jaipur. Thakur Dalel Singh of Dhula, an ancestor of the present Thakur, held the offices of *Faujdar* and *Kotwal* of Amber in the reign of Maharaja Sawai Jay Singh II (1700—1744). Another ancestor, Thakur Lachhman Singh, was killed with his son fighting against Jawahir Singh of Bhartpur. In recognition of the services rendered on this occasion a grant of villages was made to the family. The title of Rawat was conferred on another ancestor, Thakur Raghunath Singh. Rawat Ranjit Singh was a member of the *Panch Musahibat* and was subsequently *Nazim* of Shaikhawati and Torawati. The late Rawat, Bairi Sal, died on the 23rd March 1893 and was succeeded by adoption by the present *Jagirdar* who was the son of the late Thakur Arjun Sal of Thetra, and is now eleven years of age. The Rawat has no nearer relatives than those of the Thetra family.

Dudu.

(15) **Thakur Sheonath Singh of Dudu** belongs to the Kangarot branch of the Kachhwaha tribe which is descended from Jagmal, son of Raja Prithwi Raj (1488—1528). The estate, which lies 40 miles to the west of Jaipur, is exempt from payment of tribute, but serves the Darbar with horse. It was conferred originally on Thakur Anand Singh who had been employed by the Darbar as *Faujdar*. His son Pahar Singh was made a Minister of the State. Thakur Sheonath Singh who is twenty-eight years of age succeeded his father Thakur Lachhman Singh in 1884. He has two sons, one aged seven and the other an infant, and two brothers of whom one is now Thakur of Sali by adoption.

Isarda.

(16) The headship of the house of **Isarda,** to which the present Chief of Jaipur belonged previously to his adoption by the late Maharaja Ram Singh II (1835—1880), is temporarily vacant, the late Thakur Pratap Singh having died without issue, and the succession having not yet been settled. The houses most closely connected with it are those of Jhalai, Barwara, Sewar, and Baler.*

Gijgarh.

(17) **Thakur Kanh Singh of Gijgarh** is a Rahtor Rajput of the Champawat sub-clan which traces its origin to the Pokaran family of Marwar (see page 8). The *jagir* of Gijgarh, which is situated 60 miles south-east of Jaipur and serves the Darbar with horse, was originally conferred in 1775 on Thakur Syam Singh who came to Jaipur in the reign of Maharaja Prithwi Singh (1768—1779). An ancestor of the present Thakur, Ummed Singh, was killed with his followers when fighting for Jaipur in a battle near Tori. In recognition of the services rendered on this occasion the number of horses which the family was liable to contribute for the use of the Darbar was reduced by ten. Thakur Kanh Singh who is a *Tazimi* Sardar of both Jaipur and Jodhpur is twenty-five years of age and succeeded to the estate in 1876, on the death of his father Thakur Jhujhar Singh. He has no nearer relatives than the families of Pokaran and Daipha in Marwar.

Seora.

(18) **Thakur Chand Karn of Seora** is a Rahtor Rajput of the Karnot sub-clan, which traces its origin to the ruling Chiefs of Marwar. The estate, which is situated 40 miles to the west of Jaipur, serves the Darbar with horse. Thakur Chand Karn who is the son of Mukund Karn is twenty-nine years of age. He succeeded his grandfather, Samandar Karn, by adoption in 1889, Mukund Karn having died two months after Samandar Karn before his successiou was acknowledged by the Darbar. Samandar Karn was a member of the Council during the latter years of Maharaja Ram Singh II (1835—1880) and the earlier years of the present Chief. Thakur Chand Karn's near relatives are a son, Indar Karn, aged six years and an uncle, Deo Karn, Thakur of Kot Khaoda.

* Since the above account was written His Highness the Maharaja has appointed a minor named Balwant Singh of the Jagmoda Dirola branch of the Isarda family to be Thakur of Isarda. The selection was made at the instance of the two Thakuranis of the late Thakur Pratap Singh and the estate is under the management of the Court of Wards. Since his adoption Balwant Singh has taken the name of Sawai Singh, by which he is now known. The Thakur who is twelve years of age is descended from the youngest son of the first *Jagirdar* and is thus a collateral relative of the late Thakur who was descended from the eldest son. His nearest relatives are in his own family, Nathu Singh of Dheroli, his father, and Thakur Arjun Singh of Jagmoda his uncle, and in that of his adoption Thakurs Dalput Singh and Phaju Singh of Dedara.

(19) **Thakur Fath Singh of Naila,** a Rahtor Rajput of the Pilwa family of the Champawat sub-clan of Marwar, holds an estate, 12 miles east of Jaipur, and serves the State with horse. He is now about sixty years of age. His father, Thakur Jiwraj, was the first of the family to enter the service of the Darbar. Thakur Fatoh Singh was *Bakhshi of the Kilajat** when Naila was given to him in *jagir* in 1860 by the late Maharaja Ram Singh II (1835—1880), who also conferred on him the honour of the *tazim* and appointed him a member of the Council. Subsequently he held the office of Chief Minister and Vice-President of the Council till the accession of the present Chief. He now draws a pension of R600 a year. He has two sons, Rup Singh, aged thirty-six years, who is *Bakhshi of the Kilajat* and Guman Singh, aged thirty-three years. He has also a brother, Thakur Zorawar Singh of Kanaota, and a nephew, Thakur Mukund Singh of Goner.

Naila.

(20) **Thakur Mukund Singh of Goner** belongs to the same family as the Thakur of Naila (No. 19), and holds an estate 12 miles south-east of Jaipur which serves the Darbar with horse. The estate was conferred on Thakur Shimbhu Singh, the father of the present holder and brother to Thakur Fath Singh of Naila who held the office of *Bakhshi jagir* and was subsequently a member of the Council. The late Maharaja also conferred on him the *tazim*. Thakur Mukund Singh who is now forty-two years of age succeeded his father in 1886. His near relations are his son Bhojraj Singh, aged nineteen years, his brother Chiman Singh employed in Bikanir and his uncles Thakur Fath Singh of Naila and Thakur Zorawar Singh of Kanaota. He has also several cousins in Jaipur and Marwar.

Goner.

(21) **Thakur Zorawar Singh of Kanaota** is an elder brother of Thakur Fath Singh of Naila (No. 19) and received a *jagir* eight miles to the east of Jaipur and the *tazim* at the same time as his brother. The estate serves the Darbar with horse. The Thakur who holds the post of *Bakhshi jagir* is about sixty-three years of age and has three sons, Narain Singh, aged about forty-five years, General Superintendent of Girai in Jaipur, Bhim Singh, Superintendent of Girai, aged about forty years, and Gambhir Singh, aged about thirty-five years.

Kanaota.

(22) **Thakur Jiwan Singh of Surajgarh** is a Kachhwaha Rajput of the Shaikhawat sub-clan, which traces its descent from Balu, son of Raja Udai Karn (1367—1388). The estate which lies 140 miles to the north of Jaipur is subject to an annual tribute of R8,595. According to the Shaikhawat custom, the *jagir* was divided on the death of the late Thakur between his four sons. Of these two died and one succeeded by adoption to Bisau. The whole *jagir* is therefore held by Thakur Jiwan Singh. He is now thirty years of age. His father, Thakur Gobind Singh, served with the Jaipur forces under British officers in the Mutiny of 1857. His nearest relatives are Thakur Jagat Singh of Bisau and an infant son of the latter, after whom come members of the Dandlod family.

Surajgarh.

(23) **Thakur Jagat Singh of Bisau** is also a Kachhwaha Rajput of the Shaikhawat clan. He holds an estate 120 miles north of Jaipur, which yields an annual tribute of R9,885. A former *Jagirdar* of Bisau served with his contingent under British officers during the Mutiny, and his son Jawahir Singh was deputed by the Darbar to restore peace in Shaikhawati, which had been greatly disturbed by two well-known dakaits, Dang and Jawahir. Thakur Jagat Singh succeeded his father Thakur Chandar Singh in 1877. He has one infant son and three uncles, Jiwan Singh of Surajgarh and Pane Singh and Chandan Singh of Dandlod.

Bisau.

(24) **Rao Mukund Singh of Patan or Jilo Patan** is a Tunwar Rajput who holds an estate 72 miles north of Jaipur, which yields an annual tribute of R7,641. He also holds some villages in the Anupshahr Pargana of the Bulandshahr district of the North-Western

Patan.

* Warden (*lit.*, paymaster) of the Forts.

Provinces. Rao Mukund Singh who is thirty years of age, is by birth the son of Pratap Singh, a brother of the late Rao Kishan Singh. He succeeded the latter by adoption in 1878. His nearest relations are the descendants of Rao Bakhshi Ram, an ancestor separated from him by nine generations.

The following officials call for individual notice :—

Officials.

(1) **Rao Bahadur Kanti Chandar Mukharji,** C.I.E., the chief member of the State Council who, jointly with Rao Bahadur Thakur Gobind Singh of Chomu, holds charge of the Foreign, Military, and Miscellaneous Departments.

Rao Bahadur Kanti Chandar Mukharji, who is by birth a Bengali, entered the service of the Darbar in 1865 as Head Master of the Maharaja's College of which he subsequently became Principal. In the year 1876 he was appointed to the Council of the State and discharged the duties of Private Secretary to the late Chief. When Maharaja Madho Singh was vested with full powers, he nominated Babu Kanti Chandar Mukharji to be Chief Member of the Council and in 1885 conferred on him the honour of the *tazim*. Subsequently he received the grant of a village partly in *udik* and partly in *inam*. The title of Rao Bahadur and a Companionship of the Order of the Indian Empire have been bestowed on him by the British Government.

(2) **Pandit Moti Lal,** who is now a member of the Revenue Department of the Council, entered the service of the Raj in 1857 as Jaipur Vakil at Jodhpur. He has since held the appointments of Jaipur Vakil at Abu and Sadr Revenue Officer.

(3) **Haji Muhammad Ali Khan,** who is also a Revenue Member of the Council was educated at the Maharaja's College and appointed in 1870 to be *Saristhadar* of the Law Committee. He has since served in turn as *Naib Faujdar*, *Nazim* of Shaikhawati, and a Judge of the Appellate Court.

(4) **Pandit Maharaj Kishan,** whose services were placed at the disposal of the Darbar by the British Government in 1883, is the member of the Council in charge of the Criminal side of the Judicial Department.

(5) **Babu Mahendra Nath Sen,** whose father Babu Hari Mohan Sen was formerly Secretary to the Council, of which he was *ex officio* a member, is now in charge of the Judicial Department of the Council. He entered the service of the Darbar in 1865 as Head Clerk of the English Office of the Council. From 1882 to 1890 when he was appointed to his present post he was a Judge of the Appellate Court.

ALWAR.

The Chief.

His Highness Maharaja Sawai Jay Singh Bahadur of Alwar was born in 1882 and succeeded his father the late Maharaja Mangal Singh, G.C.S.I., on the 23rd May 1892. The Chief whose mother was a daughter of the late Maharaja Bherun Singh of Ratlam is a Lalawat Naruka Rajput of the Kachhwaha clan and is a descendant of the ruling house of Jaipur. The only near relatives of the Maharaja on the paternal side are connected with the family of Thana from which the late Chief was adopted by his predecessor. They are his uncle Thakur Surtan Singh of Thana, a cousin Ram Singh, the son of the Thakur, and another cousin Thakur Ganga Singh of Srichandpur.

Through the marriages of the late Chiefs, His Highness is connected with the Rahtor family of Kishengarh and the Jarechá family of Jamnagar. The Rahtor family of Bikanir, the Jhala family of Jhalawar, and the Sesodia family of Shahpura are also connected by marriage His Highness is not married. The pedigree on the opposite page shows the descent of the ruling family from the Jaipur house.

RAJA UDAI KARN (1367).

- Bar Singh (received a *jagir*).
  - Maharaj.
    - Naru (ancestor of the Narukas).
      - Rao Lala (ancestor of the Lalawats).
        - Udai Singh.
          - Lar Khan.
            - Fath Singh.
              - Rao Kalyan Singh.
                - Agar Singh.
                  - Hathi Singh.
                    - Mukund Singh.
                      - Tej Singh.
                        - Zorawar Singh.
                          - Muhabbat Singh.
                            - **Rao Pratap Singh** (1st Chief of Alwar).
                              - **Maharao Raja Bakhtawar Singh** (2nd Chief, adopted from Thana).
                                - **Maharao Raja Bane Singh** (3rd Chief, adopted from Thana).
                                  - **Maharao Raja Sheodan Singh** (4th Chief).
                                    - **Maharaja Mangal Singh** (5th Chief, adopted from Thana).
                                      - **Maharaja Jay Singh** (present Chief).
                        - Zalim Singh (ancestor of Bijnor family).
                - Amar Singh (founded the Khara family).
                - Syam Singh of Para.
                  - Nathu Singh (ancestor of the Thakurs of Para).
                  - Madho Singh of Thana.
                    - Bridh Singh.
                      - Dhir Singh.
                        - **Salah Singh.**
                          - Hanwant Singh of Thana.
                            - Hardeo Singh of Thana.
                              - Sultan Singh of Thana.
                              - **Mangal Singh** (adopted to Maharao Raja Sheodan Singh).
                          - Nand Singh of Srichandpura.
                          - **Bane Singh** (adopted to Maharao Raja Bakhtawar Singh).
                        - **Bakhtawar Singh** (adopted by Maharao Raja Pratap Singh).
                - Isri Singh of Palwa.
                - Jodh Singh of Pai.
              - Karn Singh.
              - Akhay Singh.
              - Ranchor Das.
      - Dasa (ancestor of the Dasawats).
      - Tejsi.
      - Jetha.
      - Chitar.
- Narsingh (succeeded to Jaipur).

Leading men.

The leading men of Alwar are the hereditary nobles, hereditary office-bearers, and non-hereditary officials.

Of the hereditary nobles twelve belong to the so-called **Bara Kotris** (*vide* page 72) and take their seat in Darbar on the right of the Chief, while the representatives of other Rajput houses sit with the officials on the left. The *Bara Kotris* are the families sprung from one or other of the five sons of Rao Kalyan Singh whose descendants are known as the **panch tikanas** (five families) These *tikanas*, Macheri, Khora, Para and Khora, Palwa and Pai, with their several offshoots, constitute the twelve *kotris*. In all twenty-five *jagir* families belong to this class. In addition to these, four families of Dasawat Narukas, six of Lalawat Narukas, five of Chatarka Narukas, and nineteen of Deska Narukas belong to the Chief's clan. The last-mentioned are so called, because at the invitation of various Chiefs they have come from the old home (*des*) of the Narukas in Jaipur and settled in Alwar. The others are descended from Lala, Dasa, or Chatar, sons of Nara, the founder of the house.

Outside the Chief's clan there are seventy-four families which are considered noble, but belong to other than the ruling clan: Chauhans, Gaurs, Rahtors and Jadons (Bhatis) being the most numerous. Of the nobles twenty-six have the honour of the *tazim*, that is, they are received by the Chief in Darbar standing. The remainder are not thus honoured.

The principal nobles of the State are—

1.	The Raja of Nimrana		Chauhan.
2.	The Thakur of Thana*		Naruka.
3.	Ditto	Garhi†	Do.
4.	Ditto	Bijwar*	Do.
5.	Ditto	Khora*	Do.
6.	Ditto	Pai*	Do.
7.	Ditto	Para*	Do.
8.	Ditto	Palwa*	Do.
9.	Ditto	Jaoli†	Do.
10.	Ditto	Khera*	Do.
11.	Ditto	Srichandpura*	Do.
12.	Ditto	Salpur	Rahtor.
13.	Ditto	Tatarpur	Chauhan.
14.	Ditto	Chamraoli	Gaur.
15.	Ditto	Bijwar	Chauhan.
16.	Ditto	Sukhmeri	Rahtor.

The most important estates are those of Nimrana, Garhi, and Khora.

Among the families of the twelve **Kotris** succession is by primogeniture, suitable provision being made for younger sons out of the income of the estates. Among the families belonging to other classes the estate is generally divided in equal or unequal portions among the sons, but the eldest succeeds to the rank and dignity. The *Jagirdars* are required to keep at their own expense a certain number of horsemen who serve the State for six months in each year, but some are exempted from this liability except on emergencies. The Raja of Nimrana pays a tribute in cash.

Hereditary office-bearers.

There are no hereditary office-bearers of note, but important posts have been held at different times by able *Jagirdars*. Thakurs Hanwant Singh and Hardeo Singh of Thana, Thakurs Nand Singh and Baldeo Singh of Srichandpura, and Thakur Lakdir Singh of Bijwar were members of the Council. Thakur Surtan Singh of Thana is at present *Bakhshi Fauj* (Commander of the Forces). Thakur Madho Singh of Bijwar is a member of the Alwar Branch of the Walterkrit Rajputra Hitkarini Sabha. Thakur Durjan Singh of Jadli is an honorary Captain in the Alwar Imperial Service Force. Rai Bahadur Thakur Mangal Singh of Garhi and Rao Gopal Singh of Nizamnagar are members of the State Council.

Individual persons of note.

Nimrana.

(1) **Raja Janak Singh of Nimrana,** Chauhan Rajput of the Sankat sub-clan and Kharak family, claims to be connected by descent with the celebrated Raja Prithwi Raj of Delhi. Rajdeo, sixth in descent from Madan Pal, who is said to have founded Mandawar in 1170, received the title of Raja for services performed and settled at Nimrana. The estate was formerly independent, but together with the Kishangarh *pargana* was given in 1803 by the British Government to Maharao Raja Bakhtawar Singh of Alwar. In 1861 the then Raja rebelled against Alwar, but was immediately subdued, and it was then arranged that the Raja was to exercise civil and criminal jurisdiction within his estate, but was to pay an annual tribute of R3,000 to the Chief and a *nazarana* (succession fee) of R500 on a change in the Chiefship. The rules applicable to feudatories were to apply to successions to Nimrana, a fee on succession of R500 being paid in the case of a son, brother, or nephew, and one of R24,000 in that of a remote connection. The estate which is

Those marked * belong to the twelve **kotris**. Those marked † are Dasawat Narakus.

situated in the north-west of Alwar consists of twelve villages yielding an annual income of about ₨24,000. During the minority of the present holder it is under the superintendence of the Political Agent in Alwar. Raja Janak Singh is a son of Daulat Singh and a cousin to the late Raja, to whom he was adopted in 1886 by the widows of Rajas Prithwi Singh and Isri Singh. He was born in 1877 and is being educated at the Mayo College at Ajmer. The Raja, who is unmarried, is betrothed to a daughter of Thakur Surtan Singh, the uncle of the present, and brother of the late, Chief of Alwar. He has no male relation in the family of his adoption, his nearest relatives being of the family of Kundan Singh his uncle in his own family.

These relationships are explained by the following table :—

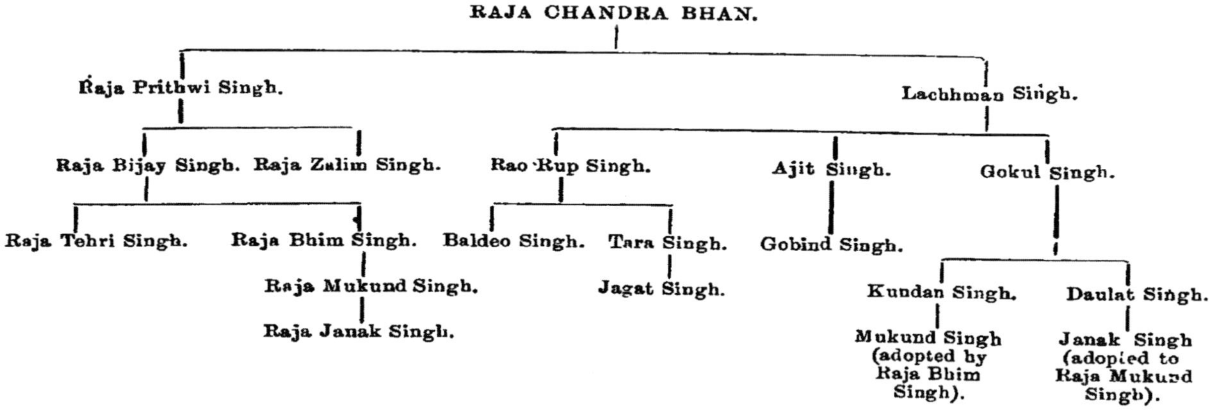

Thana.

(2) **Thakur Surtan Singh of Thana,** a Naruka Kachhwaha Rajput, is by birth the elder brother of the late Chief of Alwar and is the head of the house from which the Chiefs have, on failure of natural heirs, been adopted. The estate which consists of five villages is valued at ₨5,000 a year and keeps up twenty-one horses for the service of the State. Thakur Surtan Singh succeeded his father Thakur Hardeo Singh, formerly a member of the Council, in 1872. He was educated at the Thakur School at Alwar. He is at present **Bakhshi Fauj.** He has one son, Ram Singh, aged ten years, and a cousin, Thakur Ganga Singh of Srichand-pura.

Garhi.

(3) **Rai Bahadur Thakur Mangal Singh of Garhi,** a Dasawat Naruka Rajput of the Kachhwaha clan, holds an estate consisting of eight villages of the annual value of ₨16,000, situated in the south-east of the State and maintaining twenty horsemen for the service of the Darbar. This family, like that of Jadli, springs from Dasa, the second son of Naru. Abhay Ram and Anand Ram, descendants of Dasa in the sixth generation, are said to have left Jaipur for Delhi in search of adventures. On their way they received an invitation to stay and protect the inhabitants of Maujpur, a town now in the Lachmangarh Tahsil, from the plundering Meos. Accepting this proposal they built the fort of Garhi in the neighbouring hills and established their family there. Rai Bahadur Thakur Mangal Singh, who is one of the highest and most influential nobles of Alwar and a member of the Council of the State, succeeded the late Thakur Ranjit Singh by adoption in 1863. He was by birth the son of Thakur Sheonath Singh, a cousin of his adoptive father. Thakur Mangal Singh who is now forty years of age received the title of Rai Bahadur at the Delhi Assemblage in 1877. He has two sons, Karm Singh and Kesri Singh, aged eleven and nine years respectively and two cousins, Hanwant Singh and Hathi Singh. The family is closely connected with that of Garh in Jaipur.

Nizamnagar.

(4) **Rao Gopal Singh of Pai** or **Nizamnagar** is a Naruka Kachhwaha Rajput of the Lalawat branch. The family of Pai which was originally settled in Jaipur migrated into Alwar in 1775 after Maharao Raja Partap Singh had established his independence, and received the estate of Nizamnagar which is the present seat of the house. The estate consists of two

villages of the value of R2,000 and keeps up four horsemen for the service of the Darbar. Rao Gopal Singh succeeded his uncle Rao Kayam Singh by adoption in 1851. He is now forty-six years of age. He has three sons, Ram Singh, Narain Singh, and Nahar Singh, aged nineteen, nine, and one-and-a-half years, respectively.

Bijwar.

(5) **Thakur Madho Singh of Bijwar** is also a member of the Lalawat family of the Naruka sub-clan. He holds an estate in the south of Alwar consisting of four villages which yield a revenue of R3,000, and keeps up ten horsemen for the service of the Darbar. Thakur Madho Singh is the son of Ranjit Singh of Jamalpur, a cousin of the late Thakur Lakdir Singh of Bijwar by whom he was adopted and on whose death in 1876 he succeeded to the estate. He is now twenty-five years of age and his estate is well managed. He was educated at the Mayo College, Ajmer, and is a member of the Alwar branch of the Walterkrit Rajputra Hitkarini Sabha. Thakur Lakdir Singh was a man of great influence in Alwar, and was a member of the Council which governed the State from 1860 to 1863 during the minority of Maharao Raja Sheodan Singh. After the Chief was vested with governing powers Thakur Lakdir Singh resided at Jaipur and Ajmer. In 1866 he invaded Alwar, but was unsuccessful and had to retire. In 1870 a further insurrection took place, which ended in the formation of a Council of which Thakur Lakdir Singh was a member, under the presidency of the Political Agent. In 1876 after the death of Maharao Raja Sheodan Singh, Thakur Lakdir Singh was an unsuccessful candidate for the *gadi*, and, having refused to present the customary *nazar* to the newly-selected Chief, was banished to Ajmer where he died. Thakur Madho Singh's nearest male relatives are his cousins Gyan Singh, Raghunath Singh and Gobind Singh, the most closely allied family being that of Jamalpur in Alwar.

Khora.

(6) **Thakur Daulat Singh of Khora**, a Lalawat Naruka, holds an estate of six villages in the south-east of Alwar of the annual value of R10,000 and keeps up twenty-seven horsemen for the service of the Darbar. Thakur Daulat Singh who was born in 1865 succeeded to the estate in 1876 by adoption on the death of his uncle Thakur Mahtab Singh. The Thakur was educated at the Mayo College. His estate is well managed. His nearest relations are his cousins Devi Singh and Zorawar Singh.

None of the nobles of Alwar hold any estates in British territory.

The only officials in the State who call for individual notice are—

Shaikh Wajid Ali, a Muhammadan of Kankori, near Lucknow. He entered the service of the State in 1863 and for twenty-five years held various appointments. In 1888 he was appointed to the Council of which his intelligence and experience render him a useful member.

Munshi Balmokand Das, an Extra Assistant Commissioner and Treasury Officer, Ajmer, who was transferred to the Council on the 1st January 1893, on account of his mature and varied experience of revenue, judicial and treasury work, coupled with an excellent knowledge of English, Hindi and Urdu. The result has thoroughly justified this selection.

CHAPTER VII.

JHALA STATE.

Jhalawar.

The territory now comprised in the Jhalawar State was formerly a part of the dominions of the Chief of Kotah. The ruling family belongs to the Jhala clan, of the early history of which little is known, but which has long been settled in Kathiawar. Though, according to Colonel Tod, neither of the Solar, Lunar, nor Agnikul race, the Jhala clan claims Solar origin for itself and has always been recognized as one of the Rajput tribes. The following account of the origin of the dynasty of Jhalawar is given in Lieutenant-Colonel Abbott's Gazetteer of the State :—"About A.D. 1709, one Bhan Singh, a second son of the head of the clan, left his country with his son and a small company in order to try his fortune at Delhi. At Kotah, Bhan Singh left his son Madho Singh with the Maharao Bhim Singh, who then ruled the Kotah State, and went on himself to Delhi where all trace of him ends. His son Madho Singh won for himself the good grace of the Kotah Chief who married his eldest son to Madho Singh's sister, granted him a *jagir* of R12,000, and gave him the post of *Faujdar*, a position which implied the control of the army, the forts, and the palaces. His connection with the Chief gained him the familiar title of *Mama* which continued for some time in the family. Madho Singh was succeeded in the office of *Faujdar* by his son Madan Singh. Madan Singh had two sons, Himmat Singh and Prithwi Singh, the former of whom is said to have been famous for personal strength and prowess. Prithwi Singh had two sons, Sheo Singh and Zalim Singh, the latter of whom, being adopted by his uncle Himmat Singh, and surviving his father, succeeded to his grandfather's position in the Kotah State at the age of eighteen. Three years later, Zalim Singh was the means of securing a victory for the Kotah troops against those of the Raja of Amber (Jaipur). Zalim Singh afterwards fell into disfavour with the Maharao owing to his rivalry in the case of a favourite woman whom the Maharao wished, to place in his *zanana*.

"Leaving Kotah, Zalim Singh did good service at Udaipur. Returning to Kotah when Maharao Guman Singh was on his death-bed, the Chief sent for him and committed his son Ummed Singh and the country into his charge . . . . . The extraordinary ability with which Zalim Singh exercised his power induced Ummed Singh, after his minority ended, to leave all authority in the Regent's hands. Raj Rana Zalim Singh at last became, for all serious political affairs, the acknowledged ruler of the State; and when the British Government guaranteed by treaty with the Chief the integrity of Kotah in 1817, a supplementary article was added in 1818 which guaranteed to Zalim Singh and his heirs the authority and privileges he then possessed. This arrangement soon produced troubles; first upon the death of Ummed Singh, his successor naturally desiring to recover authority, and again on the death of Zalim Singh in 1824. After much discussion and some armed contests, the hereditary Chief of Kotah and the heir of Zalim Singh were induced by the British Government to agree to a compromise whereby certain districts of the Kotah State were separated off and ceded to the heirs of Zalim Singh, whereby the new State of Jhalrapatan was constituted under the hereditary rule of that family . . . . . The name of Jhalawar was selected for his new State by the first Chief. The arrangements were ratified by two treaties in 1838 from which year the State dates its creation . . . . . By the treaties the new Chief acknowledged British supremacy, agreed to supply troops according to his means and to pay an annual tribute of R80,000. He received the title of Maharaj Rana, was granted a salute of fifteen guns, and placed on the same footing as other Chiefs of Rajputana. When these affairs had been settled, Maharaj Rana Madan Singh, grandson of the great Kotah administrator Zalim Singh, left Kotah attended by a following of ten thousand persons, inclusive of *Jagirdars* and officials for the Dhanwara Chhaoni, a permanent camp situated between the city of Jhalrapatan and the Kotah fort of Gagraon . . . This Chhaoni thenceforth became the head-quarters of the State, and is still the place of residence of the Chief.

"Madan Singh died in 1845 and was succeeded by his son Prithwi Singh at the early age of fifteen; a Regency Council composed of the old officials of the State being appointed to conduct affairs. In 1857-58 this Chief rendered good service to Government by affording protection to British officers; in revenge the mutineers from Nimach caused the State to suffer, which led to the Government tribute for that year being remitted . . .

"Maharaj Rana Prithwi Singh was of a most good-natured and happy disposition which made him very popular with his subjects; but his good nature and easy-going disposition were taken advantage of by the several *Kamdars* (Minister) who, in turn, had the control of the State purse; the result was that the State became heavily involved, ...

"In 1873 Maharaj Rana Prithwi Singh adopted a nice boy, by name Bakht Singh, from a Jhala family, resident in Wadwan of Kathiawar, related to him in the ninth degree . . . In August 1875, Maharaj Rana Prithwi Singh died after a painful illness, much regretted by all. On the 1st June 1876 Kunwar Bakht Singh was acknowledged as the successor to the late Maharaj Rana. On the 24th June the youthful Bakht Singh, who was in his eleventh year, was formally installed, on which he took the name of Zalim Singh, in accordance with family custom, which enjoins that only the four names of Zalim Singh, Madho Singh, Madan Singh, and Prithwi Singh are to be assumed by the rulers of this house."

The Chief.

His Highness Maharaj Rana Zalim Singh Bahadur was born in 1864 at Wadwan in Kathiawar. The father of the Chief whose original name, as noticed above, was Bakht Singh, was Thakur Kesri Singh, the second son of Thakur Rai Singh, the Chief of Wadwan in Kathiawar. His Highness was educated in Ajmer at the Mayo College, and in February 1884 was invested with ruling powers over his State. The Chief having failed to administer his government in accordance with the principles laid down for his guidance, these powers were withdrawn in September 1887, since which time the administration has again been vested, as during the minority, in a British officer, who bears the style of Superintendent. Recently the Chief has been again entrusted with some departments of the administration. Maharaj Rana Zalim Singh has been twice married—(1) in 1886 to a sister of His Highness Maharaja Sir Sardul Singh, G.C.I.E., of Kishangarh, and (2) a few months later to a daughter of the Thakur of Limri of the Gohel family in Kathiawar. His Highness has no children and his nearest relatives in his adopted family are very distant cousins, Thakurs Arjun Singh and Chatar Sal. In his natural family, the Chief has two cousins in Wadwan, the present Chief of Wadwan and Ganga Singh, the son of Bechar Singh, the younger brother of His Highness's father. The following marriages have been contracted by the successive Chiefs of the house: Maharaj Rana Madan Singh married daughters of the Chandrawat Sesodia family of Rampura in Holkar's territory, of the Bhati family of Jaisalmer, of the Bhati family of Goraich in Mewar, and of the Rahtor family of Bednor in Mewar. Of these ladies, Maji Jaisalmeriji is still alive. Maharaj Rana Prithwi Singh married daughters of the Kachhwaha Thakur of Chomu in Jaipur, of the Bhati Thakur of Goraich in Mewar, and of the Solankhya Thakur of Lunarwara in Gujarat.

The present Chief's real mother belongs to the Jarecha family of Morvi in Kathiawar.

Leading men.

The leading men of Jhalawar fall into four classes: (1) and (2) nobles and officials whose ancestors came from Kotah with Maharaj Rana Madan Singh or who held their estates previously to 1838, and (3) and (4) nobles and officials whose connection with Jhalawar is of later date than the founding of the State. There is also one Charan, who holds the rank of a *Tazimi* Sardar, and who does not fall within any of these classes. Of the nobles whose ancestors accompanied Maharaj Rana Madan Singh, the three who belong to the Chief's clan, the Rao of Kundla and the Thakurs of Kolah and Fathpur, hold the principal places. The first-named is distantly, and the two latter are more closely, related to the Chief. The other nobles entitled to a place in this class are the Thakur of Sarthal, a Rahtor, Maharaja Indar Sal of Kotra, and Maharaja Balbhadra Singh, of Pipakheri, Haras, and the Thakurs of Dhanoda and Bamori, Rajawat Kachhwahas. The nobles who fall within the third class are the Thakurs of Mangal, Gajwara, and Amritkhera. All these are *Tazimi* Sardars, but, with the exception of the Rao of Kundla and the Thakur of Sarthal, none of them hold large estates. Among the nobles succession is by primogeniture, suitable provision being made for the younger sons. All the nobles pay a money tribute in alternate years to the Darbar except the Rao of Kundla and the Thakur of Dhanoda. The Thakurs of Sarthal and Dhanoda, Apji Nripat Singh of Lawasil, Maharajas Indar Sal of Kotra and Thakur Man Singh of Bamori also supply horsemen or footmen or both for the service of the State. The hereditary and some of the non-hereditary officials hold *jagirs*. None of the Jhalawar nobles have estates in British territory.

Among the leading persons of the State the following call for special notice :—

Kundla.

(1) **Rao Sawai Singh of Kundla,** a Jhala Rajput of the Halwad family in Kathiawar, holds the only *jagir* older than the founding of the State. The grant was made by the Emperor Jahangir to Har Das, an ancestor of the present holder. Har Das was at that time settled in Mewar whither his ancestors had come from Kathiawar and in return for services rendered in rescuing from the Bhils a *zanana* favourite of the Emperor, he received the title of Rao and a grant of the four *parganas* known as the Chaumahla. These *parganas* were subsequently wrested from Har Das's descendants by the Puars (Pramars) of Dhar, who left with the owners only the ten villages held by the present Rao. The remainder of the Chaumahla was afterwards ceded to Kotah by Holkar at the instance of the British Government and thus eventually became a portion of the Jhalawar State. The present value of the Kundla estate, which is held free of revenue, is estimated at R10,000. The estate is well managed and unencumbered. Rao Sawai Singh who succeeded his father in 1873 devotes himself to looking after his property and is not employed in any public capacity. He has one son, Kunwar Partap Singh, aged fourteen years, who is now being educated at the Mayo College, and one brother, Thakur Sardul Singh, who is about thirty-six years of age.

Kolah.

(2) **Thakur Arjun Singh of Kolah,** a Jhala Rajput, is descended in the sixth generation from Madho Singh, an ancestor of the ruling Chief. His great-grandfather, Govind Singh, accompanied Maharaj Rana Madan Singh to Jhalawar, and received a *jagir* of one village of the annual value of R1,501. One hundred and forty-four rupees are paid every other year as revenue to the Darbar. Thakur Arjun Singh succeeded his father in 1891.

Fathpur.

(3) **Thakur Chatar Sal of Fathpur** is also a Jhala Rajput and is closely related to the Thakur of Kolah. His grandfather, Thakur Binai Singh, came to Jhalawar with Maharaj Rana Madan Singh and received a *jagir* of two villages of the annual value of R1,325, paying R140 every other year as revenue to the Darbar. By birth the Thakur belongs to the Sadri family of Mewar, his father Thakur Himmat Singh having been adopted by Thakur Binai Singh. Thakur Chatar Sal, who succeeded his father in 1868, is now of middle age. He takes no part in the administration of the State. His only son, Kunwar Bhawani Singh, who is eighteen years of age, was educated at the Mayo College and is now employed in the State Police.

Sarthal.

(4) **Thakur Sheodan Singh of Sarthal,** a Rahtor Rajput of the Champawat sub-clan, holds the largest estate in Jhalawar. His great-grandfather, Anar Singh, owing to a disagreement with Maharaja Man Singh of Jodhpur, left Marwar for Kotah about 1806, and through the influence of Raj Rana Zalim Singh received the *jagir* of Harigarh. Owing to this connection with Zalim Singh's family, Anar Singh's son Prem Singh followed Maharaj Rana Madan Singh to Jhalawar where he received the *jagir* of Sarthal, the previous owner of which, a Hara Rajput, Nripat Singh, was granted a *jagir* in Kotah. On the death of Thakur Prem Singh, his widow adopted Bijay Singh from Ahor in Marwar, on whose death in 1888 his son, the present Thakur, succeeded to the estate. The Thakur, who is now fourteen years of age, is being educated at the Mayo College. He has two brothers, Thakurs Bhawani Singh and Bakht Singh, of whom the elder was adopted during his father's lifetime into the Ahor family. The *jagir*, which was formerly worth about R40,000, is now valued at R25,000 a year and is under the management of the Darbar, by which efforts are being made to pay off the debt with which it is encumbered. The revenue payable biennially to the State is R1,105 and forty *sawars* and ten footmen are supplied for the Raj service. The late Thakur Bijay Singh was at one time a member of the Jhalawar Council, but was removed from his pos' owing to the pernicious influence exercised by him on the young Chief.

Kotra.

(5) **Maharaja Indar Sal of Kotra** is a Hara Rajput of the Khatoli family of Kotah, in which State he still holds a *jagir*. The estate in Jhalawar, which consists of four villages of the annual value of R2,536 paying a tribute of R239 in alternate years and furnishing five *sawars* to the Darbar, was conferred on the present holder's father who came to Jhalawar with Maharaj Rana Madan Singh. The Maharaja is a man of middle age whose generous disposition has involved the estate in considerable debt. He succeeded his father in 1871 and has two sons, Kunwar Chatar Sal, aged thirty-one years, and Kunwar Durjan Sal, aged eighteen years. The latter, a youth of good promise, received his education at the Mayo College Ajmer.

Pipakheri.

(6) **Maharaja Balbhadar Singh of Pipakheri,** a descendant of the Bundi family of Karwar, is a Hara Rajput. The estate which is well managed and consists of one village of the value of R2,222 paying a tribute every other year of R222 to the Darbar, was conferred on the Maharaja's grandfather Chatar Singh who accompanied Maharaj Rana Madan Singh to Jhalawar. Maharaj Chatar Singh had rendered service to the Maharaj Rana before this time by bringing about a marriage between him and the lady of the Chandrawat house of Rampura in Holkar's territory who afterwards became the mother of Maharaj Rana Prithwi Singh. Maharaja Balbhadar Singh, who is now twenty-eight years of age, succeeded his father in 1870. When the Maharaj Rana was given charge of his State, Maharaja Balbhadar Singh was nominated a member of the Council, and the Chief, on being deprived of his powers, requested that he might be appointed as the intermediary between himself and the Political Superintendent. He held these posts up till recently and in the performance of the duties thus devolving on him displayed unvarying good temper and tact and established his reputation as an affable, courteous Rajput noble. He made himself well acquainted with the administration of the State, and his efficiency as a member of the State Council increased year by year. He now holds the appointment of Attaché to the Agent to the Governor-General in Rajputana. The nearest relatives of the Maharaja, who has no son, are his uncle Maharaj Baldeo Singh, a *Jagirdar* of Kotah, and his cousins Maharaj Nathu Singh and Maharaj Nirbhir Singh, *Jagirdars* of Bundi.

Dhanoda.

(7) **Thakur Takht Singh of Dhanoda** is a Kachhwaha Rajput of the Rajawat clan, belonging to the family of Barwara in Jaipur. Thakur Ranjit Singh, the great-grandfather of the present Thakur, migrated to Kotah, where he received a *jagir,* his ancestor Rao Ratn Singh Bahadur of Barwara having married an aunt of Raj Rana Zalim Singh. On the foundation of the Jhalawar State, he accompanied Maharaj Rana Madan Singh and received a *jagir* of five villages of the annual value of R4,261. The estate, which is still held by the family, furnishes eight *sawars* and five footmen for the service of the Darbar. Thakur Takht Singh who was educated at the Mayo College succeeded his father in 1888, and is now twenty-two years of age.

Bamori.

(8) **Thakur Man Singh of Bamori** is also a Kachhwaha Rajput of the Rajawat clan belonging to the Jhalai family of Jaipur. His grandfather, Thakur Gopal Singh, received a *jagir* in Kotah and subsequently accompanied Maharaj Rana Madan Singh to Jhalawar, where he was granted his present estate consisting of one village of the annual value of R4,413, which pays a biennial tribute of R326 and furnishes eight *sawars* and sixteen footmen to the Darbar. The estate is encumbered with debt. A sister of the late Thakur Guman Singh was married to Maharaj Rana Madan Singh. The present Thakur, who is about thirty-five years of age, succeeded his father Thakur Guman Singh in 1886. Before that time he was employed for a time in the State Police. He has three sons, the two elder of whom, Chain Singh and Ganga Singh, aged thirteen and eleven years, respectively, are being educated at the Mayo College.

Gajwara.

(9) **Thakur Anar Singh of Gajwara** is a Bhati Rajput of the ruling family of Jaisalmer. His cousin was married to Maharaj Rana Madan Singh, and he himself on coming to Jhalawar in the time of Maharaj Rana Prithwi Singh received a *jagir* of one village. The estate, which, is well managed, is valued at R948 and pays R68-11-0 biennially as tribute.

Thakur Anar Singh, a middle-aged man of retiring disposition, has two sons, Kunwars Sheodan Singh and Thakur Arjun Singh. The former, who was at one time a member of the State Council of Jhalawar, holds a *jagir* of the value of R1,000 in Jaisalmer and is in receipt of an allowance from that State. Thakur Arjun Singh has succeeded by adoption to the Nimodha estate in Jaipur. (See also page 68.)

Amritkheri.

(10) **Thakur Zalim Singh of Amritkheri** is a Bhati Rajput who holds also the *jagir* of Goraich in Mewar. Thakur Sultan Singh, the grandfather of the present Thakur, came to Jhalawar in 1841 and received a *jagir*. Maharaj Ranas Madan Singh and Prithwi Singh, both married ladies from this family, the wife of the former being a sister of Thakur Sultan Singh. The estate in Jhalawar consists of one village of the annual value of R877, and pays a biennial tribute of R47 to the Darbar. It is well managed and free from debt. Thakur Zalim Singh, who resides principally in Mewar, is about twenty-eight years of age, and bears a good reputation. He succeeded his father in 1890. He has no male issue.

Mangal.

(11) **Thakur Abhay Singh of Mangal** is a Kachhwaha Rajput of the Rajawat sub-clan, and belongs to the Muhabbatpura family in Jaipur. His grandfather Thakur Karn Singh who came to Jhalawar in the time of the late Chief drew a small allowance from the State, and subsequently received the honour of the *tazim* and a *jagir* of one village of the value of R1,198. Rupees 104 are paid biennially as tribute to the Darbar. Thakur Abhay Singh, who is twenty-one years of age, succeeded his father in 1892. He was educated at the Mayo College and his brother Phul Singh, aged ten years, is now a pupil there.

Officials.

Of the officials the following deserve to be noticed :—

(1) **Munshi Kali Charan**, a Kayastha, whose father came to Jhalawar in 1838, holds an estate of two villages of the annual value of R2,141. In the time of Maharaj Rana Prithwi Singh, Munshi Kali Charan was Persian Mir Munshi to the State. For sixteen years, he served as a Judge of the Appellate Court, and since his retirement from the judicial service in 1893 has been in charge of the State *Munshikhana*. He is a member of the Walterkrit Rajputra Hitkarini Sabha and is an honest, straightforward official of considerable experience. Of his two sons, the elder, Salig Ram, is Naib Hakim of the Civil Court.

(2) **Seth Narsingh Das**, a Mahajan by caste, is head of the Military Department (*Bakhshi Fauj*). His grandfather Seth Kanhaya Ram came from Kotah and received a *jagir* of R5,000, which on his death was reduced to R2,000. Seth Narsingh Das, who is about thirty-five years of age, is a man of good repute and quiet manner who has a fairly good hold over the troops. He has no family.

(3) **Purohit Chatur Bhuj** is a Gujarati Brahman whose grandfather Jiwan Rao accompanied Maharaj Rana Madan Singh from Kotah as family priest and received a *jagir* of the value of R7,000. The estate, which is in debt, is managed by the Darbar during the minority of the present holder.

(4) **Hakim Saadat Ahmad, Khan Bahadur,** is one of the oldest and most respected of the officials of the State. He has held many important posts, was one of the Judges of the Appellate Court during the minority and for some time afterwards, but subsequently felt himself obliged to resign his appointment. Since 1887, when the Maharaj Rana was deprived of his authority, he has been a member of the Council, and his useful work in that capacity was rewarded last year by the bestowal on him of the title of Khan Bahadur. Hakim Saadat Ahmad is now advanced in years, but has lost none of his energy and capacity for work. He has no family.

(5) **Dhabai Har Lal**, a Gujar, and a distant foster-connection of the ruling family, was assistant guardian to the present Chief when at the Mayo College, and in that capacity did good service. He was appointed a Judge of the Appellate Court in 1884, but resigned at the same time as Hakim Saadat Ahmad, like whom also he was made a member of the Council in 1887. Though illiterate, Dhabai Har Lal is a man of capacity, whose acquaintance with the administration and knowledge of Rajput customs makes him a useful member of the Council. He is now forty-one years of age. The *jagir* in the possession of the family was confiscated on the death of Dhabai Har Lal's adoptive father, but was recently restored to Har

Lal on the adoption being proved. It consists of one village of the value of R1,234. Dhabai Har Lal has one son, aged eleven years.

(6) **Pandit Ram Charan,** a Brahman by caste, has held the appointment of head of the Revenue Department since he first entered the service of the State during the minority of the present Chief. His father Pandit Rup Narayan was formerly a member of the State Council in Alwar.

(7) **Raja Sanwant Singh** of the Gangwana family in the Ajmer district (noticed on page 113) succeeded Munshi Kali Charan as Appellate Judge in 1893. He was previously a Member of the Court, but on its reorganisation in 1892 his services were dispensed with, and he remained out of employment until the recent vacancy caused by Munshi Kali Charan's retirement.

The only other person of note in the Jhalawar State is **Rao Raja Partap Sahai of Harnaoda.** The Rao Raja is by birth a Rao or bard whose ancestors formerly lived in Karauli. One of them, Chatur Bhuj, came to Gugair, now in Tonk, and received the village of Harnaoda in *jagir* from the then Khichi prince. His grandson Partap Singh was invited to Bundi by Rao Bhan Singh, and received Harnaoda and three other villages in *jagir*. He also received three villages and the title of Rao Raja from Kotah. The Kotah villages being within the *parganas* ceded to Maharaj Rana Zalim Singh, the family adhered to the new State. The *jagir* is valued at R10,000 a year. Rao Raja Partap Sahai, who is eighteen years of age, succeeded his father in 1891, and is the great-grandson of the first *Jagirdar*. He is a *tazimi* Sardar and ranks in some respects with the Rao of Kundla.

CHAPTER VIII.

JAT STATES.

[*Bhartpur—Dholpur.*]

As mentioned in the introductory chapter, Bhartpur is governed by the descendant of the landholders, who raised themselves to the rank and power of territorial Chiefs during the confusion of the eighteenth century; while Dholpur is the territory remaining with a family that had gained distinction earlier, though it first acquired political independence in the same century and under similar circumstances.

Bhartpur.

The founder of the present ruling house of Bhartpur was a Jat landholder by name Churaman, who built two petty forts in the villages of Thun and Sinsiniwar, a little south of Dig, from which he organized marauding expeditions and even ventured to harasst he rear of the Imperial army on the occasion of Aurangzeb's expedition into the Dakhan. Churaman was overcome by the Chief of Amber, Jay Singh, expelled from his territories, and succeeded by his younger brother Thakur Badan Singh, whose eldest son subsequently assumed the title of Raja, and established himself at Bhartpur where he built a large fort. Suraj Mal, who took a large part in the numerous struggles of the first half of the seventeenth century between the Mughals, the Mahrattas, the Rohillas, and Duranis, was killed in 1763 by the Mughals, while attempting to enforce a claim which he had put forward to the *faujdari* (military governorship) of Farukhnagar. His successor Jawahir Singh was defeated in a quarrel with the Raja of Jaipur, and was murdered at Agra in 1765. On his death, his next brother Ratn Singh occupied the *gadi*, but was also murdered after a very short reign. During the next two reigns, those of Nawal Singh and Ranjit Singh, the third and fourth sons of Suraj Mal, Najaf Khan stripped the Jats of all their possessions, except the fort of Bhartpur and territory yielding an annual income of nine lakhs of rupees which at the intercession of Suraj Mal's widow he allowed Ranjit Singh to keep. On the death of Najaf Khan in 1782 Sindia seized all Ranjit Singh's territories including Bhartpur, but again the widow interceded in her son's behalf, and Sindia restored eleven districts yielding ten lakhs of rupees to which three more, yielding four lakhs, were subsequently added for services rendered to General Perron.

These fourteen *parganas* now constitute the State of Bhartpur. Subsequently Ranjit Singh entered into an alliance with Sindia against Jaipur, and thereby obtained the cession of Dig, which had been held by the Emperor since its capture by Najaf Khan, and eleven *parganas* yielding a revenue of ten lakhs of rupees.

On the termination of the Mahratta war in 1803 the British Government concluded a treaty with Ranjit Singh, who with 5,000 horse had joined General Lake at Agra and thereby contributed to Sindia's defeat. In return for this service he received a grant of the districts of Kishangarh, Katawa, Riwari, Gokal, and Sahar. Immediately afterwards, however, while in alliance by treaty with the English Government, he entered into secret correspondence with Jaswant Rao Holkar who was then at war with the English Government, and offered him every kind of encouragement and support. At the battle of Dig in November 1804 the Bhartpur troops, which the Raja declared to have been assembled for co-operation with the British, were actually engaged against them and the Fort opened a damaging fire upon the British army. After the battle Holkar took refuge in this stronghold, and all the resources of the State were openly employed on his side. A siege thereupon took place. Ranjit Singh after a memorable defence, in the course of which he repelled four assaults with a loss to the besiegers of 3,000 men, finally made overtures for peace. These were accepted on the 4th May 1805 and a new treaty was concluded, by which he agreed to pay an indemnity of twenty lakhs of rupees, seven of which were subsequently remitted, and was guaranteed in possession the territories which he had held previously to the accession of the British Government. The *parganas* granted to him in 1803 were resumed. Maharaja Ranjit Singh died in 1805 leaving four sons Randhir, Baldeo,

Hardeo, and Lachhman. The eldest, Randhir, who succeeded him, died in 1823 and was followed by his brother Baldeo, who died after a reign of about eighteen months. His son Balwant, then six years of age, was recognized by the Government, but was opposed and imprisoned by his cousin Durjan Sal. A force which started from Delhi in support of the rightful heir was recalled by order of the Government who did not consider that its recognition of him involved any obligation to support him by arms. Eventually, however, when the disputed succession threatened a protracted war, it was determined to depose the usurper and reinstate Balwant Singh. After a siege that extended over nearly six weeks, Bhartpur was stormed by Lord Combermere on the 18th January 1826 and was dismantled. Durjan Sal was imprisoned at Allahabad and Balwant Singh was restored to the *gadi* under the regency of his mother and the superintendence of a Political Agent. The Rani was removed in 1826 and the ministers were formed into a Council of Regency. In 1835 Balwant Singh was put in charge of the administration and ruled till his death in 1853, when he was succeeded by his infant son, Maharaja Jaswant Singh, the late Chief.

Dholpur.

The family of the ruling Chief of Dholpur belongs to the Deswali tribe of Jats and traces its pedigree to Jet Singh, who is said to have acquired lands to the south of Alwar in the eleventh century. From Bamroli, the adopted home of one of his descendants, the family takes the name of Bamraulia. Driven from Bamroli about the year 1367 by the Subahdar of Agra the head of the house next migrated to Gwalior, where he took the part of the Rajputs in their struggles against the Emperor's officers. Eventually the Bamraulia Jats settled near Gohad, and in 1505 Surjan Deo received from Raja Man Singh Tunwar of Gwalior, a grant of the territory of Gohad, and assumed the title of Rana. After the overthrow of the Mahrattas at Panipat, Rana Bhim Singh in 1761 possessed himself of the fortress of Gwalior, but lost it six years later. In order to bar the encroachments of the Mahrattas, a treaty was made with the Rana in 1779 by the British Government under Warren Hastings, and the joint forces of the contracting parties re-took Gwalior. In the treaty of the 13th October 1781 between the British Government and Sindia, it was stipulated that so long as the Maharaj Rana should observe his treaty with the English, Sindia should not interfere with his territories. In consequence, however, of the treachery of the Maharaj Rana this stipulation was withdrawn, and Sindia re-took Gohad and Gwalior. In 1803 Ambaji Inglia, Governor of Gohad, seeing the rapid success of the British arms threw off his allegiance to Sindia, joined the forces of the British Government, and agreed to surrender the fort of Gwalior and certain districts, which the Government intended to confer on the Rana of Gohad. The districts ceded by Ambaji Inglia, with the exception of the fort and city of Gwalior, were made over to Rana Kirat Singh, who had succeeded to the *gadi* of Gohad in 1804. The possession of Gohad led to disputes between the British and Sindia, and in 1805 the Governor-General transferred Gwalior and Gohad to Sindia, and conferred Sindia's *parganas* of Dholpur, Bari, and Rajkhera on Maharaj Rana Kirat Singh. These *parganas* now form the Dholpur State. They had undergone constant changes of masters, had been seized by Raja Suraj Mal of Bhartpur after the battle of Panipat, wrested from him by Najaf Khan in 1775, taken by Sindia in 1782, occupied by the British in 1803, and made over again to Sindia in the same year.

Maharaj Rana Kirat Singh died in 1836 and was followed by his son Maharaj Rana Balwant Singh, on whose death in 1870 his grandson, the present Chief, Maharaj Rana Nihal Singh, succeeded to the *gadi*.

BHARTPUR.

The Chief.

His Highness Sri Brijindar Sawai Ram Singh Bahadur, Bahadur Jang, Maharaja of Bhartpur, was born on the 9th September 1872, and succeeded to the Chiefship on the 25th December 1893 on the death of his father Maharaja Jaswant Singh, who died on the 12th of the same month. During the minority of the late Maharaja the State was managed by the Political Agent and a Council of Regency. The Chief is a Hindu Jat of the Sinsiniwar family, the origin of which has been noticed above. The Maharaja has been married twice, the first marriage being with a daughter of a *zamindar* of Tepera in the Aligarh District, and the second with the daughter of a *zamindar* of Deoli in Bhartpur. His Highness has one younger brother, Raghunath Singh, aged seven years, and two sisters.

The next nearest relative of the Chief is his cousin, Rao Ajit Singh, who holds no *jagir* but lives on an allowance at Muttra. His Highness's other relatives are the Thakurs of the so-called **Solah Kotris**—Partap Singh, Ram Phal, Akhay Singh, Man Singh, Sita Ram, Sultan Singh, Jodh Singh, Devi Singh, Mukund Singh, Bhawani Singh, Dalel Singh, Ramkishor, Khushhal Singh, Lal Singh, Balram, and Bir Narain. In case of failure of direct heirs, the Maharaja would have to adopt from among these Thakurs, a fact which constitutes their only title to distinction. Some of them are *sipahis* and *sawars* in the State regiments. The Maharaja is related by kinship to the Chiefs of Nabha and Jhind and other Jat families and is connected with the Maharaja of Patiala, whose aunt the late Maharaja married. This lady's sister was the mother of the Maharaj Rana of Dholpur.

Leading men.

In Bhartpur where no approach to feudal institutions exists no distinction can be made between the officials and the aristocracy. With one exception, the *jagirs* are very small. The **Jagirdars** exercise no jurisdiction in their estates and pay neither revenue nor tribute to the Darbar. The officials have neither *jagirs* nor hereditary right to employment, and the son succeeds to his father's post only by special favour of the Chief. Even the Maharaja's relatives are, as already noticed, treated with no special consideration. They are styled Thakurs and hold some twenty-seven villages with an aggregate income of about R40,000. The only individual in the State calling for notice is **Faujdar Devi Singh, Jagirdar of Ballabhgarh.** This noble is the premier Sardar of Bhartpur and represents one of its oldest families, Ballabhgarh having been bestowed on the ancestor of the present holder by the Chief of Jaipur before Bhartpur came into existence as a State. The *jagir* contains fourteen villages near the Jaipur frontier. Ballabhgarh is a thriving town. Faujdar Devi Singh is the second son of Faujdar Gordhan Singh and succeeded to the estate on the death of his brother, the late holder, Faujdar Daulat Singh.

DHOLPUR.

The Chief.

His Highness Raisu-d-daula, Sipahdaru-l-Mulk, Major,* Maharaj Adhiraj Sri Sawai Maharaj Rana Nihal Singh Lokindar Bahadur, Diler Jang, Jay Deo, is a Hindu Vaishhnav Ramandi Jat of the Bamraulia family (see above). His Highness, who is the son of Maharaj Rana Kulendra Singh, was born on the 4th May 1863 and succeeded his grandfather Maharaj Rana Bhagwant Singh, on the 9th February 1873. His Highness married on the 30th April 1879 the second daughter of Shah Deo Singh of the family of Maharaja Ranjit Singh of the Panjab, by whom he has two surviving sons, one named Ram Singh, aged nine years, and the other aged one year. The relatives of the Maharaj Rana belong to a group of families which, though now only seven survive, were originally eight and consequently are known as the **Athghar.** These families are descended from one or other of the four sons of Maharaj Rana Bhag Raj, the ancestor in the eighth generation of the present Chief, who was at that time the only representative of the Bamraulia house who had issue. Of the principal family or **Gadi-ka-ghar,** the Maharaj Rana and his son are the only representatives. The nearest family to the Chief's is the Pachgaon ghar represented by Kunwar Rup Singh. The representatives of the Athghar take rank in the State only as connections of the Chief. Very few adoptions have taken place into the Gadi-ka-ghar and all of them have been from the Pachgaon family. By clan and family the Maharaj Rana is connected with the Jat races of Patiala, Jhind, Nabha, and Bhartpur. His mother was the daughter of Maharaja Narendra Singh of Patiala.

Leading men.

The leading men of Dholpur are—(1) the Rao of Sir Muttra and the Rao of Rajauni—members of the Jadon Bhati family of Karauli; (2) Jats of the Bidkheria family now represented by Faujdar Jaswant Singh and of the Bamraulia, Rajaunia, Dandak, Sandel, Bijolia, Hanselia, and Donderia families and of the Jadon Rajputs of Atar in Gwalior who also hold lands in Sindia's territory; (3) hereditary office-bearers, and (4) new officials.

Individuals of note.

Of the above the following individuals may be noticed:—

Sir Muttra.

(1) **Rao Ranjit Singh of Sir Muttra** who holds the first place in the State is a Jadon Bhati, descended from Mukat Rao, second son of Raja Gopal Das of Karauli who settled at

* This Chief is an Honorary Major in the British Army.

Sir Muttra in 1570. The present Rao, who is the son of Rao Madan Singh, is twenty-five years of age and was educated at the Mayo College, Ajmer. He has no son. Sir Muttra, which is situated in the extreme south-west of Dholpur, comprises thirty-three villages with an area of 175 square miles, of which, however, only one-fifth is culturable. The revenue of the estate is about R70,000, but the property is heavily encumbered and is under the management of the Darbar. The Rao pays an annual quit-rent to the Darbar of R20,000, and one lakh of rupees as fine on investiture.

Rajaunia.

(2) **Rao Bhup Singh of Rajaunia** is also a scion of the Karauli family. He succeeded his father in 1882 and is now thirty-three years of age. The Rao was educated at the Mayo College. He has one son, aged ten years, and a brother, both named Bhamorji. The estate, which pays a quit-rent of R1,660 to the Darbar, consists of five villages and yields a revenue of R5,000. It is in debt.

Hereditary officials.

(3) **Munshi Sundar Lal,** a Dhusar, served for some years as a Member of the State Council. His family, which came originally from Agra, has been for seventy years in charge of the *Munshikhana* (ministerial office) of the State.

(4) and (5) **Rai Bhoraprasad and Lala Brij Lal,** Head Auditors of Revenue, belong to families which entered the service of the State in 1734 and 1740 respectively.

New officials.

(6) **Rai Bahadur Bishan Sarup,** who was appointed Diwan of Dholpur in March 1891, after holding ministerial appointments for eighteen years, became Deputy Magistrate of Kekri in the Ajmer District. He held this appointment till his transfer to Dholpur in his present capacity.

(7) **Babu Uma Charan Mukharji,** a Bengali Brahman, was educated at the Agra College and was appointed tutor to His Highness the Maharaj Rana in 1877. He was for some time a member of the Council and is now Settlement Officer in the State.

(8) **Hakim Abbas Hussain and Miyan Achhu** are great-grandsons of Bakir Ali, a famous *Hakim* (doctor) in the service of Maharana Kirat Singh.

(9) **Mir Abid Ali** was formerly a member of the Council.

(10) and (11) **Mir Talib Husain and Indarbir Singh,** a Brahman of Garhwal, command the Infantry and Cavalry respectively. The latter is an aide-de-camp to the Chief.

(12) **Lala Fath Singh,** a relative of the Chief, is in charge of the Sir Muttra estate.

(13) **Kunwar Ratn Singh,** a member of the Bamraulia family, was formerly a member of the Council.

CHAPTER IX.

MUHAMMADAN STATE.

TONK.

The following account of the Tonk State is taken from Sir William Hunter's Gazetteer of India :—"The ruling family are Pathans of the Boner tribe. In the reign of the Emperor Muhammad Shah Ghazi one Tola Khan left his home in the Boner country and took service in Rohilkhand with Ali Muhammad Khan, a Rohilla of distinction. His son Hayat Khan became possessed of some landed property in Muradabad ; and to him in 1768 was born Amir Khan, the founder of Tonk. Beginning life as a petty mercenary leader, Amir Khan rose in 1798 to be the Commander of a large independent army in the service of Jaswant Rao Holkar, and was employed in the campaigns against Sindia, the Peshwa, and the British, and in assisting to levy the contribution exacted from Rajputana and Malwa. In 1806 Holkar granted to him the State of Tonk, and he had previously received the division of Sironj. In that year Amir Khan transferred himself and his army to the Raja of Jaipur, then at war with the Raja of Jodhpur; and after crushing the latter, changed sides and reduced the former. Having indiscriminately plundered both countries, he in 1809 proceeded at the head of 40,000 horsemen (being joined *en route* by 25,000 Pindaris) against the Raja of Nagpur. He was, however, warned off by the British Government, and returning to Rajputana, his bands plundered the country. Eventually in 1817, the Marquess of Hastings, with the view of putting down the Pindaris and restoring peace to Rajputana and Central India, offered Amir Khan the sovereignty of all the tracts bestowed on him by Holkar, on condition of his disbanding his army, which consisted of fifty-two battalions of disciplined infantry, one hundred and fifty guns, and a numerous body of Pathan cavalry. Finding resistance would be useless, Amir Khan acquiesced. His artillery, with the exception of forty guns, was purchased, and some of his troops enlisted in the British service. The remainder were liberally dealt with prior to disbandment, and the Rampura fort and the division of Aligarh Rampura were presented to the Nawab by the British Government as a free gift." These arrangements were embodied in a treaty in 1817. Amir Khan died in 1834, and was succeeded by his son Waziru-d-daula, who during the Mutiny of 1857 repulsed with comparatively few men an attack made on the Tonk fort by the combined forces numbering some 17,000 men, of the Nawab of Banda and Tantia Topi. In recognition of the bravery displayed on this occasion, the Nawab's salute was raised from fifteen to seventeen guns. He received a *sanad* guaranteeing the Tonk succession, according to the Muhammadan law of inheritance, on failure of natural heirs. On his death in 1864, his son Muhammad Ali Khan succeeded to the *masnad*. He was deposed three years later as a punishment for his complicity in the attack made on the uncles and followers of the Thakur of Lawa, one of the chief feudatories of the State. He was succeeded by his son, the present Chief, and the salute of the ruler of the State was reduced to eleven guns; the *ex*-Nawab being at the same time placed under surveillance at Benares, and an annual stipend of R60,000 assigned for his support out of the revenues of the Tonk State. During the reign of the present Chief the salute of seventeen guns has been restored.

The Chief.

His Highness Nawab Muhammad Ibrahim Ali Khan, G.C.I.E., Nawab of Tonk, is the eldest son of Nawab Muhammad Ali Khan and was born in 1848 (A. H. 1265). He succeeded to the *masnad* in 1866 on the deposition of his father. During his minority the administration was carried on by a Council of Regency of five members presided over by His Highness's uncle, Sahibzada Obaidulla Khan, and assisted by Captain J. Blair, an Assistant to the Governor-General's Agent in Rajputana. The Nawab was invested with governing powers on the 1st January 1870. He has five wives, of whom four belong to the Tonk family, and the fifth to that of Nawab Kalab Ali Khan, Nawab of Rampur. Eighteen sons have been born to His Highness, of whom eleven survive, namely—

(1) Sahibzada Abdu-l-Hafiz Khan, aged seventeen years, who is now being educated at the Mayo College at Ajmer.

(2) Sahibzada Muhammad Saadat Ali Khan, aged twelve years.

(3) Sahibzada Abdu-r-Rashid Khan, aged twelve years.

(4) Sahibzada Abdulla Khan, aged twelve years.
(5) Sahibzada Abdu-l-Wahid Khan, aged eight years.
(6) Sahibzada Farukh Ali Khan, aged seven years.
(7) Sahibzada Masud Ali Khan, aged five years.
(8) Sahibzada Turab Ali Khan, aged five years.
(9) Sahibzada Iftikhar Ali Khan, aged five years.
(10) Sahibzada Zabr Ali Khan, aged four years.
(11) Sahibzada Usman Ali Khan, aged three years.

The following sons are dead:—Sahibzadas Muhammad Ismail Khan, Yusuf Ali Khan, Yunas Ali Khan, Ghiyasu-d-din Khan, Alau-d-din Khan, Sadik Ali Khan, and Iftikhar Ali Khan. Of the daughters, three have recently been married.

The Nawab has eight brothers of whom three are by the same mother as himself. Six hold *jagirs* of values varying from R8,400 to R9,760 and two are in receipt of cash allowances. Four brothers have received titles from the State, and hold offices to which salaries of R175 to R200 are attached. The Nawab has also two uncles on the male side, Sahibzadas Muhammad Obaidulla Khan and Abdu-r-Rahman Khan. The former is Minister and Vice-President of the Council. He accompanied Sir Neville Chamberlain's mission to Kabul in 1878 and received a Companionship of the Order of the Star of India in recognition of his services on that occasion. He draws a salary of R800 a month in addition to his *jagir* which is valued at R18,353-10-9.

The families most closely related to the Nawab, after the above, are those of the descendants of the nine sons of Nawab Amiru-d-daula. With the exception of the Nawab of Rampur, His Highness has no relations outside his own family. Succession in the Tonk family is by primogeniture, modified only by the rule of Muhammadan law which prefers a younger son to a grandson by an elder son who has predeceased his father. The Chief of Tonk has, contrary to the usual rule of Muhammadan law, the right of adoption on failure of issue; this privilege, as already mentioned, having been bestowed by a *sanad* of the Government of India.

Leading men.

The leading men of the Tonk State are the hereditary nobles, the office-bearers, the officials, and others, such as Maulvis, Hakíms, etc. In public darbar Sahibzada Akram Khan, grand-uncle to the Nawab, is allotted the first seat to the right of His Highness in consideration of his kinship and age, and the *nazar* presented by him, which the Chief receives standing, is remitted. Next on the right come the Nawab's uncles Sahibzadas Muhammad Obaidulla Khan, C.S.I., and Abdu-r-Rahman Khan, whose *nazars* are also received by the Chief standing. After these come the Nawab's eight brothers in order of age, and lastly his cousins and other relatives.

The following are the principal nobles:—

(1) Iftikharu-l-Umara, Fakhru-l-Mulk, Sahibzada Muhammad Obaidulla Khan, C.S.I., Firoz Jang, *Jagirdar* of Sop.
(2) Sahibzada Muhammad Abdu-r-Rahman Khan.
(3) Sahibzada Muhammad Akram Khan.
(4) Azimu-l-Umara, Vikaru-l-Mulk, Sahibzada Muhammad Ishak Khan Satwat-i-Jang, *Jagirdar* of Aududa.
(5) Afzalu-l-Umara, Mumtazu-l-Mulk, Sahibzada Hafiz Hajji, Abdu-r-Rahim Khan, Muzaffar-i-Jang, *Jagirdar* of Loharwara.
(6) Mumtazu-l-Umara, Muazzamu-l-Mulk, Sahibzada Hafiz Muhammad Siddik Khan Diler Jang, *Jagirdar* of Gans.
(7) Najmu-l-Umara Ihtishamu-l-Mulk, Sahibzada Hajji Abdu-l-Wahab Khan Safdar-i-Jang, *Jagirdar* of Baori.
(8) Sahibzada Abdu-s-Samad Khan, *Jagirdar* of Dhamoda.
(9) Abdu-l Hamid Khan, *Jagirdar* of Bhambor.
(10) Sahibzada Muhammad Rafik Khan.
(11) Sahibzada Shafiulla Khan.
(12) Shamsu-l-Umra, Nizamu-l-Mulk, Sahibzada Mahmud Khan Tanmar-i-Jang, *Jagirdar* of Nawatila.

(13) Abzaju-l-Umara, Mufakhkharu-l-Mulk, Sahibzada Ahmad Khan, Shaukat-i-Jang.
(14) Sahibzada Muhammad Khan I, *Jagirdar* of Kharpa.
(15) Sahibzada Muhammad Khan II, *Jagirdar* of Jabasia.
(16) Sahibzada Ahmadulla Khan, *Jagirdar* of Armamal.
(17) Ashrafu-l-Umara, Umdatu-l-Mulk, Sahibzada Ahmad Yar Khan, Fath-i-Jang, *Jagirdar* of Napania.
(18) Sahibzada Afsand Yar Khan, also *Jagirdar* of Napania.

All the above nobles belong by birth to the Chief's family and the two last are related to it also by marriage with the daughters of Nawab Amiru-d-Daula. The largest estates are those owned by Sahibzada Muhammad Obaidulla Khan, C.S.I., and Sahibzada Muhammad Khan. As a rule no service is rendered by the *Jagirdars*, though all are expected to assist the Chief in case of necessity.

The *jagirs* are hereditary, succession fees (*nazarana*) being levied in the case of all *jagirdars* not belonging to the Chief's family. *Jagirdars* of the first class receive visits of condolence (*matampursi*) from the Chief. On failure of natural heirs adoption is allowed.

Hereditary office-bearers.

(1) **Mir Saman Shaikh Karim Baksh** is the officer in charge of gardens and other minor departments. He received from the present Chief a *jagir* of the village of Sheorampura, which yields ₹425 a year. He also holds *muafi* (revenue-free) lands and a village on *istimrari* (permanent) tenure. He pays no tribute.

(2) **Mir Shahan Rahmatulla Khan** holds in *jagir* two villages, which yield ₹3,842 and render service with five horses. He pays no tribute.

Officials.

(1) **Babu Vinayik Rao, Rao Bahadur,*** is Financial Member of the Council and Treasury Officer. He was formerly in the Public Works Secretariat of the Agent to the Governor-General for Rajputana, whence his services were transferred to Tonk in 1886. In recognition of his services in the reorganization of the Tonk finances he received the title of Rao Bahadur from the British Government as a personal distinction.

(2) **Mumhamad Najf Khan,** a pensioned Extra Assistant Commissioner from the Panjab, is Judicial Member of the Council.

(3) **Mirza Muhammad Ali Khan,** a native of Delhi, is the member in charge of Forests and Boundaries.

(4) **Fakhru-z-Zaman Saiyid Irshad Husain Khan,** the **Motamid-i-Khass,** has the rank of a *Tazimi Sardar* and holds the first place among the nobles. He holds the village of Samlatpura in *jagir*, which yields ₹1,500 a year and pays ₹118-4-9 as tribute to the Darbar.

(5) **Bakhshiyu-l-Mulk Saiyid Muhammad Usman Khan Shahamat-i-Jang** is an hereditary official and a *Tazimi* Sardar. He holds in *jagir* the village of Mauha which yields ₹2,000 a year and is exempt from service.

(6) **Dabiru-l-Mulk Muhammad Yusuf** is Mir Munshi to the Chief. He holds one village in *jagir* and one on *istimrari* tenure. These yield annually ₹4,000 and pay ₹2,230 as tribute.

Other persons of note.

(1) **Saiyid Muhammad Ismail,** a Pirzada or spiritual adviser to the Nawab, holds in *jagir* the village of Naner, which yields ₹9,000 a year and pays no tribute. As he is a minor, the management of the estate is entrusted to Bakhshi Muhammad Usman. The *jagir* was granted by Nawab Waziru-d-Daula.

(2) **Saiyid Muhammad Irfan** is also a Pirzada and occupies a rank similar to that of Saiyid Muhammad Ismail. He holds in *jagir* the village of Matuka which was also conferred by Nawab Waziru-d-Daula and yields ₹1,947. The estate is exempt from tribute.

(3) **Gauhar Ali Khan,** a minor, holds conjointly with three others the *jagir* of

* Babu Vinayik Rao died on the 7th May 1894, while these pages were in the press, from injuries received in a fire.

Himmatgarh, which yields R5,343 and pays a tribute of R113. The *jagir* was granted by Nawab Amiru-d-Daula and is under management during the minority of its owner.

(4) **Ahmad Khan** holds the *jagir* of Banwar, granted in the time of Nawab Amiru-d-Daula, which yields R3,467, pays R66-3-0 as tribute and renders service with ten *sawars*.

(5) **Ahsanulla Khan of Mirbana** holds a *jagir* conferred by Nawab Muhammad Ali Khan in consideration of the grantee's position as a Pirzada. It yields R3,025 yearly and pays R500 as tribute.

(6) **Saiyid Muhammad Yusuf,** son of Maulvi Zakariya, holds the *jagir* of Alinagar which yields R1,213 yearly and pays R213 in tribute. The estate was granted as a reward for good service by Nawab Waziru-d-Daula.

(7) **Colonel Ghaus Muhammad Khan** holds the *jagir* of Rohot, which yields R1,900 a year and pays no tribute. The *jagir* with the title of Colonel was conferred on the present holder as the grandson of Colonel Muhammad Khan, Roshanu-d-Daula, Umdatu-l-Mulk, Shamsam-i-Jang.

(8) **Bahadur Muhammad Khan** holds the *jagir* of Gangli which was conferred in the time of Nawab Amiru-d-Daula. It yields annually R2,750 and is exempt from tribute.

(9) **Fath Rai,** a Muhammadan Bhat, holds in *jagir* the village of Hari Kalan yielding R5,000 a year and paying R1,500 as tribute to the Darbar. The *jagir* was conferred by Nawab Amiru-d-Daula.

(10) **Seth Magni Ram Bhabhut Singh** of the firm of Dipchand Punamchand of Ratlam holds a *jagir* conferred by Nawab Waziru-d-daula consisting of Khari and another village yielding R1,970 and paying R10 as tribute.

(11) **Yar Muhammad Khan** holds a *jagir* consisting of Bhilwara, Undra, and two other villages yielding R2,500 a year and paying R511 as tribute. The villages were conferred by Nawab Amiru-d-Daula.

(12) **Ghulam Hazart Khan** holds the *jagir* of Pipaliya granted by Nawab Amiru-d-Daula, which yields R2,000-2-0 and pays R200 as tribute.

(13) **Thakur Balwant Singh** holds the *jagir* of Titarkheri, which existed before the foundation of the Tonk State. It yields R1,400 a year and pays R15-3-6 as tribute.

(14) **Abdu-l-Latif Khan** holds the *jagir* of Mirkhera granted by Nawab Amiru-d-Daula, which yields R1,000 a year and pays R94-9-0 as tribute to the Darbar.

(15) **Ahmad Sher Khan** holds the *jagir* of Amirgarh granted by Nawab Amiru-d-daula, which yields R2,000 and pays R188-12-0 as tribute to the Darbar.

(16) **Ghulam Akbar Khan** holds the *jagir* of Kurwansa granted by Nawab Muhammad Ali Khan, which yields R1,000 a year and pays R168 as tribute to the Darbar.

(17) **Ghulam Ghaus Khan** holds a *jagir* consisting of Chantauli and four other villages granted by Nawab Waziru-d-Daula, which yields R5,297 and pays R717-14-0 as tribute.

(18) **Muhammad Dastgir Khan** holds a *jagir* consisting of Sanaoti and three other villages granted by Nawab Muhammad Ali Khan, which yields R2,000 a year and supplies five *sawars* for the Raj service.

(19) **Raja Kalyan Singh of Devi Madho** holds a *jagir* which yields R1,600 and pays R157-8-0 as tribute to the Darbar. The *jagir* with the title of Raja and the right to carry kettle-drums and an ensign was granted by Nawab Amiru-d-Daula to an ancestor of the present holder, who was *Jamadar* of *Harkaras* (messengers).

(20) **Kazi Saiyid Abdu-l-Halim** holds the village of Deori which was granted to his ancestors by the Mughal Emperors. It yields R428-2-6 a year and pays R28-4-6 as tribute. The Kazi receives *khilats* or robes of honour at the *Ids* as a reward for conducting the services and is authorized to collect octroi in the city.

(21) **The heirs of Captain Akbar Buland Khan** hold by grant from the present Chief the *jagir* of Palri, which yields R2,607 and is exempt from tribute.

The following individuals hold lands on *istimrari* (permanent) tenures :—

No.	Name.	Village.	Income.	Tribute.	Remarks.
			R a. p.	R a. p.	
1	Rao Kesri Singh—Shaikhawat	Binota and 8 others	9,764 0 0	982 0 0	Is one of the "32" Sardars of Mewar.
2	Rup Singh—Chandawat	Mindoli	1,068 4 6	167 0 0	
3	Fath Singh—Solankhya	Biroli and 3 others	5,837 12 0	602 8 0	
4	Amar Singh—Saktawat Sesodia	Mewasa and 12 others	11,413 12 0	1,134 8 0	
5	Prithwi Singh—Rahtor	Kadmaoli and 3 others	1,890 2 0	444 0 0	
6	Lachhman Singh—Rajawat	Pilonda Khera	1,500 0 0	127 0 0	
7	Sardar Singh	Ghasana	2,843 2 9	551 0 0	
8	Lachhman Singh—Solankhya	Dinara	792 3 0	624 0 0	

All the *istimrardars* comprised in the above list belong to the Nimbahera Pargana and all save Fath Singh of Baroli and Lachhman Singh of Dinara received their estates from Mewar before the foundation of the Tonk State.

CHAPTER X.

AJMER.

The first rulers of Ajmer, of whom anything is known, were the Chauhans, by one of whom, Raja Aja, the city from which the district takes its name is said to have been founded in the year 145 A.D. The Chauhans held Ajmer without interruption till the days of Prithwi Raj, king of Delhi, who was by adoption ruler also of Ajmer. After the defeat of this monarch, the conqueror Shahabu-d-din took Ajmer and made it over to a relative of Prithwi Raj, but shortly afterwards appointed a Governor of the city to control the new Raja. After the invasion of Timurlang and the extinction of the house of Tughlak Ajmer was occupied by the Rana of Mewar, on whose assassination it fell into the hands of the Muhammadan kings of Malwa. These held it from 1469 to 1531, when the kingdom of Malwa was annexed to that of Gujarat. The Chief of Marwar, Mal Deo, took advantage of the opportunity to seize Ajmer, which was held by the Rahtors for twenty-four years. Akbar conquered it in 1556. For one hundred and ninety-four years from that time Ajmer remained an integral portion of the Mughal Empire and the centre of a *subah* (province) which comprised the whole of Rajputana. In 1720 Ajit Singh, the son of Raja Jaswant Singh of Marwar, seized Ajmer and killed the Imperial Governor. He was expelled by Muhammad Shah, and his son Abhay Singh was appointed Viceroy of Ajmer. In the struggles which took place between Ram Singh, the successor of Abhay Singh, and the latter's uncle, Bakht Singh, the Mahrattas under Jay Appa Sindia were called in by Bakht Singh. After Bakht Singh's death his son Bijay Singh opposed the Mahrattas, and Jay Appa was assassinated at his instigation. Eventually Ajmer was ceded to the Mahrattas as *Mundkati* or compensation for the blood of Jay Appa and was held by them till 1787 when, after the defeat of the Mahrattas at the battle of Tonga by the coalition of the Rahtors and Kachhwahas under the Raja of Jaipur, the Rahtors retook the city. Three years later the Mahrattas under De Boigne recovered Ajmer which they held till 1818. At the close of the Pindari war in that year, Ajmer was ceded by Daulat Rao Sindia to the British by whom it has since been held.

Leading men.

The leading men of Ajmer fall into three classes:—(1) **Istimrardars**, (2) **Jagirdars**, and (3) **Seths**. The Seths are the bankers of Ajmer and live in the city. The *istimrardars* and *jagirdars* hold so much of the land of the district as is not *khalsa*. As might be expected from the history of Ajmer the landholders are all Rajputs or Muhammadans, but it is remarkable that, though the Chauhans held the district for over a thousand years, no single representative of the clan is now to be found within its borders. Almost all the Rajput estate-holders are Rahtor descendants of the ruling house of Marwar. The only exceptions are the Sesodia family of Sawar in the south, the petty *istimrardar* of Manoharpur, the *jagirdar* of Rajgarh, and one or two other small *jagirdars*. These last are all Rajputs of the Gaur clan. The Gaur Rajputs for a time held a prominent position in Ajmer. In the days of Prithwi Raj three brothers, being then on a pilgrimage from Gaur in Bengal to Dwarka, were engaged by that monarch in a successful expedition against Daya Singh of Nagor, and subsequently each of them married a daughter of the king. One, Raja Bachraj, settled in Ajmer. In the course of time Junian, Sarwar (now in Kishangarh), Deolia, and the adjacent country fell into the hands of the Gaur Rajputs and to the head of the clan Humayan gave a *mansab* of R7,000. In the time of Akbar, Raja Bithal Das founded the town of Rajgarh and called it after the name of his grandson Raj Singh. The son of the latter took Srinagar from the Puar (Pramar) Rajputs who have now disappeared from the district. This was the climax of the prosperity of the Gaurs, for soon afterwards they were ejected from Rajgarh and all their territory by Kishan Singh, a Rahtor. After twenty-five years of dispossession, Gopal Singh recovered Rajgarh and the Gaurs were in possession when the country fell into the hands of the Mahrattas. The Mahrattas in 1817 resumed Rajgarh and the twelve villages attached to it, as the Raja was unable to pay a contribution of R10,000 as *fauj kharch* (war expenditure). On the establishment of British rule, these villages were restored on condition of payment of *nazarana* (succession fee), but as the *nazarana* was not, or could not be, paid, the whole estate, with the exception of one small village, was resumed and remained *khalsa* till 1874, when it was presented in *jagir* to the representative of the ancient house.

Istimrardars.

The **istimrardars** are so called from the fact that they hold their estates in perpetuity on condition of paying an annual revenue to Government, which is not liable to enhancement. They are divided into two classes—*tazimi* and non-*tazimi*. All are entitled to seats in Darbar. Of the nineteen principal *istimrari* estates, the holders of fifteen, — Bhinai, Sawar, Masuda, Pisangan, Junian, Deolia, Kharwa, Bandanwara, Mehrun, Para, Deogaon-Bhagera, Govindgarh, Tantoti, Barli, and Bagsuri, — enjoy the honour of the *tazim*. Of these, the first four and the *istimrardar* of Kharwa are the heads of their respective houses, from which the remainder are offshoots. The Rahtors of Ajmer are descended from one or other of the Chiefs of Marwar, of whom the following are in this connection the most important:—Rao Jodha, 1453 (Masuda and Bagsuri), Rao Maldeo, 1531 (Bhinai), and Raja Udai Singh, 1583 Gangwana (*jagir*) Pisangan, Mehrun, Junian, and Govindgarh. The families of Deolia, Bandanwara, Deogaon-Baghera, Tantoti, and Barli are offshoots of the house of Bhinai, and the **istimrardar** of Para is a descendant of the family of Pisangan.

In all the *istimrardar* families, with the unimportant exception of Karel where sub-division is still the rule, succession is by primogeniture, the provision for younger sons consisting generally of a grant for life of a well and a few *bighas* of land. In early times, as in Karel at present, all sons shared alike except the eldest whose portion was generally larger than that of the rest, but the disruption of estates which ensued was so inconvenient that it was dropped in favour of an assignment, known as *gras*, of single villages to younger sons, an arrangement which in its turn has given place to that now prevailing.

The following account is given by Mr. LaTouche of the origin of the *istimrar* tenures:—"The tenure of the feudal Chief was originally identical with that of the Chiefs in the Native States of Rajputana. The estates were *jagirs* held on condition of military service and liable to various feudal incidents. Colonel Tod, in his Rajasthan, Volume I, page 167, thus sums up the result of his inquiries into these tenures—'A grant of an estate is for the life of the holder with inheritance for his offspring in lineal descent or adoption with the sanction of the Prince, and resumable for crime or incapacity; this reversion and power of resumption being marked by the usual ceremonies on each lapse of the grantee, of sequestration (*zabti*), of relief (*nazarana*), of homage and investiture of the heir.' From all that can be discovered the original tenure of the mass of the *istimrar* estates in Ajmer is exactly described by the above quotation. The estates were life-grants, but, like all similar tenures, they tended to become hereditary."

The *istimrardars* are by law incompetent to make alienations lasting beyond their own lives. Like the other estates in Rajputana, those of Ajmer were originally held on service tenures and were subject to certain feudal liabilities. In lieu of these burdens the Mahrattas substituted fixed cash payments and exacted certain cesses. The latter were abolished by the British, and in 1873 it was finally decided that the assessments then levied should be fixed in perpetuity, subject only to the condition of payment of a *nazarana* on succession.

Jagirdars.

Of the **jagirdars** two, those of Rajgarh and Arjunpura, are Gaur Rajputs, and one, Gangwana, is a Rahtor. The remainder are chiefly Muhammadans, the principal being Diwan Ghiasu-d-din Ali Khan, a descendant of Khwaja Muayyinu-d-din Chishti and Inayatullah Shah, the descendant of a saint who lived in Herat.

Seths.

Ajmer is the residence of the heads of several important firms of **Seths** who have branches throughout Rajputana and in other parts of India. The principal occupation of the Ajmer Seths is the purchase and sale of *hundis*.

Tazimi Istimrardars.

(1) **Raja Udai Singh of Bhinai,** a Rahtor Rajput, descended from Rao Jodha, the founder of the city of Jodhpur, is the premier Thakur of the district. Chandra Sen, the grandson of **Rao Mal Deo of Marwar (1531),** came to Ajmer, and having by stratagem intoxicated Madlia,

the chief of a band of Bhils who ravaged the country near Bhinai, slew him and dispersed his followers. For this service Bhinai and seven other *parganas* were bestowed on him in *jagir* by the Emperor Akbar. The *jagir* consisted of 84 villages which were subsequently divided in the proportion of forty-six to thirty-eight between Udai Bhan and Akhay Raj in the fourth generation from Chandra Sen, the former making Bhinai and the latter Deolia his head-quarters. Udai Bhan being at that time childless adopted Narsingh Das, a son of Akhay Raj, but on the subsequent birth of a son, Kesri Singh, three villages were assigned to Narsingh Das from whom is descended the present Thakur of Tantoti. Kesri Singh obtained Bhinai and twenty-four villages, and a younger brother Suraj Mal, who became the ancestor of the house of Bandanwara, received ten villages. The twenty-five villages of Bhinai yield a revenue of about R80,000 a year. Three of them have been assigned to the minor Thakur of Sholian, Sarana, and Santola as maintenance and one, Kotri, to a Charan. Santola is held in mortgage by the Maharaja of Kishangarh. The Bhinai estate, which is well managed, pays a revenue to Government of R7,717. The title of Raja was bestowed on the head of the Bhinai house in 1783 by the then Chief of Jodhpur as a reward for military service.

The present Raja, who is six years of age, succeeded his father Raja Mangal Singh Bahadur, C.I.E., in July 1892. Raja Mangal Singh, who was an Honorary Magistrate and Subordinate Judge, received the title of Raja Bahadur as a personal distinction on the 1st January 1877, and was admitted two years later to the Companionship of the Order of the Indian Empire.

The pedigree on the opposite page shows the various branches of the Bhinai family and gives the descent of the *tazimi* lines.

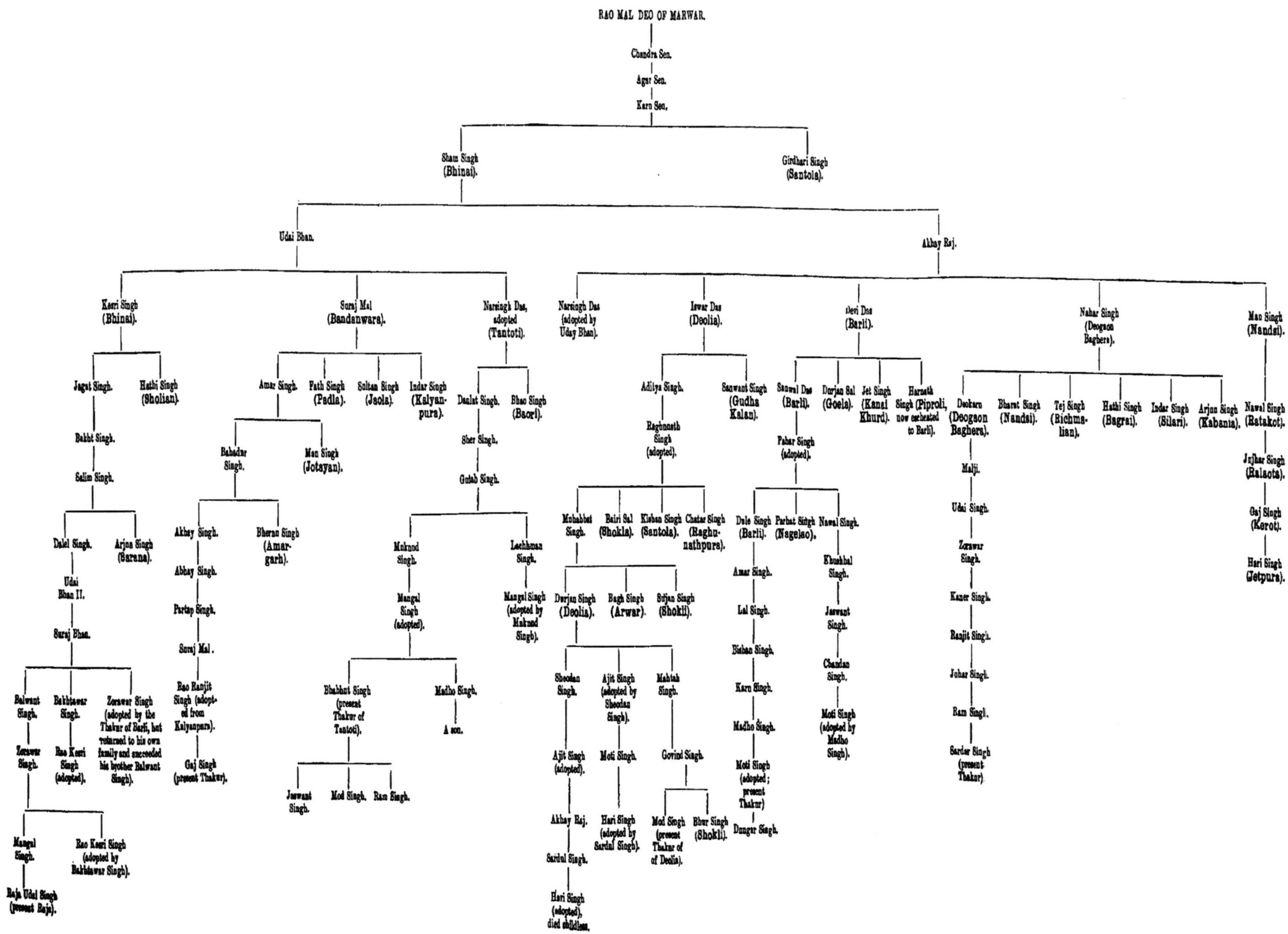
RAO MAL DEO OF MARWAR.
Chandra Sen.
Agar Sen.
Karn Sen.
Sham Singh (Bhinai).
Girdhari Singh (Santola).
Udai Bhan.
Akhay Raj.
Kesri Singh (Bhinai).
Suraj Mal (Bandanwara).
Narsingh Das, adopted (Tantoti).
Narsingh Das (adopted by Uday Bhan).
Iswar Das (Deolia).
Devi Das (Barli).
Nahar Singh (Deogaon Baghera).
Man Singh (Nandsi).
Jagat Singh.
Hathi Singh (Sholian).
Amar Singh.
Fath Singh (Padla).
Soltan Singh (Jaola).
Indar Singh (Kalyanpura).
Daulat Singh.
Bhao Singh (Baori).
Aditya Singh.
Sanwant Singh (Gudha Kalan).
Sanwal Das (Barli).
Durjan Sal (Goela).
Jet Singh (Kanai Khurd).
Harnath Singh (Piproli, now escheated to Barli).
Deokaran (Deogaon Baghera).
Bharat Singh (Nandsi).
Tej Singh (Bichmalian).
Hathi Singh (Bagrai).
Indar Singh (Silari).
Arjun Singh (Kabania).
Nawal Singh (Ratakot).
Bakht Singh.
Bahadar Singh.
Man Singh (Jotayan).
Sher Singh.
Raghunath Singh (adopted).
Pahar Singh (adopted).
Malji.
Jujhar Singh (Ralaota).
Salim Singh.
Gulab Singh.
Udai Singh.
Gaj Singh (Kerot).
Akhay Singh.
Bheran Singh (Amargarh).
Muhabbat Singh.
Bairi Sal (Shokla).
Kishan Singh (Santola).
Chatar Singh (Raghunathpura).
Dule Singh (Barli).
Parbat Singh (Nagelao).
Nawal Singh.
Dalel Singh.
Arjun Singh (Sarana).
Mukund Singh.
Lachhman Singh.
Zorawar Singh.
Hari Singh (Jetpura).
Abhay Singh.
Amar Singh.
Khushhal Singh.
Udai Bhan II.
Mangal Singh (adopted).
Mangal Singh (adopted by Mukund Singh).
Durjan Singh (Deolia).
Bagh Singh (Arwar).
Sujan Singh (Shokli).
Kaner Singh.
Partap Singh.
Lal Singh.
Jaswant Singh.
Suraj Bhan.
Ranjit Singh.
Suraj Mal.
Bishan Singh.
Chandan Singh.
Johar Singh.
Balwant Singh.
Bakhtawar Singh.
Zorawar Singh (adopted by the Thakur of Barli, but returned to his own family and succeeded his brother Balwant Singh).
Rao Ranjit Singh (adopted from Kalyanpura).
Bhabhut Singh (present Thakur of Tantoti).
Madho Singh.
Sheodan Singh.
Ajit Singh (adopted by Sheodan Singh).
Mahtab Singh.
Karn Singh.
Moti Singh (adopted by Madho Singh).
Ram Singh.
A son.
Zorawar Singh.
Rao Kesri Singh (adopted).
Gaj Singh (present Thakur).
Madho Singh.
Ajit Singh (adopted).
Moti Singh.
Govind Singh.
Sardar Singh (present Thakur).
Jaswant Singh.
Mod Singh.
Ram Singh.
Moti Singh (adopted; present Thakur)
Mangal Singh.
Rao Kesri Singh (adopted by Bakhtawar Singh).
Akhay Raj.
Hari Singh (adopted by Sardul Singh).
Mod Singh (present Thakur of of Deolia).
Bhur Singh (Shokli).
Dungar Singh.
Sardul Singh.
Raja Udai Singh (present Raja).
Hari Singh (adopted), died childless.

Sawar.

(2) **Thakur Ummed Singh of Sawar** is a Sesodia Rajput of the Saktawat family who holds an estate of thirty-three villages yielding an income of about R30,000 and paying R7,215 as revenue to Government. The estate forms a portion of a *jagir* granted by the Emperor Jahangir to Gokul Das, grandson of Sakat Singh and great-grandson of Rana Udai Singh of Mewar. Thakur Ummed Singh who succeeded his father, Raja Madho Singh, is now twenty-nine years of age. He was educated at the Mayo College and knows Hindi and English. He is also an Honorary Magistrate and Munsif within the limits of his estate. He has no children and the nearest family is that of Tankawas. The title of Raja was conferred on Thakur Madho Singh as a personal distinction in 1877. The following pedigree shows the descent of the family from Gokul Das and the connected branches :—

GOKUL DAS.

- Sundar Das (Sawar).
  - Pratap Singh (Sawar).
    - Raj Singh (Sawar).
      - Indar Singh.
        - Sakat Singh.
          - Bhup Singh.
            - Udai Singh.
              - Ajit Singh.
                - Jaswant Singh.
                  - Madho Singh.
                    - Ummed Singh (present Thakur).
                - Zorawar Singh (Tankawas).
    - Chatar Singh (Chandthali).
      - Bahadur Singh (Chosla).
  - Jay Singh (Piplaj).
  - Ram Singh (Basundni).
- Ajib Singh (Deokheri).

Masuda.

(3) **Rao Bahadur Singh of Masuda**, a Rahtor Rajput of the Mertia family, holds the largest and richest estate in the district, consisting of twenty-six villages yielding a revenue of about a lakh of rupees and paying R8,555 as revenue to Government. Several Mer villages in Merwara which were formerly held by the Thakur of Masuda have under a recent arrangement been declared *khalsa*, the Rao receiving R4,000 a year as compensation. According to a badly authenticated tradition the town of Masuda received its name from Masud Ghazi, a son of Salar Sahu, who founded it in the time of Sultan Muhammad. The *pargana* of Masuda was given as a *jagir* by the Emperor Akbar to Hanwant Singh and his brothers as a reward for the expulsion by them of the Puar (Pramar) Rajputs who had attacked the imperial *thana* (outpost). Hanwant Singh was the son of Jagmal and great-great-grandson of Rao Jodha of Marwar through the latter's son Duda. For four generations the estate was not divided. Since that time, as may be seen from the annexed pedigree, divisions have been frequent.

Rao Bahadur Singh, who is the adopted son of the late Thakur Sheonath Singh, is now thirty-seven years of age. He was educated at the Mayo College and knows English and Hindi. He has no children. He is an Honorary Magistrate and Munsif within the limits of his own estate. He received the title of Rao as a personal distinction in 1877 and was made a Companion of the Order of the Indian Empire in May 1893. His grandfather Devi Singh rendered assistance to the British in their conquest of Merwara in 1817-18.

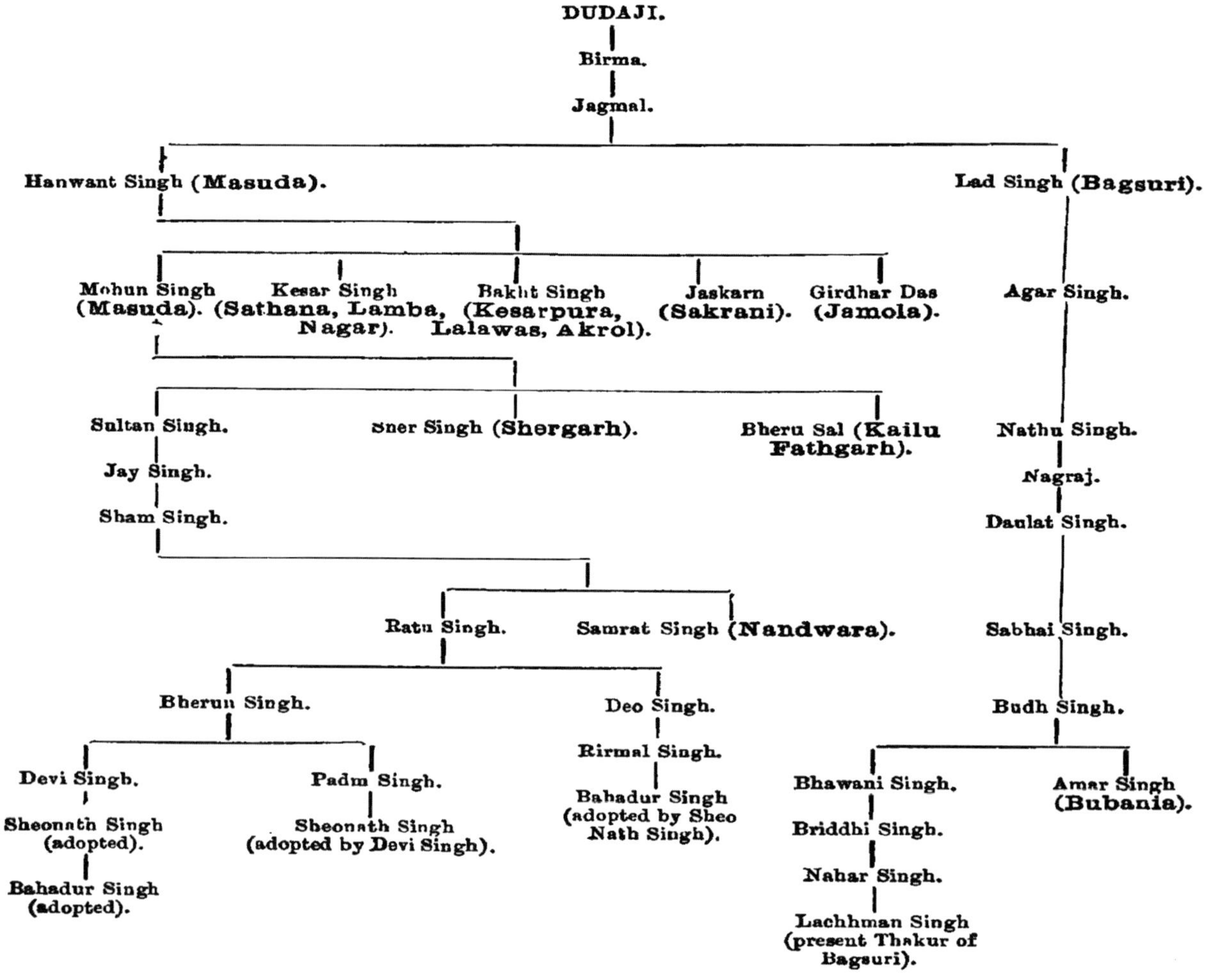

Pisangan.

(4) **Raja Kandarp Sen of Pisangan,** a Rahtor Rajput of the Jodhawat family, holds an estate consisting of eleven villages to the west of Ajmer, of which the annual income is about R23,200 and the revenue payable to Government R4,563. The founder of the estate was Kesri Singh, a grandson of Raja Udai Singh of Marwar, who, having come to Ajmer to seek his fortune, ejected the Puar (Pramar) Rajputs from Pisangan. His son Sujan Singh conquered Junian from the Gaur Rajputs and Mehrun from the Sesodias. In the division of property which took place on Sujan Singh's death, Pisangan was assigned to the youngest son, as a reward, it is said, for his having avenged the death of an uncle. The title of Raja, which is held by courtesy by the *istimrardar* of Pisangan, was granted by a *sanad* of Maharaja Man Singh of Marwar in 1806 to Nathu Singh in recognition of services rendered by the latter in the famous marriage dispute between Jodhpur and Udaipur. The title was also conferred as a personal distinction by the British Government on the late Thakur Partap Singh in 1877. The present Raja, who is now thirty years of age, was the son of Thakur Mahipal Singh of Khawas and was adopted by Raja Partap Singh in 1883. He has one son Ramchand Das. The following pedigree shows the descent of the Pisangan, Junian, and Mehrun families :—

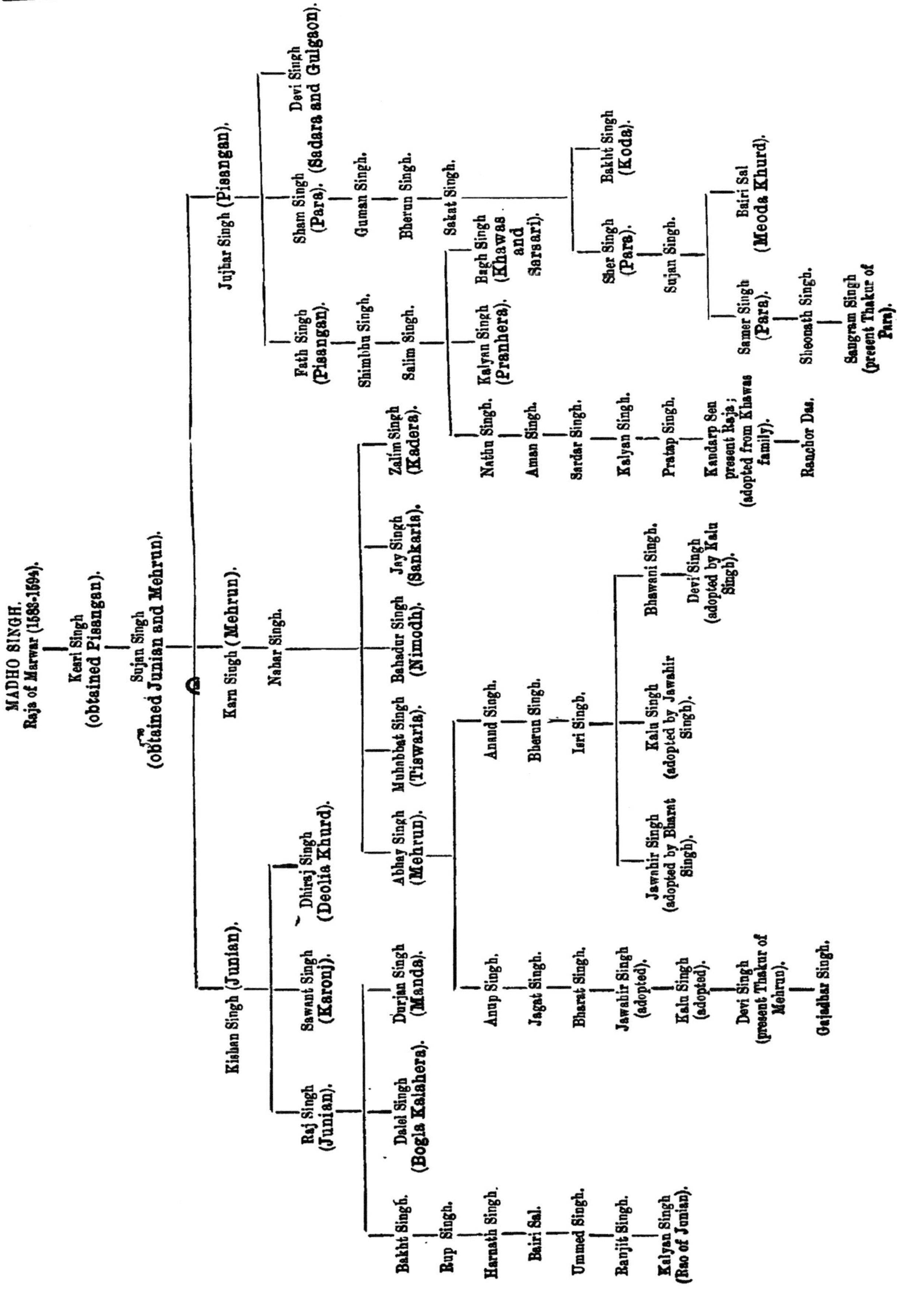
MADHO SINGH. Raja of Marwar (1583-1594).
Kesri Singh (obtained Pisangan).
Sujan Singh (obtained Junian and Mehrun).
Jujhar Singh (Pisangan).
Karn Singh (Mehrun).
Kishan Singh (Junian).
Fath Singh (Pisangan).
Sham Singh (Para).
Devi Singh (Sadara and Gulgaon).
Shimbhu Singh.
Guman Singh.
Salim Singh.
Bherun Singh.
Sakat Singh.
Nathu Singh.
Kalyan Singh (Pranhera).
Bagh Singh (Khawas and Sarsari).
Sher Singh (Para).
Bakht Singh (Koda).
Aman Singh.
Sardar Singh.
Kalyan Singh.
Pratap Singh.
Kandarp Sen present Raja; (adopted from Khawas family).
Ranchor Das.
Sujan Singh.
Samer Singh (Para).
Bairi Sal (Meoda Khurd).
Sheonath Singh.
Sangram Singh (present Thakur of Para).
Nahar Singh.
Zalim Singh (Kadera).
Jey Singh (Sankaria).
Bahadur Singh (Nimodh).
Muhabbat Singh (Tiswaria).
Abhay Singh (Mehrun).
Anand Singh.
Bherun Singh.
Isri Singh.
Bhawani Singh.
Devi Singh (adopted by Kalu Singh).
Kalu Singh (adopted by Jawahir Singh).
Jawahir Singh (adopted by Bharat Singh).
Anup Singh.
Jagat Singh.
Bharat Singh.
Jawahir Singh (adopted).
Kalu Singh (adopted).
Devi Singh (present Thakur of Mehrun).
Gajadhar Singh.
Sawant Singh (Karonj).
Dhiraj Singh (Deolia Khurd).
Raj Singh (Junian).
Durjan Singh (Manda).
Dalel Singh (Bogla Kalahera).
Bakht Singh.
Rup Singh.
Harnath Singh.
Bairi Sal.
Ummed Singh.
Ranjit Singh.
Kalyan Singh (Rao of Junian).

Junian.

(5) **Rao Kalyan Singh of Junian** is a Rahtor Rajput belonging to the same family as the Raja of Pisangan (*q. v.*). The Junian estate consists of sixteen villages yielding an annual income of ₹35,000 and paying ₹5,723 as revenue to Government. The *istimrardar* of Junian is hereditary *bhumia* of Kekri and provides as such for the watch and ward of that town. He holds also one village in Jaipur and one in Kotah in *jagir*. Rao Kalyan Singh, who is now thirty years of age, is the son of Kunwar Ranjit Singh and succeeded his grandfather Thakur Ummed Singh in 1868. He was educated at the Mayo College and knows English and Hindi. Kalyan Singh, on whom his present title of Rao was bestowed as a personal distinction in 1877, has married a sister of the late Maharaja Mangal Singh of Alwar.

Deolia.

(6) **Thakur Mod Singh of Deolia,** a Rahtor Rajput, descended from Akhay Raj, the son of the founder of the Bhinai family, holds an estate of five villages yielding an income of about ₹32,000 a year and paying ₹3,380 as revenue to Government. During the Marwar ascendency Deolia supplied thirty-six horsemen to the service of the State and the holder enjoyed besides the Ajmer *jagir* an estate of the value of ₹36,000 in Marwar and received ₹35 a day from that State. The Marwar *jagir* and the daily allowance were continued till 1806. Thakur Mod Singh, who is now twenty years of age, and was educated at the Mayo College, succeeded the late Thakur, Rao Hari Singh. The estate was transferred to him in the month of February 1893 on his attaining majority. The Rao had nominated the Thakur of Kaibania as his successor, but Thakur Mod Singh being the nearest of kin to the deceased, his claim was recognized by the Government of India as being the stronger in accordance with the usage prevalent in the family. The late Thakur Hari Singh, on whom the title of Rao was conferred as a personal distinction in 1877, was an Honorary Magistrate and Munsif within the limits of his own estate. The descent of the Thakur and of the minor connected families is shown in the pedigree of the Bhinai family at page 103.

Kharwa.

(7) **Rao Madho Singh of Kharwa** is a Rahtor Rajput of the Sakat Singhot family, descended from Rao Jodha. He holds an estate consisting of fifteen villages and yielding an estimated revenue of ₹30,000 and pays ₹2,318 annually to Government. The estate is said to have been conferred by Akbar on Sakat Singh, a son of Raja Udai Singh of Marwar, as a reward for saving the Emperor from drowning. For seven generations no division took place, but at the present time three villages belonging to Kharwa are held by three subordinate *istimrardars* and one by Charans. Seventeen villages which formerly belonged to Kharwa were incorporated in Merwara on the constitution of that district, and under an agreement recently sanctioned the Rao receives ₹1,000 a year from the British Government in full satisfaction of his claims to these villages.

Madho Singh, on whom the title of Rao was conferred as a personal distinction in 1877, is an Honorary Magistrate and Munsif within the limits of his estate. He has one son, Kunwar Gopal Singh.

The following pedigree shows the descent of the Rao of Kharwa and the connected minor *istimrardars* from Raja Udai Singh :—

UDAI SINGH.
- Sakat Singh.
  - Karn Singh.
    - Hukma Gir.
      - Kalu Singh.
        - Fath Singh.
          - Amar Singh.
            - Ram Singh.
              - Suraj Mal.
                - Deo Singh.
                  - Pratap Singh.
                    - Ram Singh.
                      - Rao Madho Singh.
                        - Kunwar Gopal Singh.
                    - Sham Singh (Bhawani Khera).
                  - Gulab Singh.
                - Chatar Singh (Deogarh).

Bandanwara.

(8) **Rao Ranjit Singh of Bandanwara,*** a Rahtor Rajput of the Bhinai family (*q.v.*) holds an estate of twenty-one villages situated to the south of the Nasirabad Cantonment. The estimated income of the estate, including the subordinate *jagir* of Amargarh which pays revenue to the Rao, is R27,000, and the yearly revenue payable to Government is R5,356.

Suraj Mal, the second son of Udai Bhan of Bhinai, was the founder of the Bandanwara family, and at one time held, in addition to the Bandanwara *jagir*, the villages of Ramsar and Srinagar. These were subsequently resumed by Maharaja Ajit Singh of Marwar and are now *khalsa*. The Rao, who is forty-nine years of age, succeeded by adoption to Suraj Mal II, the late Thakur, at the same time changing his name from Bharat Singh to Ranjit Singh. He belonged originally to the Kalyanpura branch of the family, and was adopted in 1852. He has one son, Kunwar Gaj Singh, who was educated at the Mayo College and is twenty-three years of age. The Rao, on whom his present title was conferred as a personal distinction in 1877, is an Honorary Magistrate and Munsif within his own estate.

Mehrun.

(9) **Thakur Devi Singh of Mehrun** is a Rahtor Rajput of the Pisangan and Junian family who holds an estate of thirteen villages, yielding an income of about R20,000 and paying a fixed revenue to Government of R5,360. The origin of the estate has been described in the account of Rao Kalyan Singh of Junian. In 1811 the Thakur of Kadera, Lal Singh, made an attack on his cousin Jagat Singh, Thakur of Mehrun, on the ground that insufficient land had been assigned to him for maintenance. The attack was successful, and Jagat Singh and his son, Bharat Singh, after a promise of safety, were treacherously murdered. Lal Singh made himself master of Mehrun, but was forced to give up his conquest by the Raja of Shahpura, and Bharat Singh's widow was placed in possession of the estate. She in 1842 adopted her cousin Jawahir Singh, who was subsequently succeeded by his brother Kalu Singh. The present Thakur, who is now twenty-seven years of age, and has one son, Gajadhar Singh, was adopted by Kalu Singh.

* Rao Ranjit Singh died on the 4th April 1894, while this account was in the Press, and has been succeeded by his son Gaj Singh.

Para.

(10) **Thakur Sangram Singh of Para** is a Rahtor Rajput and is the head of a junior branch of the Pisangan family (*q.v.*). The estate, which consists of six villages, pays a revenue of R2,492 to Government. To the villages originally separated from Pisangan and assigned to the first Thakur, Jhujhar Singh, two were subsequently added by himself and one by his son. Thakur Sangram Singh, who is twenty-six years of age and was educated at the Mayo College, succeeded his father Thakur Sheonath Singh. He has three younger brothers and no children.

Deogaon-Baghera.

(11) **Thakur Sardar Singh of Deogaon-Baghera,** a Rahtor Rajput of the Deolia branch of the Bhinai family (*q.v.*), holds an estate consisting of three villages which yields a revenue of R28,000 and pays R5,925 to Government. The founder of the estate was Nahar Singh, the third son of Akhay Raj, who having obtained Nandsi as maintenance from Deolia expelled the Gaur Rajputs from Deogaon and the Sesodias from Baghera. Of the villages which he thus obtained, he bestowed three on the Thakur of Junian who had assisted him in his enterprise and whose son had been slain in battle. As will be seen from a reference to the Bhinai pedigree, Nahar Singh was the father of a numerous progeny, whose descendants hold many villages in subordination to Deogaon-Baghera. Thakur Sardar Singh, who is thirty-five years of age, succeeded his father Thakur Ram Singh in 1879.

Gobindgarh.

(12) **Thakur Sankar Lal Singh of Gobindgarh,** a Rahtor Rajput, descended from Raja Udai Singh of Marwar, holds a small estate of two villages and three hamlets to the west of Ajmer. The annual income is about R10,000, and the revenue paid to Government is R2,418. The founder of the family was Gobind Das, a grandson of the Mota Raja (Udai Singh) of Marwar. The present Thakur, who is fifteen years of age, is receiving his education at the Mayo College, the estate being managed by the Court of Wards. The Thakur succeeded by adoption to his eldest brother in 1891. The following pedigree shows the descent of the family :—

- GOBIND DAS.
  - Jaswant Singh.
    - Lal Singh.
      - Jet Singh.
        - Hari Singh.
          - Akhay Singh.
            - Samrat Singh.
              - Ajit Singh.
                - Sheonath Singh (adopted).
                  - Lachhman Singh.
                    - Raghunath Singh.
                      - Thakur Sankar Lal Singh (present Thakur).
                    - Zorawar Singh.
                    - Sankar Lal Singh (adopted by Raghunath Singh).
            - Mohkam Singh.
              - Sheonath Singh (adopted by Thakur Ajit Singh).

(13) **Thakur Bhabhut Singh of Tantoti,** a Rahtor Rajput of the Bhinai family (*q.v.*), holds an estate of three villages of a total annual value* of R15,000, which pays R3,318 annually to Government. The Thakur, who holds *bhum* lands in three villages, has also a *jagir* village in Marwar. The present Thakur, who is fifty years of age, has three sons and one brother. He succeeded his father Thakur Mangal Singh.

Tantoti.

(14) **Thakur Moti Singh of Barli,** a Rahtor Rajput of the Deolia branch of the Bhinai family (*q.v.*), holds an estate consisting of twelve villages, of which the revenue is estimated at R30,000 and which pays R3,398 annually to Government. The village of Pipaliya, which formerly belonged to Barli, now forms a part of the Bhinai estate, having after much litigation been made over to Zorawar Singh, the grandfather of the present Raja of Bhinai, who had been adopted by Bishan Singh, the then Thakur of Barli, early in the present century. The condition of the adoption was that in the event of Bishan Singh having no son Zorawar Singh should be heir to Barli, or, should a son be born, should obtain Pipaliya. A son was born, but until compelled, the Barli Thakur refused to make over Pipaliya. The present Thakur Moti Singh, who is about twenty-eight years of age, succeeded Thakur Madho Singh in 1886 as being the nearest qualified claimant.

Barli.

(15) **Thakur Lachhman Singh of Bagsuri** is a Rahtor Rajput of the Masuda family (*q.v.*). The Bagsuri estate consists of two villages and a hamlet yielding an annual revenue of about R12,000, and pays R1,410 to Government. The founder of the estate was Lal Singh, the brother of Hanwant Singh, who obtained Masuda by grant from the Emperor Akbar. The present Thakur, who succeeded his father Thakur Nahar Singh, is twenty-three years of age, and has no children. He was educated at the Mayo College, where he gained considerable credit. The name is said to be derived from *bagh* and *sur*, Lal Singh having seen a pig and a tiger fighting on the spot where the fort was built by him on the assurance of the augurs that it would be impregnable.

Bagsuri.

* The estate includes the village of Baroi held by a cousin.

Jagirdars.

Rajgarh.

(1) **Raja Chandra Singh,** *Jagirdar* of Rajgarh, is a Gaur Rajput of the Bithaldasot family (see page 101). The estate consists of two villages and yields an annual income of R5,000. The Raja succeeded his adoptive father Raja Devi Singh in 1887. He has no children. The title of Raja is held by courtesy by the head of the family and was conferred on Devi Singh by the British Government as a personal distinction in 1877.

RAJA BITHAL DAS.

- Anand Singh.
  - Raj Singh.
    - Prithwi Singh.
    - Kesri Singh.
    - Nahar Singh.
    - Sujan Singh.
    - Nirbhay Singh.
    - Ummed Singh.
    - Gopal Singh.
    - Chiman Singh.
    - Chatar Singh.
    - Devi Singh.
    - Chandra Singh (adopted from the Danta family; present jagirdar).
  - Atma Ram (Danta).
- Arjun Singh (descendants in Rajgarh).

The Diwan.

(2) **Diwan Ghiyasu-d-din Ali Khan,** Sajjada Nashin-i-Dargah-i-Khwaja Sahib, is a Muhammadan Saiyid and a lineal descendant of Khwaja Muayyanu-d-din Chishti, who is said by tradition to have come to Ajmer from Sanjar in Khorasan to establish a shrine. According to the account given by Mr. La Touche (Settlement Report, page 51): "the Khwaja Sahib is said to have died in the year 1235 at the age of ninety-seven and to have come to Ajmer at the age of fifty-two, shortly before the invasion of India by Shahabu-d-din. Many marvels are related of him in the Akbaru-l-Akhyar and other works, and it is difficult to extract the historical facts of his career from the mass of romantic legends which have gathered round his name. It was at Medina that a voice came from the tomb of the prophet calling for Muayyanu-d-din and directing him to go to Ajmer and convert the infidels. He obeyed the call and on his arrival at Ajmer rested on the spot now known as the Kangara Masjid in the Dargah where at the time the king's camels were tethered. From this he was ejected and went and took up his abode on the hill which overlooks the Ana Sagar, the margin of which lake he found covered with idol temples. The idolaters enraged at the slaughter of kids by the Mussalmans conspired to massacre them, but when they came in sight of the Khwaja, remained rooted to the spot and though they tried to ejaculate *Ram! Ram!* could only articulate *Rahim! Rahim!* In vain did the idolaters, led by the great sorcerer Ajaypal and the *deota* Shadideo, renew their attacks. They were defeated on every occasion and finally begged forgiveness of the Khwaja

and invited him to come and take up his abode in the town. He consequently chose the site of the present Dargah." This shrine which commands the most profound veneration from Indian Muhammadans and was visited on foot by the Emperor Akbar as a pilgrim, is endowed with a *jagir* in Ajmer of fourteen villages yielding a revenue of about ₨22,000 and with another in His Highness the Nizam's territories. The income is shared equally by the Diwan, the Dargah, and the *Khadims* (servants). The Diwan is the manager and head of the spiritualities of the shrine, and besides large offerings which he shares with the *khadims*, holds a *jagir* in Ajmer and another in Jaipur. The annual income of the *jagir* is about ₨6,000. The estate is at present involved in debt and its management is, under a special regulation, vested in the Court of Wards. The Diwan received the title of Shaikhu-l-Mushaikh as a personal distinction in 1877. Mir Imam-ud-din, a cousin of the Diwan, is a Revenue Extra Assistant Commissioner in the Ajmer District.

Nawab Kumhar Baori.

(3) **Nawab Shamsu-d-din Ali Khan,** popularly known as Nawab Kumhar Baori, holds a *jagir* valued at ₨10,000 a year and consisting of four whole and seven half villages. Tahawwur Khan, the ancestor of the Nawab, accompanied Aurangzeb to Ajmer on his expedition against Dara, but was put to death on suspicion of treachery. His son Sheru-d-din received a *jagir* from the Emperor Farukhsiyar. The present Nawab is a student at the Mayo College and his estate is under the management of the Court of Wards. Succession is by primogeniture.

Gangwana.

(4) **Raja Bijay Singh, Jagirdar of Gangwana,** is a Rahtor Rajput, descended from Kishan Singh, the founder of the Kishangarh State. Maharaja Raj Singh of Kishangarh (1706—1748) died leaving four sons, of whom the eldest, Fath Singh, became the ancestor of the Fathgarh family (*vide* page 22). The second, Sanwant Singh, succeeded to Kishangarh. The third, Bahadur Singh, on the failure of heirs to Sardar Singh, son of Sawant Singh, became the ancestor of the present Chief of Kishangarh. The fourth, Bir Singh, got a share in Karkeri and left two sons, Amar Singh and Surat Singh. It was intended by Sardar Singh that Amar Singh should succeed him, but Bahadur Singh, with the help first of the Maharaja of Jodhpur and subsequently of Holkar, expelled Bir Singh and his family from all their possessions except Ralaota and procured the adoption of his own son Birad Singh. Bir Singh having joined the Mahrattas was killed at the battle of Panipat and his two sons received a *jagir* of six villages, three, subsequently confiscated by the Mahrattas, being assigned to Amar Singh, and Gangwana, Untra, and Magra to Surat Singh. Of Surat Singh's two sons the elder received Ralaota and the younger, Arjun Singh, the Gangwana *jagir* out of their father's inheritance. Arjun Singh's sons, Balwant Singh and Sher Singh, divided the Gangwana estate, of which moieties are held by their descendants. The whole income of the *jagir* is about ₨5,000. In the elder branch, that of Raja Bijay Singh, primogeniture now prevails. Raja Bijay Singh, who was born in 1863, succeeded his father Raja Balwant Singh in 1878. Of the shareholders in the other moiety of the *jagir*, Raja Sanwant Singh is Appellate Judge at Jhalrapatan. His uncle Raja Amar Singh, whose sister was the mother of Maharana Sajjan Singh of Udaipur, is Commander-in-Chief of the Mewar Forces. The title of Raja is enjoyed by the members of the family by courtesy and was conferred as a personal distinction in 1877 upon Raja Balwant Singh.

Dudiana.

(5) **Mir Inayatulla Shah,** a Muhammadan Saiyid Pirzada, holds a *jagir* consisting of Dudiana and half Dilwara. The former is held by the *Jagirdar* as *Sajjada-nashin* of the shrine of Khwaja Madud Chishti in Herat with which, however, all connection has ceased for two centuries. The whole *jagir* is of small value and being involved in debt is under the management of the Court of Wards. Mir Inayatullah Shah, who is now sixty-five years of age, succeeded his father in 1832 and was at one time an Honorary Magistrate of Ajmer. He has three sons, Muhammad Ismail Ali Khan, aged thirty-four years, Muhammad Yakub Ali Khan, aged twenty years, and Muhammad Ayub Ali Khan aged eleven years.

Jharwasa.

(6) **Mir Mihrban Ali, Jagirdar of Jharwasa and Bhatiani,** holds a third share in a *jagir* of which the whole value is about ₨3,500 and which is enjoyed revenue-free. Mir Mihrban Ali, who was recognized as *Jagirdar* in 1888, succeeded his grandfather Mir Nizam Ali who was

an Honorary Magistrate, a member of the *Jagir* Committee, and President of the Committee of the Dargah Khwaja Sahib.

Seths.

(1) **Rai Bahadur Seth Samir Mal,** a Mahajan, Oswal, is considered the leading Banker of Ajmer. He belongs to the Lodhi family, of which the origin is ascribed to a Chauhan Rajput of Nandoli in Marwar who being born without arms and legs received the nick-name of *Lodha* (a clod) and subsequently obtained his limbs by the favour of a Jain ascetic. An ancestor of the family migrated to Alwar, and a further migration took place two generations ago to Jaipur and subsequently in 1818 to Ajmer where the firm was established under the style of Kanwal Nayan Hamir Singh. Seth Samir Mal, who is sixty years of age, is the Vice-President of the Municipal Committee at Ajmer. He was Honorary Magistrate in the city for many years, but has lately resigned this office. He received the title of Rai Bahadur in 1890. His brother-in-law is Mahta Panna Lal, Diwan of Mewar (see page 36). Seth Samir Mal and his brother Seth Ummed Mal are in high repute in Ajmer.

(2) **Rai Bahadur Seth Mul Chand Soni** is the proprietor of the banking firm of Jawahir Mal and Ganbhir Mal. He is now sixty-one years of age, has enjoyed the distinction of Rai Bahadur since 1881, and is universally esteemed for his loyalty and integrity. He is an Honorary Magistrate and a member of the Ajmer Municipal Committee and District Board. Seth Mul Chand's father, Jawahir Mal, was an inhabitant of Kishangarh whence he migrated to Ajmer seventy-six years ago and made a large fortune by trading in opium. Seth Mul Chand is assisted in his business by his son Seth Nemi Chand. The firm has branches at Jaipur, Udaipur, Kotah, Karauli, Dholpur, Calcutta, Bombay, Mandsor, Agra, Gwalior, Nimach, and other places.

(3) **Rai Seth Chand Mal,** a Jain Oswal, belongs to a family which three generations ago, being then settled at Riyan, received the hereditary style of Seth from the Raja of Marwar. Seth Hamir Mal, the father of the present representative, was well known in his time, and Seth Chand Mal's position and services as a member of the Municipal Committee of Ajmer and of the District Board and as an Honorary Magistrate gained him in 1877 the title of Rai. The firm which own several *zamindari* villages in the Central Provinces are Government treasurers at Peshawar, Jalandhar, Hoshiyarpur, Kangra, Sambhar, Sagar, and Morar, and have branches at Bombay, Jabalpur, Narsinghpur, Mirzapur, Sagar, Rae Bareli, Damoh, Jalandhar, Hoshiyarpur, Peshawar, Gwalior, Jodhpur, Jhansi, Indore, and other places.

(4) **Bakhshi Khuman Singh, C.S.I.,** a pensioned official of Maharaja Holkar's service, is now residing at Ajmer, where he holds landed property. Born of a poor Gehlot family, he was taken in 1834, when only four years old, by his father Khet Singh from his birthplace Bhilara, in Mewar, to Indore. Khet Singh entered Holkar's service and the son, after studying privately and at the *madrasa* was, when fourteen years of age, appointed a Commandant in the army. In 1852, when the Maharaja received his powers, Khuman Singh was appointed *Bakhshi* and was subsequently presented with a *jagir*. In recognition of his loyalty and good service during the Mutiny he was given a *khilat* of the value of R5,000 by the Viceroy at a Darbar held at Jabalpur in 1861. He was afterwards a member of the Board of Education. He visited England, the Continent of Europe, and Egypt in 1870, and was nominated a Companion of the Star of India in 1877. Two years later he was appointed Commander-in-Chief and Minister by Holkar from whose service he has now retired. Of his two sons, Fath Singh and Ram Singh, the former has held posts of importance at Indore.*

* Bakhshi Khuman Singh has recently gone to Indore since this account was written, and it is not known if he will return to Ajmer.